Unsung Hero

The Story of Colonel Young Oak Kim

Woo Sung Han

Translated by
Edward T. Chang

Published
by
The Young Oak Kim Center
For Korean American Studies
UC Riverside
©2011

This book is an English translation of *The Beautiful Hero, Young Oak Kim*, the Korean original edition, published in The Republic of Korea. Copyright © 2008 by Woo Sung Han. This edition was translated and prepared by Edward T. Chang in consultation with Woo Sung Han.

Unsung Hero: The Story of Colonel Young Oak Kim English version copyright © 2011 by Woo Sung Han. All rights reserved.

Young Oak Kim Center for Korean American Studies at UC Riverside Web site:
http:www.yokcenter.ucr.edu.

Biographies

Woo Sung Han was Deputy Editor of the Foreign Desk, Business Desk and City Desk of the Korea Times Los Angeles. Han was also the first Knight Fellow of Stanford University as an ethnic journalist. He is the author of the Korean book the *Beautiful Hero Young Oak Kim*. Han has been a writer and journalist for most of his professional career and has won numerous awards including the Korea Journalist Award, the Associated Press News Executive Council Award, and the New California Media Award. He was nominated for a Pulitzer Prize in 2001.

Edward T. Chang is Professor of Ethnic Studies at the University of California Riverside. He is also the Director of the Young Oak Kim Center for Korean American Studies at UC Riverside. Chang has written several books and articles on the struggles of ethnic minorities.

ISBN 978-0-615-47372-7

Table of Contents

ACKNOWLEDGEMENTS I

INTRODUCTION III

PREFACE XIX

CHAPTER 1: LIBERATION OF ROME 1

CHAPTER 2: IMMIGRANT FAMILY 13

CHAPTER 3: IRONY OF A KOREAN AMERICAN OFFICER IN A JAPANESE AMERICAN UNIT 28

CHAPTER 4: FIRST BATTLE 38

CHAPTER 5: SAMURAI KIM 51

CHAPTER 6: SNIPER 67

CHAPTER 7: BEGINNING OF A LEGEND 82

CHAPTER 8: A BEAUTY AND A HERO 97

CHAPTER 9: THE LEANING TOWER OF PISA 101

CHAPTER 10: SMOKESCREEN 109

CHAPTER 11: PENICILLIN 121

CHAPTER 12: IDA 142

CHAPTER 13: CHAMPAGNE CAMPAIGN 149

CHAPTER 14: BACK IN UNIFORM 166

CHAPTER 15: TO FATHER'S COUNTRY 174

CHAPTER 16: HORSE TRADING 191

CHAPTER 17: SOYANG RIVER................................. 203

CHAPTER 18: WILD GRASS...................................... 219

CHAPTER 19 MASON AND MCCAFFREY 229

CHAPTER 20: WALKING ON THE RIDGE 252

CHAPTER 21: NIGHT MARCH 268

CHAPTER 22: FRIENDLY FIRE................................. 289

CHAPTER 23: OSAKA HOSPITAL 305

CHAPTER 24: BACK TO KOREA 313

CHAPTER 25: ORPHANAGE...................................... 333

CHAPTER 26: THE IRON TRIANGLE....................... 341

CHAPTER 27: BLUE HOUSE 353

CHAPTER 28: CANDLELIGHT 358

INDEX 371

BIBLIOGRAPHY 376

ABOUT THE YOK CENTER 381

HOW TO ORDER 382

Acknowledgements

When I first read the story of Colonel Young Oak Kim in Korean, it read like a novel. Remarkably it was a true story! I've decided that it is important to reach out to a wider audience by translating this Korean book into English. Author and award-winning journalist Woo Sung Han, interviewed Young Oak Kim numerous times, and visited many sites, consulted thousands of military documents, and interviewed various people, to corroborate the story. Han spent almost seven years writing this book on Young Oak Kim because the story truly moved his heart. I decided to translate this book because I strongly believe that this story will not only inspire the young and old, men, women, students of all races and ethnicity, but also push them to take action for racial equality and social justice. As a director of the newly established Young Oak Kim Center for Korean American Studies at the University of California Riverside, I am particularly interested in inspiring young Asian Americans to slay their passivity and not only take more actions for their individual success in life but also for social and community causes. Hopefully, the story of Young Oak Kim will inspire millions of people to work toward racial equality, social justice, and peace.

Young Oak Kim's legacy is beginning to shine like a candle in the dark. In his honor, the Young Oak Kim Center for Korean American Studies was established at the University of California Riverside in 2010. Also, the Los Angeles Unified School District named one of its junior high schools the Young Oak Kim Academy in 2009. All 5th graders in Korea learn about the legacy of Young Oak Kim as his story is now included in their Korean textbooks.

Grateful acknowledgment is made to individuals who helped this translation project from beginning to end.

It is not possible to mention all the names of those who provided generous support for the YOK Center and this book translation project. However, I would like to express my sincere thanks and appreciation to Dr. Mike Hong, Mr. Yeung Kim, and Mr. Jay Kim for their generous support. I'd like to acknowledge contributions from Ambassador Byung Hyo Choi, President Ku Hong Lee, and the Overseas Koreans Foundations for their support. Many other individuals also provided both financial support and words of encouragement for this book translation project.

Carol Park and Katherine Yungmee Kim provided invaluable editorial suggestions and corrections to improve the quality of this book. Mary Song and Pat Gallagher also read parts of this manuscript and provided critical editorial comments as well. I also thank Woo Sung Han's wife (Young Sook) and my wife (Janet) for their unconditional support, understanding, and patience.

Introduction

Korean Diaspora in America
By Edward T. Chang
(Director of the Young Oak Kim Center for Korean American Studies, UC Riverside)

On December 27, 2005, I visited Colonel Kim for the last time as he lay unconscious and in a coma at the Cedars-Sinai Medical Center in Los Angeles. I told him that his biography, written in Korean, had just been published in Korea. Out of hope that he understood my words, I thought that his right index finger moved slightly. I wished I had visited him sooner and had the chance to talk to him about his life in-depth, but it was too late. Two days later, he passed away.

I first met Young Oak Kim when he worked as a volunteer for the United Way of Los Angeles in the early 1980s. I knew him as a second-generation Korean American who was a retired U.S. Army officer. He was a soft-spoken, kind, and quiet person, and he was very efficient in getting things done. I did not know much about him beyond this. He never bragged about his war experiences in Italy, France or Korea. It never occurred to me at the time that he was a war hero.

More importantly, he was a champion of human rights. He dedicated his life, after retiring from the Army, to underprivileged, disadvantaged and dispossessed persons. He cared deeply about social justice and rights for women, children, minorities and orphans. Colonel Kim's actions were decisive and he always sought out ways to unite people, organizations and institutions.

Colonel Kim often spoke of "hope and courage" to young people. He was a brilliant strategist, as he understood when, where, how and with whom he should pick his fights. He firmly believed that people with heart would join a movement if it were a just cause. Colonel Kim was a war hero, but he was also against unnecessary conflict. He was one of the highest decorated soldiers to sign the petition against the war with Iraq. From his point of view, war was particularly cruel to women and children, and should be avoided at all costs.

Colonel Young Oak Kim stood tall in modern American and world history, but it seems very few knew who he was. Later, I found out that Colonel Kim was a highly respected leader of the Japanese American community. Ironically, while Colonel Kim was well-known and respected by Japanese Americans, hardly anyone knew who he was in the Korean American community. He possessed a big heart and he was able to break down the historical wall between Korea and Japan. During the war, he decided to fight alongside Japanese American soldiers.
They came together as Americans against a common enemy.

I hope his story inspires many people to work toward social justice and peace. It is with this conviction that I proudly introduce Colonel Young Oak Kim to readers of the English language. To understand who he is and what he has done, it is important to locate him within the context of Korean American history.

Korean diaspora in America[1]

Discriminatory immigration laws curtailed Asian and Korean immigration to the United States prior to the passage of the Immigration Act of 1965. As a result, the Korean population in America remained small for some

---

[1] The earlier version of this section was first published in *The History of Korea*. National Institute of Korean History, Seoul. Korea, 2008: 222-235.

time. According to 1970 census figures, there were only 69,000 documented Koreans living in the Untied States. The history of Korean immigration to the United States can be divided into four distinct periods: the first wave (1885-1902), the second wave (1903-1924), the third wave (1950-1964), and the fourth wave (1965-Present). The characteristics of each wave of Korean immigration are distinct and unique in terms of political and socioeconomic backgrounds, as well as the motive for emigrating from Korea.

The Early Korean Immigrant Community (1885-1924)
      The Treaty of Amity, Commerce and Navigation between Corea (The Great Joseon) and the United States (also known as the Korean-American Treaty) was signed on May 22, 1882, and took effect on June 4, 1883. The signing of the Korean-American Treaty in 1882 opened formal relations between the two nations. A Korean diplomatic mission led by Min Yong-ik arrived in San Francisco in 1883, and Yu Kil-jun (1856–1914), a member of the mission, remained in the United States to study at the Governor Dummer Academy (predecessor of the Governor's Academy) in Byfield, Massachusetts. After the failed Coup d'Etat of 1884 (Kapsin Chongbyon), So Jae Pil (Philip Jaisohn)[2] and So Kwang-bom fled Korea, and came to the United States as political exiles in 1885. Political exiles and student leaders shaped the "highly political" nature of the early Korean immigrant community

---

[2] So Jae Pil changed his name to Philip Jaisohn by spelling his Korean name backward. Philip Jaisohn became the first American-educated Korean to receive a medical degree at Columbian Medical College (predecessor of the George Washington University) in June 1892. He also became the first Korean to marry an American, Muriel Armstrong in June 20, 1894.

as they contributed, sacrificed, and dedicated their lives to the independence movement. In addition, records shows that 165 ginseng (Insam) merchants, 3 women, 2 children, and 20 elders (age 45 and above) ventured to the United States between 1899 and 1902).[3] Korean immigrants who arrived prior to 1903 should be considered the pioneers of the Korean American community as they shaped the "highly political" nature of the early Korean immigrant community. Political exiles and student leaders contributed, sacrificed and dedicated their lives to the Korean independence movements in the United States.

However, the first official documentation of Korean immigration to the U.S. is widely considered to begin with the arrival of 102 Korean laborers in Hawaii on January 13, 1903 (Choy 1979; Patterson 1988). To commemorate the official beginning of Korean immigration to the United States, the Korean American community, together with the U.S. government, designated January 13 as Korean American Day. Between 1903 and 1905, a total of more than 7,000 immigrants arrived in Hawaii from Korea. However, it is important to note that many Koreans arrived in America before 1903 as diplomats, ginseng merchants, students and political exiles.

Both internal and external factors contributed to the second wave of Korean immigration to the United States. Internal factors included exploitation of the working classes by the ruling Yangban elite, natural disasters such as famine and flood, and political instability in Korea.[4]

This period of Korean immigration was also greatly shaped by the internal conditions that occurred during the

---

[3] Sun Joo Bhang, *Hanin Miju IjuEui Sijak: The Beginning of Korean Immigration to the U.S.* in A History of Korean Immigration to the U.S. Seoul: National Institute of Korean History, 2003: 55.

[4] Edward T. Chang. *Following the Footsteps of Korean Americans.* Cerritos, CA: Pacific Institute for Peacemaking, 1995: 15.

Japanese invasion and occupation of the Korean peninsula. The hardships resulting from Japanese imperialism made the country inhospitable for many Koreans. By 1905, Korea became a "protectorate" of Japan, and the Japanese subsequently colonized the country in 1910. External influences, such as American missionaries and recruiting agents sent by the Hawaiian Sugar Plantation Association (HSPA), played a critical role in the transportation of Korean immigrants to Hawaii during the early 1900s. The HSPA actively pursued a "divide and conquer" strategy to lower wages and control the labor force in Hawaii. To balance the dominance of Japanese labor in Hawaii's sugar plantations, Korean workers, along with Chinese, Portuguese, Filipinos and others, were recruited as fieldhands and sugar refinery workers. The first Koreans to immigrate to Hawaii were mostly young (in their twenties), urban, single male workers, with a large percentage (close to 40 percent) being Christian converts.[5] Korean immigrant churches not only provided spiritual salvation, but more importantly a place to discuss and strategize the independence of Korea. The churches served the important function of regularly bringing together the Korean American community, which was spread out in mostly rural areas, and organizing support for Korean independence. They were centers for educational forums and debates concerning Korea's future.

Almost ten percent of these early Korean immigrants were women.[6] These women were called "picture brides" because they came to the U.S. to become the wives of Korean bachelors after an exchange of

---

[5] Chang, 1995. "Koreans in Hawaii." Pp. 937 – in The Asian American Encyclopedia, edited by Franklin Ng. New York: Marshall Cavendish Corp.

[6] Wayne Patterson, *The Ilse: First-Generation Korean Immigrants in Hawaii, 1903-1973*. Honolulu: University of Hawaii Press, 2000: 5.

photographs by post. The average age difference between a bride and groom ranged from ten to fifteen years. At the time, "anti-miscegenation" laws prohibited marriage between whites and non-whites; therefore, Korean bachelors were unable to find brides in the United States.[7] Many Korean bachelors had to work for over ten years to save enough money to finance marriages with women living in Korea. Approximately 800 to 1,000 Korean picture brides arrived in Hawaii to begin married lives in a foreign country.[8] Korean women often worked as cooks, janitors and laundresses on the plantations where the workers lived.[9] With the arrival of these Korean picture brides, the Korean immigrant community became much more stable and family-oriented. Some Korean immigrants came as a family unit.

Young Oak Kim's parents came to the United States right after Korea was colonized by Japan in 1910. To escape from Japanese oppression and continue independence activities, they decided to migrate to the U.S. Young Oak Kim was born in 1919 as the eldest son of Soon Kwon and Nora Koh in Los Angeles.

Independence Movement

Korean Americans were passionately opposed to Japan's occupation of their homeland and displayed their protest through a variety of means. Three Korean immigrant leaders in particular embodied the different strategies that people adopted to fight the Japanese while in

---

[7] Chang, p. 39.
[8] In-Jin Yoon, In-Jin. *The Social Origin of Korean Immigration to the United States from 1965 to the Present.* Honolulu: East-West Population Institute, 1993.
[9] Yo-jun Yun, "Early History of Korean Immigration to America," in *The Korean Diaspora*, ed. by Hyung-Chan Kim. Santa Barbara: Clio Press, 1979.

the United States. Park Yong-man advocated direct military confrontation, Syngman Rhee, focused on diplomacy, and Ahn Chang Ho emphasized education and developing patriotic leadership.[10] Following Park's suggestion of armed confrontation was difficult, because Koreans in the U.S. were considered "aliens ineligible for citizenship" and were not allowed to use firearms, leaving them to train using wooden models of rifles.[11] On the other hand, Syngman Rhee's bid for diplomatic efforts along with Ahn Chang Ho's emphasis on developing educational resources and patriotic leadership held both promise and practicality.[12]

The March 1, 1919 Mansei Movement was a pivotal historical event that ignited Korean independence activism all over the world, including in the United States. Koreans throughout the country demanded "self-determination" and independence from Japanese rule through mass demonstrations. Between March 1919 and December 1920, Korean Americans raised over $200,000 to support the independence movement in Korea.[13] One of the most significant examples of Korean immigrant fierce antagonism that Korean immigrants felt towards Japanese occupation occurred in 1908 with the assassination of Durham Stevens, an adviser to the Korean government who was later found to be a shill for the Japanese.[14] Stevens was labeled a traitor to the Korean people, and a Korean immigrant named Chang In-hwan shot and killed him.

---

[10] Bong-Youn Choy, *Koreans in America*. Chicago: Nelson Hall, 1979; Takaki, p. 281
[11] Chang, p. 83.
[12] Ronald Takaki, Strangers from a Different Shore. p. 281.
[13] Bong-Youn Choy. *Koreans in America*. Chicago: Nelson Hall Press, 1979.
[14] Choy, p. 146.

While many participated in anti-colonial activities, they also worked to acclimate themselves to life in the U.S.

The early Korean American community focused much of its attention toward independence of the homeland while adjusting to immigrant life. A small number of Korean immigrants in Hawaii left the islands and went to the mainland to seek better lives. Most worked as field hands on farms or laborers in California cities like San Francisco, Los Angeles, Riverside, Dinuba, Reedley and Willows. Despite the hardships endured due to their marginalized status in the American community and workplace, Korean immigrants in the United States were adamantly dedicated to the independence of Korea from Japanese rule. The development of an independence movement and the establishment of community churches became characteristic of the early Korean immigrant community, both in Hawaii and on the mainland.

The Korean Aviation School

During the early 20th century, only a few nations (Great Britain, Russia, France, Japan and the U.S.) established air schools to train combat pilots. It is in this context that Roh Baek Rin, defense secretary of the Korean Provisional Government in Shanghai, decided to establish the Korean Aviation School in the United States. The creation of the Korean Aviation School in Willows, California was highly unusual in that it was a military policy implemented by the Korean Provisional Government in China to establish a training facility for Korean combat pilots on American soil. The Korean Aviation School commenced in February of 1920 at Willows, California, a small town located 230 km north of San Francisco.

The Korean Aviation School ran for at least a year and a half and trained several young Korean men as pilots.[15] It was part of a dream of establishing an independent Korean air guard. The Korean Provisional Government in Shanghai appointed at least two Korean pilots from the Korean Aviation School as officers in the later developed Korean Air Force.[16]

The Korean Provisional Government in Shanghai appointed Ro Baek Rin as its Defense Minister.[17] With commitment and financial support from businessman Kim Chong Rim, Ro decided to establish the Korean Aviation School in California.[18] Both Ro and the Korean immigrant community agreed on the importance of building up an air force to achieve independence for Korea. The Korean community in the United States highly valued the importance of an air force when they saw how effectively the U.S. fleet of fighters and bombers carried out missions during World War I.

The number of students at the Korean Aviation School began to increase. According to the New Korea

---

[15] *50-Year History of the Korean Air Force Academy*. The Korean Air Force Academy. Korea, 1999: 25. According to this source, the Willows Korean Aviation School graduated 25 cadets in July 1920, 41 cadets in June 1922, and 41 cadets in 1923, but it seems to be in error since the School shut down sometime in middle of 1921.

[16] *The Independence Newspaper* (February 4, 1920) reported that Ro's declaration used the term "liberation army" as it reads "20 million Koreans should organize and participate as a member of liberation army systematically." Sun Pyo Hong, "Military Independence Movement of Korean American Community" in *Korean American Community and Independence Movement I*. Committee to Commemorate the 100th Year History of Korean Immigration to the U.S. Seoul: Pak Young Sa, 2003.

[17] Sun Pyo Hong, "Military Independence Movement of Korean American Community" in *Korean American Community and Independence Movement I*. Committee to Commemorate the 100th Year History of Korean Immigration to the U.S. Seoul: Pak Young Sa, 2003.

[18] *Willows Daily Journal*. February 19, 1920.

(March 19, 1920), 24 young men enrolled in the program. The number of students increased from 15 to 24 within a month and grew to 30 by June 22. The Willows Daily Journal (March 1, 1920) quoted Ro Baek Rin as saying that the "Korean Aviation School is a continuation of the March 1st Movement of 1919, and Korean pilots will be mobilized to fight against Japan."

Regardless of its strong community support and early successes, the Korean Aviation School faced major problems when Kim Chong Rim's rice farm was flooded in October of 1920, devastating his business. It appears that Kim Chong Rim contributed around $50,000 to the Korean Aviation School in 1920, and its worth at the time is estimated to be between $2.8 million to $8 million in today's value. The Korean Aviation School was unable to reopen when Kim Chong Rim's rice farm failed.

Although the Korean immigrant community was sometimes divided between supporters of Syngman Rhee and Ahn Chang Ho, Kim Chong Rim— considered one of the most influential donors and leaders of the Korean American community at that time—provided financial support to both leaders. He was one of the core financiers of the Korean National Association established by Ahn Chang Ho, but he also maintained close relations with Rhee, having served as a chair at the national meeting of the Comrade Association in 1946. More than 400 guests attended Kim Chong Rim's eldest son's wedding ceremony in 1946, attesting to his extensive connections within the community. As previously mentioned, Kim Chong Rim tried to venture into new businesses, but never really succeeded. He passed away in 1973 in Los Angeles.

There are many prominent second-generation Korean Americans who made significant and valuable contributions to American society. Notable second-generation Korean Americans include: Sammy Lee, two-time Olympic gold medalist (1948 and 1952); Mary Lee Shon, a well-known and respected educator in the Los Angeles Unified School District; David Hyun, an architect who designed and managed the "Japanese Village Plaza" in Little Tokyo, Los Angeles; Philip Ahn, the eldest son of Ahn Chang Ho and renowned Asian American actor, who has his name placed on the Hollywood "Walk of Fame"; and Alfred Song, who was the first Asian American elected official in the State of California.

The Third Wave (1950-1964)

The Korean War (1950-53) had a profound impact on the lives of the Korean people. This war took a heavy toll, as approximately 450,000 (not counting North Koreans) were killed, including about 33,000 Americans. The division of the Korean peninsula along the 38th parallel in 1945 led to the outbreak of the Korean War. This separation into two Koreas has left lasting effects on thousands of families. Family members have been forced apart for generations due to the closing of national boundaries. The Korean War also had a direct impact on immigration to the U.S. It was not until the Korean War that sizable numbers of Koreans were able to emigrate to the U.S. At the beginning of the Korean War in 1950, the total number of Korean Americans living in the U.S. is estimated to be approximately 17,000.[19]

Between 1950 and 1964, almost 6,000 Korean women entered as wives of U.S. servicemen ("war brides"), which accounted for roughly 40 percent of all Korean immigration to the U.S. during this period.[20] One estimate

---

[19] Eui-Young Yu, "Koreans in America: an Emerging Ethnic Minority," *Amerasia Journal*, Vol. 4. 1977: 117-131.
[20] Pyong Gap Min. "Korean Americans," in *Asian Americans: Contemporary Trends and Issues,* ed. by Pyong Gap Min. Thousand Oaks, CA: Sage Publications, 1995.

is that these Korean women are responsible for almost half of all Korean immigration to the U.S. since 1965, by sending for their relatives living in Korea.[21] In addition, the 1951 Refugee Act allowed orphans and refugees to enter the U.S. Five thousand children came in as adoptees to families in the U.S. Thus, both war brides and adoptees comprised about two-thirds of all Korean immigrants to the U.S. at that time.[22] Approximately 6,000 students entered the U.S. through admissions to colleges and universities during this period as well.[23]

The Fourth Wave:
New Urban Immigrants (1965-Present)

South Korea and the United States share a complex military, economic, political and cultural link. Direct military and political ties have existed between the two nations as U.S. troops have been stationed in South Korea since 1945. The Korean American community grew rapidly with the passage of the 1965 Immigration and Nationality Act. The Korean American population increased from 69,130 in 1970 to 1,076,872 in 2000. Korean immigrants who arrived after the passage of the 1965 Immigration Act are commonly known as "new urban immigrants" because many of them came from middle class, urban and professional backgrounds. Drastic changes in the Korean economy in the 1960s and 1970s that turned war-torn Korea into a rapidly growing industrial, capitalist

---

[21] Daniel BooDuck Lee. "Marital Adjustment Between Korean Women and American Servicemen" in Hyung Chan Kim and Eun Ho Lee, eds., *Koreans in America: Dreams and Realities*. Seoul: Institute of Korean Studies, 1990.

[22] In-Jin Yoon. "Korean immigration to the United States." Pp. 894 – 906 in *The Asian American Encyclopedia*, edited by Franklin Ng. New York: Marshall Cavendish Corp, 1995.

[23] Warren Y. Kim. *Koreans in America*. Seoul: Po Chin Chai Printing Company, 1971.

economy had a direct impact on immigration to the U.S. Many more Korean people qualified for white-collar jobs than there were jobs to fill in Korea.

Contrary to popular belief, however, the Korean American community is not homogeneous, but bi-modal in areas of language, nativity, generation, identity and class backgrounds. Language usage divides Korean Americans into three identities: Koreans in America, 1.5 generation, and second-generation Korean American. A majority of Korean immigrants speak the Korean language (80.7 percent), and the 1.5-generation Korean Americans are often bilingual. A majority of the second-generation Korean Americans, however, can only speak English (80.3 percent), although increasing numbers of the second generation are learning the Korean language and culture.[24] In addition to language, the occupational structures of the Korean American community attest to divisions within the community. Among employed Korean Americans 16 years and older, 43.9 percent were in "management, professional and related occupations," and 14.6 percent were in "service." Sales and office occupations accounted for 28.9 percent. Therefore, it is important to note that the Korean American community is polarized along generation and identity, language and class backgrounds. Korean American women today are much more likely to be working outside the home (50.8 percent) and for long hours.[25] The average Korean American woman works outside the home 51 hours per week; 80 percent of Korean women work outside the home full-time.

---

[24] This data is based on U.S. Census Bureau's 2006 American Community Survey.

[25] U.S. Census Bureau's 2006 American Community Survey found that 50.8% of Korean American females 16 years and over were employed and 2.9% were unemployed.

Church and Ethnic Entrepreneurship

Two distinct characteristics set Korean immigrants apart from other Asian groups: a church-centered community and entrepreneurship. The church is the most dominant institution in the Korean American community. Studies have shown that approximately 70 percent of Korean immigrants are regular churchgoers. Korean American churches are the most important social, cultural and economic institutions that serve the needs of Korean immigrants. Church is not only a place where recent Korean immigrants go to worship, but it also provides a venue where they may can share their immigrant experiences and cope with language and cultural barriers in a new society.

Since Korean immigrants view small business as an avenue for success in America, Korean immigrants have been actively developing and cultivating a niche in the small business sector.

According to In-jin Yoon, Korean Americans ranked the highest in self-employment rates in 1990.[26] A combination of factors facilitated high self-employment rates among Korean immigrants. Cultural misunderstanding, language barriers and unfamiliarity with American society put Korean immigrants at a disadvantaged position in the U.S. labor market. Korean immigrants also found it difficult to find jobs that were commensurate with their education level.

Lessons from the L.A. Civil Unrest of 1992

The proliferation of Korean-owned businesses in African American neighborhoods during the 1980s exacerbated conflicts between Korean American

---

[26] In-jin Yoon, *On My Own: Korean Businesses and Race Relations in America*. Chicago: University of Chicago Press, 1997.

businessmen and African American customers. The culture clash fueled antagonism between Korean immigrant merchants and African American residents. Volatile relations between Korean American and African American communities in Los Angeles exploded into the mass destruction of property and loss of life on April 29, 1992. The eruption of violence in Los Angeles destroyed approximately 2,280 Korean-owned businesses and caused a total of $1 billion in damage, of which $400 million was shouldered by the Korean American community.[27]

The Los Angeles riots of 1992 are commonly known as Sa-ee-gu (4-29) in the Korean American community. Many consider Sa-ee-gu as the most important historical event, a "turning point," "watershed event," or "wake-up call" during one hundred years of Korean American history. Sa-ee-gu profoundly altered the Korean American discourse, igniting debates and dialogues in search of new directions, which continue to this day.[28] Sa-ee-Gu also exposed many problems and challenges for the Korean American community: a lack of leadership and political power, generation split, and lack of contact with other communities. Korean Americans have learned many valuable lessons from the 1992 Los Angeles Civil Unrest. First, the Korean American community did not passively accept this event. Within a matter of days, more than 50,000 Korean Americans in Los Angeles came together for a "Peace March." This historic event is said to be one of the largest gatherings in all of Asian American history. Also, the 1.5 and second generations played a critical role

---

[27] Edward Taehan Chang, "The Post-Los Angeles Riot Korean American Community: Challenges and Prospects. *Korean and Korean American Studies Bulletin*. Vol. 10 No. 1 & 2, 1999: 6.

[28] Edward T. Chang, *What does it mean to be Korean Today? Part II. Community in the 21st Century*. Amerasia Journal. Vol. 30 No. 1, 2004: vii.

in the community during and after the civil unrest. It was the younger generation that articulated Korean American voices to the society at-large by getting involved in politics and the media. For 1.5 and second generation Korean Americans, the civil unrest gave them a new sense of belonging and ethnic pride as they participated in relief efforts and peace marches.

Political empowerment has become one of the most important goals for the Korean American community. Preoccupied with Korean homeland politics, many Korean immigrants had traditionally shown little interest in politics in America, until they were confronted with the agonizing reality of their lives during and after the civil unrest. The Korean American community lacked the critical resources and grassroots and political organizations to assume this new role as an Asian American community grounded in the realities of post-1992, multiracial Los Angeles. Korean immigrants painfully learned the lessons of what it means to be Korean American in a multicultural and multiracial context. They realized the importance of breaking out of ethnic isolation and actively reaching out to other communities to forge working and harmonious relations. In doing so, Korean Americans have begun to embrace a new role in proactively participating in an inclusive, multiracial and multiethnic America. As the Korean American community rebuilt itself from the ashes of Sa-ee-gu, it must also continue to rebuild the political consciousness and awareness of itself as a vital and contributing entity involved within a larger society.

Colonel Young Oak Kim's story is part of Korean American, Asian American, and American history and serves as an example that will inspire millions of people to reach out and seek peace and humanity.

Preface

Several years ago, a publisher asked me why I was writing a biography on Young Oak Kim. "Who is he?"

I took a moment before answering.
"I have a son. I'd like my son to live like him."

The reason I'd like my son, my daughter and other young people to live like him is not only because he was a legendary war hero who received multiple decorations from several countries, but also because he represented the underprivileged, lighting himself like a candle in the dark. Yet, he never boasted about his amazing accomplishments. So while the brightness of his light still glows across North America, Europe and Asia, most people remain incognizant of its source.

Despite that fact, there are a few people who do know of the source. Some of the older residents of Bruyères—a little town nestled in the Vosges Mountains in France—are such individuals. After the Allied Forces had liberated Paris in 1944, they continued their push towards Germany; the Vosges Mountains, located in northeastern France, were the last line of Germany's defense. Subsequently, the Vosges were where many fierce battles were waged. When I visited the area to examine the battlefields where Colonel Kim fought during World War II, an official from the French forestry department invited me to dinner at his house. Thanks to him, for the first time in my life, I was privy to an authentic, candlelit French home-cooked meal, served with excellent wine. He had also invited several of the elderly residents of the area to dinner. Just as we were about to begin our feast, the host asked me to briefly introduce myself to the other guests. As nobody spoke English, I had no choice but to speak in my poor French.

"I'm a Korean American journalist," I explained. "I came here to write a story about Colonel Kim, an American soldier of Korean ancestry, who fought here during World War II."

I had used the title "Colonel Kim," because that was how he was known and referred to in the United States. Everybody was silent. I had hoped that perhaps I might meet someone who recalled his name, but I was disappointed. I thought that it was possible that they did not understand my French, and I regretted not having paid more attention to my studies of the French language, which had been my major in college. Just then, a thought hit me, "Wasn't he a captain during World War II? Perhaps..." So I modified my introduction.

"I came here to cover 'Captain Kim,'" I said. "He was a U.S. soldier of Asian ancestry who fought here during World War II."

As soon as the name "Captain Kim" left my mouth, an elderly woman, who had been sitting quietly to my left, softly exclaimed, "Ah, Capitaine Kim!"

"Do you know him?" I asked, unable to hide my excitement. But before she could respond, an elderly man to my right said, "I, too, grew up hearing the name."

As my earlier excursions to the battlefields in Italy had not yielded a single person who could recall Colonel Kim, let alone his unit, I had gone to France with little hope. So I was overwhelmed by the French villagers' recollections. However, the same folks who remembered 'Capitaine Kim' as the war hero who had liberated them also believed that he had been of Japanese ancestry.

In Biffontaine, a smaller town just a few miles away from Bruyères, the townspeople dedicated a small copper plaque with Colonel Kim's name on the wall to the right side of their church entrance. The plaque was in appreciation for all of the Allied soldiers who had shed their blood to liberate them from the Nazis.

"To the left of this church's entrance, Captain Young O. Kim, one of the heroes of the 100th Battalion, was captured by the German forces and successfully escaped with Mr. Chinen," the plaque reads. (Mr. Chinen was a U.S. Army medic).

The plaque made me think of many things. From 1943 to 1944, Korea was still suffering under the tyranny of Japanese occupation. It was during this period that Kim relentlessly tested the line between life and death in Italy and France and became a legend. A second-generation Korean American, born to a Korean independence movement fighter who had moved to America, Kim became a U.S. Army officer and successfully led a cadre of Japanese American soldiers against the Nazis in the European Theater of Operations. At the time, he was merely 24 years old.

While retracing his footsteps in France, Italy and the United States for a number of years, I was often startled, albeit refreshingly, by what I encountered. Many people I met over the course of my research shed tears over Kim. I had asked Mr. Raymond Nosaka, a second-generation Japanese American who fought in World War II as one of Kim's squad members, what he thought of the fact that Kim did not receive the Medal of Honor from the United States. With tears filling his eyes, Mr. Nosaka replied, "The U.S. government is out of its mind. They should have asked those of us who actually fought side by side with him."

Captain Arthur Wilson, a Caucasian American soldier who fought in the Korean War with Kim, held my hand tightly with both his hands with tears streaming down his face, when I explained my project. Some time passed before Captain Wilson, with tears still on his face, implored, "Please write a beautiful story about him."

I also spoke with Colonel John Covach, a second-generation Hungarian American, who immediately upon commission as second lieutenant had been dispatched to Korea to participate in the Incheon Landing. Later, he fought under Kim's command, and eventually went on to serve in the Vietnam War. When he heard I was coming to Washington D.C. to inquire about Kim, Colonel Covach drove his Cadillac to Dulles International Airport to greet me personally and take me to his home to share a meal prepared by his wife. Although we had never met before, the good colonel practically commanded me to stay at his home whenever I visited Washington D.C. When I did indeed visit his home again for additional research, he stayed true to his word and extended his hospitality by opening the doors to a pristine room normally kept for extended visits by his married daughter.

Aside from Kim's comrades-in-arms and the rural denizens of France, there were innumerable others whose accounts of personal encounters with Colonel Kim astonished me. At the award ceremony of the Moran Medal of Korea, the second-highest civilian decoration of Korea, Kim expressed his desire to see the orphans he had cared for during the Korean War. His wishes were wired by the Yonhap News Agency, the Korean version of the Associated Press, to Korea. I was answering the phone for Kim because the article carried my telephone number, and the first call came in from Korea. A woman recounted her story in tears, repeatedly stressing, "Please tell him that I can't express enough how grateful I am to him." Many other calls followed from the U.S. and Korea.

There were times when I was more astonished by those who did not know Colonel Kim than by those who had had the good fortune to know him. Kim established the

Korean Health Education Information and Research Center in Los Angeles, a successful non-profit health organization for low-income people. Its average annual budget is $4.5 million and it is highly regarded by the U.S. federal government. Kim founded and/or developed many non-profit community service organizations in California. However, only a few individuals seem to be aware of this. Needless to say, this is likely due to Kim's silence and modesty concerning his own accomplishments.

What is it about Kim that makes individuals shed tears even after fifty to sixty years have passed? Why have so many of them opened up and shared their stories? In February 1997, I drove 50 minutes from Los Angeles to meet Kim at his humble office in Torrance. After a brief exchange of greetings, I got straight to the point and asked for his permission to write a book about him. He responded that he hadn't lived a life worthy of a biography and refused. After almost an hour passed, I thought of giving up. But I stood up, put both hands on my side of his desk and bent my upper body halfway towards him.

"Colonel Kim, everyone dies. You will die too. So far, you've done many wonderful things for other people, particularly for Koreans. Before you die, please do one last thing for them."

He didn't say anything, but he looked directly into my eyes.

"What is that?" he asked.

"Very simple. Let me bring your story to a broader audience."

He fell silent again.

"Okay, do whatever you want," he finally said.

This is how my journey into his life began. He didn't scold me for my rudeness—for mentioning his own death, and upon our first meeting, at that. Later on, I discovered that several professional writers had already offered to write his biography. More than fifty proposals for a documentary or feature film based on his life had already been made. After refusing all of this, he had agreed to everything at our first meeting. Back then, I was just a nameless reporter for an ethnic newspaper published in the Korean community in America; I hadn't yet become the award-winning journalist that I am today. As Kim was exceptionally keen and intelligent, I can only hope that he read my sincerity beyond the rudeness I displayed and still regret to this day.

I came to America as an immigrant in 1987 and became a reporter in Los Angeles the following year. Four years later, I witnessed the 1992 Los Angeles Civil Unrest. One of the weakest Asian American communities, the Korean American community brutally became a race relations scapegoat. The mainstream media depicted Korean Americans as ruthless people who could shoot an African American child to death over a one-dollar bottle of orange juice. We were portrayed as selfish immigrants who cared only for money without service for community or country. It was a sad attempt to find a quick fix for the explosively escalating tensions between whites and blacks. Something had to be done to reveal that this was not the entire truth.

Historically, from Korea's independence to the Korean War and even up to the present, America's influence on Korea has obviously had its many pros and cons. Aside from any analysis of the situation from any party's unilateral stance, both countries will continue to be deeply enmeshed with one another. Hence, these countries need to be proactive, and for this to happen, a relationship needs to be forged upon mutual understanding and respect. Each country needs to get to know the other more precisely.

The same goes for the relationship between Japan and Korea. This relationship is even more historically rooted and perhaps much more complicated than the one between the U.S. and Korea. Nevertheless, the relationship between Korea and Japan should not be solely tied to the past. The relationship between the two countries will continue to play a very important role in northeast Asia and world politics. This relationship should also be based on mutual understanding and respect. Each country needs to get to know the other more precisely.

After emigrating to the U.S., I recognized a huge schism between domestic Koreans and Korean Americans. I don't know whether the same situation can be equally applied to other immigrant groups. Korea is a small country, which encourages emigration, yet domestic Koreans have ambivalence towards their emigrants, particularly towards Korean Americans. A famous Korean novelist once said, "Emigrants are like rats that jump off a sinking ship first."

As a reporter who wrote for a Korean ethnic newspaper in America, how influential a message could I deliver to mainstream America or to Korea and Japan across the Pacific Ocean? I made a list of Korean Americans, living or dead. In order for the name to stay on my list, that person's real life needed to satisfy the following four criteria:

No. 1: Did he or she substantially contribute to America?

No. 2: Did he or she substantially contribute to Korea?

No. 3: Can his or her story help improve the relationship between the U.S. and Korea?

No. 4: Can his or her story help improve the relationship between Japan and Korea?

Because I was born and educated in Korea, my opinions were from a distinctly Korean perspective. But after immigrating, I realized that America and Korea were different in many aspects. In some ways, Korea was better.

In other facets, America was better. Neither country was better than the other; they were just different.

The concept of a hero also differed. America is a society where other people's accomplishments are willingly accepted and such individuals are respected. I believe Americans have a well-defined notion of a hero. There are many heroes in America, not because there are inherently many heroic Americans, but because Americans create heroes and embrace them. However, Americans don't call just someone a hero because that individual made a lot of money and gave large donations. Instead, Americans readily call an individual a hero if he is a policeman, a fireman, a Private First Class, or a CIA or FBI agent, who was killed in the line of duty. Americans call them heroes and erect statues or name streets or buildings after them. In short, Americans call someone who shed his or her blood for country or community in crisis a hero. He or she doesn't need to be a president or a general. Therefore, when I was searching for someone who has substantially contributed to America, priority was given to someone who shed blood for America during a time of crisis. In accordance with the aforementioned four criteria, I began striking one name after the other off my list. With this particular definition of an American hero in mind, there was only one name that remained on my list: Young Oak Kim.

Reporters are people who are trained to capture many decades of an individual's life in one short interview. In other words, they are trained to process a lot of information over a very short period of time. This was the case for me as well. After deciding to write about Young Oak Kim, I tried to be "smart" in order to write efficiently. Knowing he was a war hero, I asked him, "How many military decorations did you receive?"

"I'm not sure," he said. "When I go home, I'll count them and let you know."

I asked the question because I thought that behind each decoration there would surely be a heroic and entertaining story. His answer was unexpected. So I asked myself, How could a soldier not know how many decorations he's received? I semi-doubted and semi-believed him, but since there was no obvious reason why I shouldn't believe him, I accepted his response and simply waited. After several interviews, I asked him again.

"Did you count your decorations?"

"No, I forgot."

At that moment, I felt that he would never give me an exact answer. By then, I had a better understanding of what kind of person Kim was. One day, I visited his home in the suburbs of Las Vegas, Nevada. Upon entering his house, I intentionally looked around in search of his decorations or awards, but nothing was displayed. Not only were there no military medals, there was also absolutely nothing to indicate he had ever been a soldier. I asked him again, "Where do you keep your decorations?" He led me to his garage and asked me to pull out an old dust-covered box from a corner. Then, he asked me to open it. The box was full of many smaller boxes. I could see that both the big and small boxes had not been opened for quite some time. He pointed towards a box on top and asked me to open it. When I wiped off the dust and opened it, he said, "That's a Silver Star."

Stunned, I realized that I could not approach his story in an "efficient" way, and that his story would take an enormous amount of my time and energy. When I first began my research, I knew he was a hero of World War II, but I had no idea he had been one of such stature. He was the star of the liberation of Rome and Pisa. United Press International aired the story of his courage and boldness during the liberation of Rome all over the world. His brilliant strategy during the battle of Pisa made it possible for the troops to cross the Arno River without a single casualty and liberate Pisa. In the battle of Bruyères, he even risked his own life to save enemy lives. When I began my research, it was a little known fact that Kim had fought in the Korean War.

I was constantly surprised by the evidence that he had been in every significant moment of the making of Korea's modern history. He played a key role in shaping Korea's borders. In 1951, his legendary victories moved the frontline to the north by approximately thirty-seven miles. The Defense Ministry of Korea officially acknowledged this in 2005. Of course, he didn't do this single-handedly; it was achieved by all the U.N. and Korean soldiers who shed blood together. Another piece of hidden history is the fact that, while fighting as a battalion commander on the frontline, Kim managed to care for hundreds of war orphans during the Korean War.

However, I devoted myself to this research because Kim's humanitarian acts and community service after he retired from the U.S. Army have been just as significant as his military accomplishments. Half of the real story lies in his humanitarian accomplishments. While silence and modesty were the essence of his personality, they were real obstacles for me. He never bragged about himself, and many times, he would share a story with me only after being bombarded by my single-minded repetitive questions. His reticence was even more evident when it came to dramatic stories. It was only afterwards that I realized that true war heroes don't like to recollect horrible battle scenes. When I told people I was writing his biography, everybody who knew him readily accepted my interview request. The only exception was one particular commander of the 2nd

Battalion, 31st Infantry Regiment, who stated that he didn't want to talk about the Korean War ever again.

Because Kim's community service was relatively recent, and because most of the work he was involved in was successfully executed, he left an indelible mark in Southern California and my research in this area was not difficult. But discovering exactly what had happened in the Korean War was never easy. War is a world where complete chaos prevails and veterans who fought in the same battle often have memories that are entirely different. Some don't recall the battle at all. The U.S. Army attempts to leave detailed battle records, and although these were instrumental to me, they didn't always tell the truth. Because of this, verifying the accuracy of those records was one of my toughest tasks.

When it came to battles, my primary sources of information were Kim's testimonies, other veterans' testimonies, memos and memoirs, U.S. Army units' command reports and battlefield bulletins and newspapers. Secondary sources were local newspapers, magazines, books, theses and experts' testimonies. I made it a rule to visit actual sites as much as possible. In the case of the Vosges Mountains in France and the Soyang River in Korea, I had to go back twice, because I realized something didn't fit quite well after I had started writing at home.

I am not a professional book writer, and I know I haven't such talent, so I tried hard to write a documentary. This book is strictly nonfiction. The names of people and places, times and weather conditions are all real. The conversations in quotations are not products of my imagination. Because of this, some pieces of the story are not connected very smoothly. I was tempted to use my imagination (and was actually prompted to do so), but I did not. I acknowledge the lack of smoothness in the story, but I still chose to publish what I had. Because I knew the hero, who was suffering from cancer and had gone through his third surgery, would leave us soon.

There is one more thing I'd like to add. Although it was very late, Korea officially decided to award Young Oak Kim the Taeguk Order of Military Merit, the highest military decoration of Korea in 2005. France had awarded him the Legion d'Honneur, the highest military decoration of France in 2003. Italy had already awarded him the Military Valor Cross, the highest military decoration of Italy back in 1946.

The United States, however, has not yet given fair recognition to its own hero, who fought in three different countries, in two separate wars, and has received the highest decorations from three other countries. The U.S. has awarded Young Oak Kim one Distinguished Service Cross, two Silver Stars, two Region of Merits, two Bronze Stars and three Purple Hearts, but not the Medal of Honor. I truly believe that America is the best country in the world, but when it comes to racial equality, America still has a long way to go. If there is one more addition to America's injustices, it is our lack of interest in what this beautiful hero has done for all of us.

This book was not written as just another military tribute to a soldier. It is part of a civil rights campaign. The "Go For Broke Monument" erected in Los Angeles in 1999 carries the names of each and every Japanese American soldier who fought for this country in World War II. The Japanese American community hails this monument as a prominent symbol of our civil rights movement rather than just a simple war memorial. I agree. The story of Young Oak Kim is not a story of a war hero with decorations on his chest like ornaments on a Christmas tree. Nor is it a story about someone who accidentally turned out to be a humanitarian activist after retirement. To America, Kim's story answers the question of whether Korean Americans, and Asian Americans in the broader sense, are valuable assets to this country. To Korea, his story answers the question of whether Korean emigrants are really those who jump off a sinking ship first. His story also depicts what kind of relationship is desired between the U.S. and Korea, as well as between Japan and Korea.

In this book, readers will be treated to a wonderful human being. He was born in an era of darkness, became a legendary war hero, dedicated his life to the socially underprivileged, and eventually became someone we could hold a candle to—all while overcoming severe racial discrimination, poverty and physical disability.

"If young people can have hope and courage from my story, that's enough for me."

Citing his humble statement here, I present his story to all the young people of today and tomorrow.

Los Angeles, December 2005

Part I
World War II

Chapter 1
Liberation of Rome

The Allied Forces landed in Italy in September 1943, but the Gustav Line remained unbroken six months later. Stretching from the Mediterranean Sea to the Adriatic Sea across the mid-southern section of Italy, the Gustav Line was the key German defense against the Allied advance northward. The Allied Forces made a bold move—a surprise landing at Anzio, a port just south of Rome, above the Gustav Line. Although using just two divisions, the attack was a major success, threatening the Gustav Line from the north while positioning Allied Forces for an immediate attack on Rome, which was defended at the time by only a handful of Germans. Nevertheless, the general in charge of the operation, Major General John Lucas, was overly cautious and delayed the attack on Rome. This delay allowed the Germans to redeploy forces from northern Italy to Rome and Anzio. Had the Allied Forces immediately followed the Anzio landing with an attack on Rome, the city would have fallen without bloodshed within hours. Instead, the Allied Forces and the Germans dug in and their positions hardened to a stalemate.

This was the situation when Lieutenant General Mark Clark devised his plan. Clark, a politically savvy soldier with ambitions of martial glory, decided to launch an all-out attack on Rome before the start of the Normandy Landings. His plan was for the Allied Forces to attack Rome from the relatively steep south side rather than attacking through the flatlands in the southwestern part of Rome. Since the south side was dimpled with the Mussolini Canal and many small swamps, this was the best way the Allied Forces could attack with tanks.

German tanks were feared instruments of war at the time. More powerful than American tanks, they could turn an Allied attack into a suicide mission if they were stumbled upon unexpectedly. The Allies had recently lost track of the position of the German tank division. It was critically important to locate this division before proceeding. Failure to locate the deadly tank division could turn the Italian front against the Allies.

The strategy for obtaining this information was simple enough: capture German prisoners of war. Fifth Army Headquarters issued several orders to get POWs. Major General Charles Ryder, commander of the 34th Division and a man who usually did not issue unreasonable orders, pressed his men to capture German soldiers immediately. On several occasions, Americans sent platoons and once an entire company to get POWs. All attempts failed.

Now it was the 100th Battalion's turn. As the battalion intelligence officer, First Lieutenant Young Oak Kim felt it was his responsibility to capture German prisoners. He went to see Lieutenant Colonel Gordon Singles, his battalion commander.

"If you send me out, I will bring back Germans," he said.

"That's crazy," replied Singles, refusing to approve the risky plan.

"I promise to come back alive," Young Oak said.

Although Singles was against it, Young Oak insisted. Young Oak already had a plan. He felt that previous patrols had failed because they had gone out at night, when the enemy was most alert. His thought was that it would be easier to capture German POWs during the day. The Germans would never anticipate that the enemy would attempt to cross into their territory in broad daylight. Young Oak followed German soldier activities through his binoculars and discovered that they went to sleep right after breakfast. The Allied Forces had been alerted to guard against German infiltration at night, but were allowed to relax during the day. The Germans were no different. Young Oak also believed that too many men had been sent out on previous patrols. So he decided to infiltrate German territory with just one other soldier.

The battalion headquarters, regimental headquarters, division headquarters and Fifth Army Headquarters did not want to approve Young Oak's suicide mission. But, 10 days after he had first submitted his plan to Singles, they finally let him go. Once Young Oak received approval, he began to work out the specifics. He requested and received hundreds of aerial photographs from the division every day. He studied them carefully, and double-checked the terrain and German positions with his binoculars. This was his element. He was born with a very special talent for map reading. He could recreate maps into 3-D images in his mind and had a photographic memory. It was a gift from heaven for an infantry officer. Young Oak began etching all the details of the German camp into his memory.

The Allied Forces were positioned in the middle of the Anzio plain while the German forces occupied the mountain areas. This allowed the Germans to monitor Allied movements. The forces were separated by a "no-man's land"—a treeless plain split lengthwise in front of each position. Each side had also buried thousands of land mines in the area to prevent even wild dogs from crossing safely. It seemed impossible to cross this stretch. In addition, each side had dug long trenches behind its barbed wire. Behind the trenches were numerous individual foxholes, and behind those were underground bunkers. At night, both sides positioned themselves in the long trenches and retreated in the early morning. Soldiers, however, remained all day inside the individual foxholes. Since each side shot at anything that was seen moving, any movement into or out of the individual foxholes was attempted only at night.

Young Oak would have a tough nighttime journey to the other side. He would have to cross in this order: Allied side's underground bunker, individual foxholes, long trench, barbed wire, and then the Allies' minefield. Once he entered enemy territory, he would have to pass through the enemy minefield, barbed wire, and the trench. Once through to the other side, he would have to hide himself until sunrise, and then, when the sun rose, move quickly to capture German POWs.

Because of the danger involved in the mission, Young Oak wanted to call for a volunteer. After a meeting, Young Oak came back to the battalion intelligence section, and calmly announced to the room, as if he were looking for a picnic companion for the next day, "I have to capture German POWs. Does anyone want to go with me?" He was always like that. He never raised his voice, regardless of the circumstances, and his cool attitude inspired confidence and trust in his men. As soon as he was done talking, all four men in the section volunteered: Sergeant Yoshio Minami, Private Irving Akahoshi, Private James Kubokawa, and another soldier. Due to the severe casualties in the battalion during previous battles, only four soldiers had remained in the intelligence section. Sergeant Minami, Private Akahoshi and Private Kubokawa all hailed from Honolulu, Hawaii and called themselves the "Three Musketeers." Originally, they had been assigned to an antitank unit. When they heard Young Oak's platoon needed replacements after its first battle in Italy, all three requested transfer to his unit. When Young Oak was wounded and evacuated to a field hospital during the battle at Santa Maria Olivetto, they did not want to stay in the 2nd Platoon under the new platoon leader, and all three men volunteered for the intelligence section. These men, among others, felt a powerful loyalty toward Young Oak. Young Oak told the men that he would think it over, and dismissed them.

The next morning, Young Oak announced his decision to leave Sergeant Minami behind in case he was captured or killed in action. Sergeant Minami was the best man to take over the intelligence section in his absence. Private Kubokawa changed his mind and decided to drop out, as he was the only son in his family. The other soldier was married, so he was excluded from consideration. Young Oak was left with Private Akahoshi. Sergeant Minami, usually quiet and obedient, looked at Young Oak resentfully when he heard the final decision. Private Akahoshi was born in Kumamoto, Japan as the youngest of four sons and four daughters of very poor parents. He was drafted a month before the Pearl Harbor attack. His next older brother enlisted after Pearl Harbor and was fighting against Japan in the Pacific. Private Akahoshi volunteered for the mission because he liked the idea of infiltrating enemy territory with just one other soldier. Young Oak knew that Private Akahoshi, while extremely shy, was not one to back down. In Young Oak's mind, Private Akahoshi was the right man for the mission.

On May 16, Young Oak chose a route secured by B Company, commanded by Captain Sakae Takahashi. Young Oak requested that Captain Takahashi cut just enough barbed wire on their side for one person to go through. He also asked for the mines to be cleared on the path where they were to cross. At 10:30 p.m. Young Oak and Akahoshi were supposed to meet with the company's best Browning Automatic Rifle men at the farmhouse that was being used as B Company's command post. The BAR men were needed to protect Young Oak and Akahoshi when they returned from German territory. As planned,

Young Oak and Akahoshi arrived at the farmhouse at 10:30 p.m. It was early summer, but nights in Italy were still cold. Both had to wear heavy underwear. Each carried only a pistol, a Thompson submachine gun, and two grenades. Young Oak, Private Akahoshi and Captain Takahashi's party immediately left the farmhouse. Hours later, they arrived at the American trench behind the barbed wire. From there, only Young Oak and Private Akahoshi were to advance. Captain Takahashi looked at Young Oak for a while, then shook his hand to bid him farewell. With a firm grasp of his hand, the captain hugged Young Oak with tears in his eyes and mumbled,

"Young, you are crazy. This could be our last..." his voice trailed off.

Young Oak wanted to say something back to him, but couldn't. He was preoccupied with the immediate task of crossing the minefields. He gestured to Private Akahoshi to begin their mission.

After Young Oak and Private Akahoshi had passed through the Allied side, they entered the German minefield. They crawled forward slowly, using their hands and fingers to scan the ground in front of them for mines before proceeding. In the darkness, they could hear the sounds of the B Company soldiers returning to their positions. The BAR men were supposed to stay in the foxholes to wait for Young Oak and Private Akahoshi to return. That itself was a dangerous gamble as well. The BAR men were ordered not to eat anything to prevent them from making noise. Young Oak and Private Akahoshi continued to crawl forward, carefully using their hands to sweep the ground in front of them before moving. Germans used two types of mines at the time: mines that exploded immediately when someone stepped on them and mines that exploded when someone touched the attached wires. The Germans planted the mines very cleverly.

In the pitch dark, it took 40 minutes for them just to crawl through the narrow German minefield. When they reached the barbed wire fence they could observe the movements of German soldiers. They carefully cut the barbed wire. The cutting sounds were masked by strong winds, and they made their way through the fence. Once through, they were in enemy territory, close enough to the enemy that they felt they could touch their helmets. At that moment, they had no choice but to lie on the ground silently and wait in the dark. The cold penetrated their bodies from the ground, but they couldn't move or cough.

At about 2:00 a.m., the German soldiers returned to their camps in a single line. Young Oak and Akahoshi followed them, staying 10 to 15 yards behind. The heavily armed Germans paid no attention to anything behind them, probably because they were returning to their base after a long night. Sometimes, the German soldiers randomly shot toward the direction of U.S. troops from their foxholes, presumably to prevent any American encroachment. But American protocol was the opposite; soldiers were ordered not to shoot at unidentified objects so they could keep their positions hidden. For Young Oak and Akahoshi, it was a blessing as they were able to precisely locate enemy positions. As a result, they knew they had passed through two German positions. Young Oak and Akahoshi saw German soldiers enter the underground bunker. Young Oak and Akahoshi retreated to a small ditch Young Oak had identified in aerial photographs. They used the ditch as a hideout as they waited for dawn. Their target was a pillbox, located at a place that Young Oak called "Twin Tree," because German soldiers manned two machine gun nests side-by-side, between two trees. From the position of the pillbox and machine gun nests on the low hill, Young Oak expected that there would be a German headquarters nearby. For the purposes of this mission, Young Oak wanted to capture German soldiers who worked at the headquarters. His plan was to carry out a surprise attack on the pillbox, capture two German POWs, and kill the others. Since the Germans were heavily armed, it was a risky plan.

As dawn approached, the winds carried sounds of Germans talking and metal clanking. Young Oak and Akahoshi could clearly hear the voices of German soldiers and the noise they made cleaning their weapons. They signaled to each other that everything was going according to plan, waited patiently and held their breath. Young Oak slowly pulled out his left arm to glance at his watch. It was about 9:00 a.m.—time for the Germans to eat breakfast and go to sleep. As Young Oak signaled to Private Akahoshi, he hoped his calculations had been correct. The entire mission was based on Young Oak's belief that the Germans would never expect just one or two enemies to infiltrate their base, especially during the day. Young Oak and Akahoshi exited the ditch into wheat fields and began to crawl, low enough so that their faces almost touched the ground. They could not breathe deeply, for fear that this would raise their backs too high, so they crawled in wide arcs. They crept slowly, stopped frequently to check for danger, then inched forward again, repeating this painstaking process until they eventually reached the rear of the pillbox.

Private Akahoshi could not help but imagine Young Oak's body exploding from a mine into pieces. It was highly unlikely, since their body weight was evenly distributed on the ground, but Akahoshi was wary. He also thought about what he would do if Young Oak's body flew into the air. In his mind, two possible scenarios could ensue: he could rush out with his machine gun drawn and shoot toward the German soldiers, or he could run away. Private Akahoshi chuckled to himself about these wild thoughts, although the American soldiers who were observing them found little humor in the situation.

The American soldiers, including Lieutenant Colonel Singles, were scarcely breathing while watching the movements with their binoculars. B Company commander Takahashi, enveloped in the events as they unfolded in front of him, found his breathing matched that of Young Oak's and Private Akahoshi's. It took a while for Young Oak and Akahoshi to crawl about 250 yards. Fortunately, strong winds concealed the trail of bent grass they left behind. The wheat had grown knee high, covering them completely.

Suddenly, Young Oak could hear the sound of snoring. He froze in his place. Two German soldiers were sleeping inside a small dugout nearby. Young Oak snuck in a half-circle around the dugout while Akahoshi approached it from the front. The two German soldiers were sound asleep, unaware they were being observed by the enemy. The dugout was too small for a person to stretch his legs, so the two soldiers had their legs folded under them and their heads against the wall sleeping with their mouths open.

Young Oak and Private Akahoshi quickly stuck their submachine guns into the mouth of each German. The German soldiers awoke to the chill of metal in their mouths, fear spreading quickly over their faces. Young Oak signaled them to put down their weapons and raise their hands, and the German soldiers nodded quietly. When they laid down their rifles, Akahoshi quietly kicked them away. Akahoshi placed his submachine gun on his back, grabbed a grenade fastened to his chest, and looked at Young Oak. As Young Oak nodded, Akahoshi laid the grenade on the ground without removing the safety pin. This was to let other Germans know that the two soldiers had been captured by Americans. Akahoshi felt it would be unfair for the enemy soldiers to be mistaken for deserters.

Young Oak and Akahoshi ordered the German soldiers out of their dugout and then made them crawl toward no-man's land. One German soldier crawled in front, followed by Private Akahoshi, followed by the other German soldier. Young Oak brought up the rear. With their prize in hand, Young Oak and Akahoshi chose a direct route back to headquarters. Since their number had increased to four, the chance of them being spotted by Germans was greater. Fortunately, the Germans paid no attention to what was happening in their own territory. The four kept crawling until they had passed the barbed wire on the American side. It was much easier for them to cross the minefield during the day. Once on the other side, they pushed the prisoners into the foxholes where the BAR men were waiting. Immediately, Young Oak reported to Singles that they had accomplished their mission. Now all they had to do was wait until evening.

At around 7:00 p.m., it grew dark, and soldiers returned to their respective foxholes. When Young Oak and Akahoshi returned to B Company headquarters, a jeep dispatched from division headquarters was waiting.

The two German guests were a sergeant and a private. They did not reveal much, but the Americans were able to gain a very important piece of information before the interrogation even began: the Germans' uniforms and unit insignia revealed they were not part of the tank unit.

The Allied Forces became excited about the news of the capture of the two German soldiers. As soon as Young Oak returned to his unit, he reported to regimental headquarters, division headquarters, corps headquarters and army headquarters. The battalion commander was still high in spirits when Young Oak returned to his unit.

"Congratulations, Young, you just got a Distinguished Service Cross!" he said.

"Unbelievable. Only the paper work will take more than three months," Young Oak replied.

"It's true. I just got a call from General Clark. If you were here three minutes earlier, you could have received the call yourself. General Clark also wanted to deliver his personal congratulations."

A UPI war correspondent reported the daring mission of Young Oak and Akahoshi to the world. A month later, Lieutenant General Clark himself presided over the award ceremony. As he pinned the medal on Young Oak's chest, the general recognized him.

"Aren't you the same lieutenant whom I gave a Silver Star to a few months ago?" he asked.

"Yes, sir," Young Oak replied.

"Why are you still a first lieutenant?"

"I didn't get the promotion order, sir."

Lieutenant General Clark immediately called over his aide, took off the aide's captain's bars, and pinned them on Young Oak's collars. After ordering his aide to take care of the necessary documents for the promotion, Lieutenant General Clark turned back toward Young Oak.

"This is a mistake," Clark said. "You should have received a Medal of Honor. I will not repeat the same mistake again. I apologize."

The day after the capture of the two German soldiers, Division Commander Ryder visited battalion headquarters to meet Young Oak in person. Major General Ryder congratulated Young Oak on what he had accomplished and slipped a word to Young Oak that Allied Forces were planning a full-scale attack based on the information obtained from the two German POWs. The attack that Major General Ryder mentioned was "Operation Buffalo," which began on May 23, 1944. Because of

Operation Buffalo, the Allied Forces smashed the last German line of defense and liberated Rome on June 4—two days before the Normandy invasion.

The government of Italy presented Young Oak with a Bronze Cross of Military Valor immediately after the liberation of Rome. In 1946, the Italian government reevaluated his accomplishments and awarded him a Cross of Military Valor, its highest military decoration at the time.

Chapter 2
Immigrant Family

Young Oak's parents arrived in the United States early last century, around the time of Japan's colonization of Korea. Young Oak's father, Soon Kwon Kim, was from Incheon. He graduated from Kyungshin High School, which was founded by American missionaries. As the shadow of Japan loomed over Korea, he decided to go to America. After several unsuccessful attempts, he finally smuggled himself into the country on his third try. Perhaps his determination came from the missionaries at his school who likely filled the young Mr. Kim's imagination with stories of America.

He arrived in Hawaii in or before 1906 and worked hard on a sugar plantation to save enough money to go to the mainland. At the time, most Asian immigrants who journeyed to the mainland from Hawaii first landed in Seattle. Mr. Kim and his cohorts worked on local farms to make money for travel and made their way south, eventually reaching Los Angeles. Young Oak's mother, Nora Koh, was born in Suwon, and graduated from Ewha Woman's University. She majored in theology and taught Bible classes in Seoul for several years. She wanted to continue her education in America, but instead went on to become a professor in Korea. Eventually, she arrived accompanied by American missionaries in Seattle in June 1916. The immigration officer insisted that her husband be notified of her whereabouts. Despite her objections, they sent a telegram to Mr. Kim. As a result, she was forced to join her husband in Los Angeles and give up her dream of continuing her education. Their life in Los Angeles was not what she had hoped for; she toiled as a manual laborer.

Regardless of background, most Koreans who came to America worked as manual laborers and lived paycheck to paycheck. Still, many were able to save enough money and build up enough credit to open grocery stores, fruit stores and laundromats. Some tried to start up restaurants, but the small number of Koreans in America limited their clientele.

Initially, Young Oak's parents worked as manual laborers, but they were able to save money to acquire a grocery store in downtown Los Angeles. They bought the store from another Korean immigrant couple who had, in turn, purchased it from a Caucasian owner. The previous Korean owners had succeeded in purchasing the store by working diligently, but they encountered many problems due to their limited English. They could not communicate with salesmen or comprehend their utility bills. Since they were unable to run the business effectively, they sold it to Young Oak's father, who had studied English in night class and spoke it fluently.

Mr. Kim and Nora had six children in all: four boys and two girls. Young Oak had an older sister, but he was the eldest son. He was born in 1919. His father gave him a Korean name: Young Oak. Young Oak grew up helping out in his parents' grocery store, which was located in a wealthy white neighborhood in downtown Los Angeles and included Hollywood personalities among its patrons. Young Oak often delivered items to these customers.

At the time, only a few privileged people had access to a telephone. Since the store had a telephone, it was a sign that the store was doing very well. His father's English was an asset, but it was his mother who worked hard to maintain the business. Despite the store's success, his family was always short on cash. Young Oak and his siblings disliked their father because they believed they were poor because of him.

Young Oak's father liked to drink. Mr. Kim would invite his friends over almost every weekend. Since most were single and lonely, his mother would always prepare Korean food and serve alcohol for her husband's guests without complaining. The men spent all night drinking, eating and talking. Young Oak could not understand why his father continued to hold these Saturday soirees every week when it created extra work for his mother. His mother was tired enough, working seven days a week in the store. From Young Oak's point of view, his father had failed in his duty to support the family. He was a failure as a businessman, husband and father.

What Young Oak and his siblings were too young to know was that their father was very active in the Korean independence movement. According to the New Korea, a newspaper published at that time, Mr. Kim was the wealthiest Korean in Southern California in terms of business capital. Yet the family was always short on cash because his father had promised to donate more money to the movement than he was earning.

The people who came every Saturday night were members of the Dongjihoe (Comrades' Association). The Dongjihoe was established in Hawaii by Syngman Rhee, who later became the first president of the Republic of Korea. The Dongjihoe moved its headquarters to the mainland, and in 1929, the Dongjihoe established its headquarters in Los Angeles. Many Korean leaders belonged to the Dongjihoe, including Alfred Song, the first Asian American elected to the California State Legislature, and Soon Ki Lee, father of Dr. Sammy Lee, two-time U.S. Olympic gold medalist in diving. Its members called their financial contributions for the "Patriotic Fund," an independence movement campaign. Some members even delayed marriage so they could contribute to the fund.

Mr. Kim subscribed to two English newspapers and, as a result, he became knowledgeable about American politics and international relations. Although he could not vote—Asian immigrants were not eligible to become naturalized citizens at the time—he knew each candidate's background and pledges. At the dinner table, Mr. Kim often spoke about politics, heavily influencing the environment in which Young Oak and his siblings grew up.

"It seems to me Korea will not gain independence during my lifetime," Mr. Kim told his children. "Therefore, it will be almost impossible for you to go back to Korea. You should learn to live as Americans. Learn how to think and act like Americans." For this reason, Young Oak and his siblings ate American dishes at least once a day.

Since Young Oak's father was busy with politics, his mother was responsible for running the business. Small businesses usually stayed open for long hours, seven days a week. She opened the store at 6:00 a.m. and closed it at 10:00 p.m. Nora was a devoted Christian, but she could not attend church on Sundays because she had to work at the store. Nevertheless, she had her husband go to church with the children every Sunday. Although Mr. Kim was not a devoted Christian, he attended church on Sundays because he could talk about his favorite subject—politics—with other Koreans. These conversations often continued long after the service ended.

The Korean community was very small in the 1920s, with about 1,000 immigrants living in Southern California. There were three important tasks for Korean immigrants at the time: working, attending church, and participating in independence activities. In particular, Korean immigrants considered attending church and rallying for independence to be on the same path. However, disagreement over how to achieve independence divided the Korean immigrant community. Supporters of Mr. Syngman Rhee attended one church, while those who supported Mr. Ahn Chang Ho attended a rival church. These two leaders of the Korean immigrant community disagreed over how to achieve independence for Korea and often clashed.

Young Oak's father was a strong supporter of Syngman Rhee. When Rhee came to Los Angeles, he often stayed at Young Oak's house. Rhee, who had no children of his own, had considered adopting Young Oak's younger sister. When Ahn Chang Ho died of tuberculosis after being tortured by the Japanese police in Korea in 1938, Rhee sent Young Oak's father as his delegate to the funeral service.

Although Young Oak's mother was the most devoted Christian in the family, she was the only person who was unable to attend church. Still, she prayed for 30 minutes every morning upon rising and again every evening before going to bed. Some of Young Oak's fondest memories of his mother were of her praying or working at the store. In stark contrast to how Young Oak viewed his father, Young Oak viewed his mother as a devoted wife and a successful businesswoman, and the sacrifice she made in giving up her studies was never lost on him.

Persimmons were one of her favorite fruits. At the time, they were brought in from Central California. She could not afford to buy persimmons for each family member, so she often bought just three or four of them and would place them on the windowsill so they could dry in the sun. Young Oak liked to watch the greenish persimmons turn orange as they ripened. At times his mother would scold him for eating one before it was ripe. Around the dinner table, Young Oak and his family would enjoy these ripened persimmons together.

Once, when Young Oak was 12 years old, his mother assumed he had done something wrong, although he denied it. Convinced that she was right and wanting to teach him a lesson, she went out and got three thick sticks and whipped him on the calves, hitting him so hard that the first stick broke.

"Why are you not remorseful and why won't you say you won't do it again?" she chastised him.

"I didn't do it," Young Oak pleaded.

He refused to cry or apologize for something he had not done. Nora whipped him more. But this time, she begged Young Oak to apologize.

"Just say 'I'm sorry' and I won't do it again," she said.

"No," he responded. "I did not do it."

Believing that Young Oak was lying, his mother continued to whip him. Young Oak's calf began to bleed. After breaking her third whip, his mother embraced Young Oak's calf, and began to cry.

"You are a very stubborn boy," she sobbed.

Young Oak remained silent.

"Other children would have begged for forgiveness and cried out loud. But you refused to cry or apologize until your calf bled. My arms are tired from whipping you. I do not know what to do. You won. This is the last time I will whip you. I will not do this anymore. When you grow up, you will either become a hero or a felon."

No one else knew what happened between Young Oak and his mother that day. They never talked about the incident again. Later, Young Oak's older sister Willa heard what had happened from her mother.

With the exception of his parents, Young Oak's older sister Willa was the most influential person during his childhood. When the Kims had their first daughter, they named her Willa because it was the closest pronunciation to the Korean word wolla, which means "Moon of Los Angeles." Although Young Oak's father was knowledgeable about American political and social issues, he knew very little about American customs and ways of thinking. Willa taught Young Oak how to speak and dress properly. She was always regarded as extremely bright and later she became an internationally renowned costume designer, winning two Tony Awards and two Emmy Awards.

After the Great Depression of the 1930s, many intellectuals turned to socialist political philosophy. In her early twenties, Willa became enchanted by such ideals and tried to persuade Young Oak to learn more about them. However, since childhood he was not the kind of person to take another's opinion without studying the issue himself. He expanded his knowledge on socialism by not only listening to Willa and her friends but by also reading many books on socialism, including Karl Marx's *The Communist Manifesto*. However, he came to different conclusions than Willa.

Sometimes, Young Oak had to pay a small price because of Willa's involvement with socialist activities. A year after she graduated from high school, Willa was involved with the "China Relief" bazaar held at the Shrine Auditorium in Los Angeles. The bazaar was organized to support the government of China. The previous December, Japan had killed hundreds of thousands of Chinese civilians in Nanjing. This event was widely known as the Nanjing Massacre. Young Oak decided to accompany Willa to help her sell items to raise funds. Along the way, he was arrested by the police for violating a city ordinance. He was fined $25, but the charges were later overturned because the ordinance violated federal law.

When Young Oak attended Central Middle School in Los Angeles, he was not aware that he was a minority, since the diverse student body included Caucasian, Chinese, Japanese, Mexican and Jewish children. However, the situation changed completely when he started attending Belmont High School. Most students were white and they overtly discriminated against minority students. The school allowed minority students to participate in regular school subjects and sports activities, but they were strictly prohibited from participating in other extracurricular activities.

"Where are you from?" many students asked Young Oak.

"Korea."

"Where is Korea? Is it China or is it Japan? Is it a country? We can't find it on the map!"

"Korea is Korea!" Young Oak would reply.

His parents had educated him to take pride in being a Korean, so he possessed a strong Korean identity. And yet, he felt somewhat depressed every time he had to answer questions like this. In particular, he felt angry when people asked if Korea was the same as Japan. His parents had told him many times not to associate with any Japanese students at school. He was also not allowed to eat Japanese food. Although his family did not eat out often, when they did go out, they dined at either Mexican or Chinese restaurants—never at Japanese restaurants. The family also did not dine at American restaurants, where they were usually treated badly or met with unwelcome stares from white customers. Owners did not display open hostility toward his family, but they intentionally poured extra salt on their food. Italian restaurants were similar, as they did not want Asian customers in their restaurants for fear of losing white customers.

The lessons Young Oak learned while navigating his way through high school were similarly tinged with racial overtones. White student bullies often picked on Asian or Jewish students, rather than on Mexican or Italian students, because Asians and Jews were deemed physically weak. The bullies became even more aggressive if the Asian and Jewish students tried to avoid them. So Young Oak never backed down against them. They were physically bigger and stronger, but he never gave up in a fight. Eventually they left him alone and became friends with him.

America was—and remains—a land of immigrants, but minorities faced much more overt discrimination at the time. Not all minorities experienced the same racial discrimination, though. The degree of discrimination varied across Asian groups.

The Chinese arguably faced the worst discrimination, despite the fact that they made valuable contributions in the development of the Western frontier. Chinese immigration stopped completely with the passage of the Chinese Exclusion Act of 1882. The Chinese also could not testify against white persons in court.

Japan's victory in the Sino-Japanese War in 1894 and Russo-Japanese War in 1905 made Japan a major superpower in the world. Unlike the Chinese, who faced complete exclusion, Japanese immigrants were able to bring "picture brides" to the U.S., after Japan signed the Gentleman's Agreement with the United States in 1907.

The status of Korean immigrants was a bit more unclear, as Korea became a colony of Japan in 1910. The Japanese government decided to prohibit Korean immigration to the United States in order to protect the economic interests of Japanese immigrants in Hawaii. This was one of the main reasons why the number of Korean immigrants remained small and the Korean American community did not grow, both in terms of quantity and quality, during the early 1900s.

In general, however, Asian Americans were heavily regulated and often restricted from participating in American mainstream culture. Discriminatory restaurant owners and school bullies aside, the Alien Land Law of 1913 prohibited Asian immigrants from leasing or owning land in California. In a capitalist economy, accumulating wealth without the ability to own land is difficult. Therefore, Asian immigrants had to work extra hard and long hours in order to become wealthy.

For Korean immigrants, education was one of the most important reasons for coming to America. Young Oak's mother insisted that he attend college and that was the main reason he went to Belmont High School—a college preparatory school. He graduated from Belmont and attended Los Angeles City College, but he was not happy at all. He knew other students who did very well in college, but still ended up working at vegetable stores, laundromats or butcher shops. Because of racial discrimination, Asian Americans were not given opportunities to pursue professional occupations, regardless of whether they had a college degree or not. Against his mother's wishes, Young Oak dropped out of college after his freshman year, and began to wander. He found employment as a farm hand, salesman, meat-cutter, rickshaw puller, and automobile mechanic, but he was unhappy with these situations. Finally, with the outbreak of World War II, Young Oak volunteered for the Army. But the Army rejected him because at the time Asians were not allowed to serve in the military. Though a natural-born American citizen, he was denied the opportunity to serve simply because of his race.

However one day he received a draft letter from the Army. Congress had passed legislation subjecting Asian Americans to the draft. He was enlisted as a private in the U.S. Army in January 1941. Three months after his enlistment, his father died of liver cancer, without seeing his dream of Korean independence come true.

After Young Oak completed basic training in the 17th Regiment, 7th Division, an officer told him that he could be assigned as a cook, mechanic, or supply clerk. Young Oak didn't understand. He wanted to become a combat soldier, not a cook or clerk.

"How come I can't become a combat soldier?" he asked.

"What? Are you out of your mind? You have the wrong eyes. Slanted eyes won't make a real soldier."

It really did not matter that Young Oak had hit all 10 bullseyes during his first target practice—an impressive feat considering he had never touched a gun—his ethnicity was all anyone needed to know.

"Anyway, think about it," the training officer said. "We have too many cooks and clerks. You know where you'll be assigned."

This meant that Young Oak would be assigned as a mechanic.

"I don't know anything about machines," Young Oak said.

"Don't worry. We will send you to mechanics school."

Perhaps they decided to send him to mechanics school because he had attended auto mechanic school prior to his enlistment. In any case, Young Oak began his military career as a mechanic. Soon afterwards, the 7th Division was transformed into a mechanized unit and Young Oak began fixing buses, trucks, jeeps and other equipment. He quickly became a skillful mechanic.

Of course, serving as a mechanic—however skilled—was not what Young Oak had in mind when he originally volunteered, and was eventually drafted into the Army. However, fate intervened. On December 7, 1941, Japan launched an attack on Pearl Harbor. The United States now had no choice but to enter World War II. A year after Pearl Harbor, Young Oak's company commander handed him a packet of documents while he was training in the desert.

"Sign them," said the commander.

"What's this?" Young Oak asked.

"You are going to Fort Benning."

Fort Benning was where the U.S. Army Officer Candidate School was located. The Army was suffering from a shortage of young officers.

"I haven't fired a single shot since basic training," Young Oak said.

"Don't worry. The war is going to end soon. You are smart and highly educated. I think you will become a good officer. It's a waste if you stay here."

Young Oak became the first Asian American to attend Officer Candidate School in U.S. military history. He had experienced racial discrimination throughout his life, and he had never expected that an Asian would be given the opportunity to become an officer.

An officer in the American military was considered elite. His doubts were so heavy that he felt he might be rejected by the OCS despite the company commander's recommendation. But when he was accepted, he made a simple promise to himself: "I will do my best. I will never be kicked out for not trying."

Young Oak began his training in November 1942. He was lucky to be selected and admitted into the Officer Candidate School in Fort Benning, Georgia, a school where he wasn't just the only Asian, but the only minority. As Young Oak progressed in his training, he gained confidence in himself, no longer believing the myth of white superiority.

The training revealed that Young Oak was a born soldier. In particular, he possessed a talent for accurately reading maps and a keen sense of direction. He could visualize maps in 3-D, somehow knowing exactly where he was, even in unfamiliar territory. For an infantry officer, these skills are a matter of life or death. Fortunately, Young Oak possessed this extraordinary skill—in 3-D, no less.

Still, it was not easy to complete the three-month training. Anyone who didn't meet the requirements was disqualified and kicked out. Others quit because they couldn't endure the rigorous training. At the Officer Candidate School, soldiers were grouped into teams of four. Young Oak's team was the only one that successfully completed training with all its original members. After successfully graduating from OCS in January, his classmates were assigned to different units, but he did not receive any orders. He had to remain at Fort Benning for a few more days without doing anything. He hated wasting his time and complained to his supervisors.

"You are assigned to the 100th Infantry Battalion," he was told. "But they are in the process of relocating to Camp Shelby. Therefore, you should wait a few more days."

Young Oak felt strange that the unit's name was the "100th Battalion." Traditionally in the U.S. Army, three infantry battalions belonged to one infantry regiment, and each battalion was called 1st, 2nd or 3rd battalion. So the name "100th Battalion" was very unusual, as it didn't seem to belong to any regiment or division. But he didn't ask questions. As a soldier, he had been trained to follow orders. In any event, it would be another 10 days before the 100th Battalion arrived at Camp Shelby.

"If that is the case, can I leave here now and join the unit when they arrive at Camp Shelby?" Young Oak asked. The OCS did not want him to sit idle at the school, so they accepted his request. He went to Arkansas to see some friends.

When Japan attacked Pearl Harbor, the United States openly questioned the loyalty of Japanese Americans and interned them with the president's issuance of Executive Order 9066. Nearly 120,000 Japanese Americans were forced to abandon their homes and properties and were sent to internment camps.

Although his mother had prohibited Young Oak from being friends with anybody of Japanese ancestry, he had some Japanese American friends anyway, and they were being held in Arkansas.

"Internment camps," Young Oak quickly realized, in fact closely resembled "concentration camps." The camp was surrounded by barbed wire and dominated by observatory towers with searchlights and machine guns. He was stunned to see the machine guns pointing towards the inside. With his officer uniform on, Young Oak requested to enter the camp. The security guards did not know what to do.

"You'd better go back to Little Rock," they suggested to him, politely.

"I just got off the last bus and there are no rooms available there," he responded.

The security guards got on the phone. Young Oak waited at the checkpoint for a while. Finally, a guard appeared.

"You may go in, sir," said the guard.

The conditions in the internment camp were rough. There was very little privacy. Small cottages were shared by several families. Blankets stood as walls separating families. They all used a common bathroom and they had to eat their meals in a mess hall. Young Oak spent about a week with his Japanese American friends and their families. He became a hero in the eyes of the Japanese Americans, particularly for the young children in the camp. They never missed watching the American soldiers, who were cruel to the internees, but were polite to Young Oak, always calling him "sir."

Chapter 3
The Irony of a Korean American Officer in a Japanese American Unit

Racial minorities were assigned to segregated units during World War II. The 100th Battalion was one such segregated unit. The approximately 1,500 men in the battalion were mostly second-generation Japanese Americans. Almost all the officers were Caucasians or Japanese Americans. The Army did not fully trust the loyalty of these second-generation Japanese American soldiers and secretly transferred the unit from Hawaii to the mainland after the Pearl Harbor attack. The existence of the 100th Battalion was confidential. Since October 1942, the unit was training to be deployable to the frontline with only a 10-day notice.

Young Oak, the son of a Korean immigrant who dedicated his life to expelling the Japanese from his homeland, was assigned to this Japanese-American unit. It was truly ironic. Most likely the Army mistook Young Oak for a Japanese American. When Young Oak's mother came to America, she carried a Japanese passport because Korea was occupied by Japan at the time. So the Army wrote that his mother tongue was Japanese when Young Oak was drafted.

After Young Oak bid farewell to his friends, he went to Camp Shelby Mississippi. The 100th Battalion had already arrived and most of the soldiers were away for field training. Only a few soldiers remained at the base. During the winter, rain is plentiful in Mississippi. Young Oak's first day there, a Sunday, was no exception. It rained endlessly. On his first day in the camp, he met two significant people, the first being Captain Katsumi Kometani.

Young Oak had arrived in the late afternoon and had nothing else to do, so he spoke with Captain Kometani for several hours. He learned that Captain Kometani was a dentist. This was unusual because dentists were not normally assigned to an infantry battalion; they seldom took part in military training. When the 100th Battalion was first established, however, the parents of the Japanese American soldiers wanted a person like Captain Kometani to watch out for their sons. The Army granted their wishes, and Captain Kometani was specially assigned to the 100th Battalion. The soldiers often sought Captain Kometani's counseling with their problems. He became a father figure for the soldiers as he tried to mediate problems between them and the officers. He was always fair to everyone regardless of rank and was always supportive. The 100th Battalion was a special unit with a unique system that eventually added to its effectiveness on the battlefield.

The other significant person Young Oak met at the training camp was Sergeant Mike Miyaki. Prior to Young Oak's arrival, Captain Kometani knew Young Oak would be assigned to B Company so he introduced the B Company supply sergeant Mike Miyaki to Young Oak on the same day.

At around 8:00 a.m. the next morning, Young Oak was awakened by a soldier who told him, "The lieutenant colonel has returned just to meet you." This was Lieutenant Colonel Farrant Turner, the battalion commander, who had returned to the base early when he heard that Young Oak had arrived. Young Oak entered his office, stopped in front of his desk, saluted and said, "Lieutenant Young Kim reporting for duty, sir."

Turner looked up at him and said, "You know, I don't think you realize that this is a Japanese unit. You're Korean. Historically, the Japanese and Koreans don't get along. I'll have you transferred."

"Sir, they're Americans, and I'm an American. We're going to go fight for America, so I want to stay."

The battalion commander looked surprised.

"All the other officers who preceded you and who were not Japanese wanted out. The process has been set up. I can have you transferred first thing in the morning."

"No, sir, I want to stay."

The battalion commander, still surprised, smiled and said, "Well, you can stay, but you're going to be on probation to see how well you get along with the men."

With that Young Oak saluted him and turned around. At that moment, he made a promise to himself: "I will stay, but I will not act cowardly toward other officers and soldiers in order to stay." As a 24-year-old officer, Young Oak believed in the U.S. Constitution and American ideals. His view later changed, but at that time he was young. He was assigned to B Company and was appointed the second platoon leader by the company commander, Captain Clarence Johnson.

It was not an easy task for a Korean American officer to lead a unit full of Japanese American soldiers at a time when Korea was a colony of Japan. A crucial element on the battlefield is mutual respect and trust. Soldiers must trust each other, since the actions of their fellows may determine their own life or death.

It took a considerable amount of time for Young Oak to gain the trust of the men. When he was first assigned as the platoon leader, the soldiers were at field training, so he was unable to meet with them right away. When he eventually saw them, he found that they were undisciplined and thoroughly unprepared for combat. They looked totally unfit to be soldiers. Many failed to wear their uniforms properly; shirts were not tucked into pants, and pants were not tucked into boots. Their hair was long and many wore beards. Instead of wearing military boots, some wore flat shoes and some were even barefoot! Many who wore shoes didn't bother to tie their laces. They were totally undisciplined.

Young Oak dismissed them after a simple greeting. He was at a loss for words. Over the next two days, he let Sergeant Takashi Kitaoka take charge, while he listened in on the soldiers' conversations and observed them closely. He then summoned Sergeant Kitaoka, who graduated from the University of Texas with a law degree and later became a judge after the war. On the morning of December 7, 1941, Kitaoka had just gotten out of bed at home in Honolulu, when he heard the bombs and news of the attack on the radio. The next day, he was ordered to join the army. He was a very intelligent person, seven years older than Young Oak. He was the only platoon soldier who had a good relationship with Young Oak from the beginning.

"What the heck are you guys doing?" Young Oak asked him.

"In fact, we do not know, sir," replied Sergeant Kitaoka.

"Well, that is why I'm asking."

"We've been conducting basic military training, but this is our third basic training session. These men were drafted into the Hawaii National Guard prior to Pearl Harbor. They received their first basic training in the National Guard. Later, they were sent to the 100th Battalion and received the same basic training at Camp McCoy. Now, again, this is our third basic training."

The officers and enlisted men of the 100th Battalion were all tired of repeating the same basic training every day. In the morning, they marched to a comfortable location to hear the morning lecture, got some sleep, and returned to camp after lunch. That's all they did, nothing new.

It was evident that they were receiving the wrong training. The attitudes of the officers were a problem as well. The officers were mostly ROTC graduates or former members of the Hawaii National Guard. They were familiar with basic training, such as marching and military drills. However, they themselves had never received combat training. Therefore they had very little choice but to keep repeating the basic training ritual. And yet, both white and Japanese American officers had too much pride to acknowledge that they lacked knowledge of real combat training.

After the conversation with Kitaoka, Young Oak went to see the company commander. Captain Johnson was a reasonable man with an ROTC background and had served in the Hawaii National Guard before he was assigned to the 100th Battalion. Young Oak expressed his desire to change the training method.

"That is a very good idea," affirmed Commander Johnson. "But, frankly, I don't really know anything about infantry. I'm over 50 years old. I am really worried, however, that they will be sent into battle without adequate preparation. I know we need to change the training method, but how?"

"I have a plan," Young Oak said.

Young Oak suggested changing from individual training to squad, platoon, company, and battalion group training during the next week.

"It looks good," said the commander, "even though I don't really know. If we were to implement a new military training system, we should change it for the entire company. It doesn't make any sense to change just for one platoon. One problem is that you are the most junior second lieutenant in this company. They won't listen to you, so let me try to explain it to two other second lieutenants and First Lieutenant Candy. If Candy agrees with you, then let's do it. I will issue a special order for the other officers and send them to town to enjoy their time off. As for you, revise a week's military plan to a four-month plan and report back to me. I will take a look at it first and approve your plan if it looks good."

"Candy" was a nickname for First Lieutenant Ernest Tanaka. Some people said he earned this nickname because his parents owned a candy store in Hawaii. Others said he got the nickname because he liked candies. Lieutenant Candy opposed Young Oak's plan, but the other second lieutenants liked it. Young Oak finalized a new training manual and submitted it to the company commander and it was approved quickly. Although Lieutenant Candy initially opposed the new plan, he became a strong supporter of it later.

The new regimen was rigorous, beginning at 8:00 a.m. and ending at 5:00 p.m. Young Oak had changed the contents of the training, focusing primarily on simulating real combat situations. All soldiers were expected to take over the squad leader's role, while squad leaders practiced the role of assistant platoon leader or platoon leader, and platoon leaders assumed the role of company commander. They also practiced attacking hills and pillboxes. In order to simulate the real combat experience of attacking enemies under heavy machine gun fire, Young Oak borrowed supplies from division headquarters. Soldiers repeated this new military training until they became sick and tired of it, but before long, they were able to assume new roles seamlessly. The squads no longer had to wait for a direct order from a platoon leader when attacking. When moving under fire, as one squad was shooting, the other two squads moved into new positions. If another squad was shooting, then the other squads moved. This was the product of the training manual Young Oak devised. B Company was the only unit that adopted the new training. The other units ridiculed B Company, but Young Oak was a strongly believed that hard training would save lives in real combat.

After successfully changing the training regimen of his men, Young Oak began to work on their attire. They looked like they had lost the war before even fighting it. Young Oak wanted his men to look like real soldiers: appropriately dressed, clean shaven, shoes polished, and uniforms pressed. This was what he expected as a young officer who had just graduated from Officer Candidate School.

The soldiers complained about the hard training, but they accepted it. However, they refused to adhere to the Army dress code. The Japanese American soldiers from Hawaii simply didn't feel comfortable wearing military boots. They also had no interest in cleaning clothes or polishing boots. They complained that their feet hurt when they wore boots that were too tight. They didn't like to tuck their shirts into their pants. Camp Shelby is located on the Mississippi River and the area is very hot and humid. Most soldiers simply wanted to be comfortable, so they ignored Young Oak's attempt to follow military dress codes. Young Oak eventually gave up on his attempts to change their physical appearance.

As a brand new and demanding officer, Young Oak received several nicknames. One of them was "Yeobo." In Korea, husband and wife call each other Yeobo. The Japanese-American soldiers were aware that Koreans didn't like Japanese. So when Young Oak declined to be transferred out of the battalion in the beginning, the battalion commander's concern about possible friction between him and his men was well-founded. Yeobo was a derogatory term to call a Korean.

His second nickname was "90-Day Wonder," a slang term for those who had graduated from Officer Candidate School with a mere three months of training. By comparison, becoming an officer through ROTC or West Point takes four years. The third was "Kotonk." This was a native Hawaiian slang term for mainlanders. Kotonk mimicked the sound of an empty coconut and symbolically meant "stupid mainlander." Even among the Japanese American soldiers, there was division between the mainlander and Hawaiian divisions. The last one was "G.I. Kim." He was called G.I. Kim because of his harsh, disciplinary military training.

The soldiers pretended to converse with each other, but made sure they spoke loudly enough so that Young Oak could hear them. He could hear the derogatory nicknames, but pretended not to. He thought this was the best way to protect his authority. As he ignored their provocation, they became more aggressive and took more direct action. Whenever they spoke to him, they used Pidgin English. The Japanese American officers began to do this as well.

Pidgin English is a combination of the native Hawaiian language, Japanese, and other languages. It is grammatically incorrect and involves simply mixing different languages. Outsiders couldn't comprehend what they were saying. Young Oak had never heard of Pidgin English. He couldn't understand how some of them had become officers without learning how to speak proper English. Pidgin English was a source of inspiration and unity among the Japanese-American soldiers from Hawaii and was eventually used effectively on the European front because Germans were unable to understand it.

Conflicts always exist in any human relationship. Young Oak and his men came from different and, at times, mutually hostile backgrounds, but they knew they were jointly confronted with important and urgent issues. They were united in a common mission—if orders came, they would be brothers in war. Before joining the war, the men justified and rationalized their military role as defenders of democracy and freedom. But once they were on the front line, they would have to fight to survive. More importantly,

Young Oak and his men knew that many soldiers would never return home alive.

They shared other common experiences. As Asian Americans, they had encountered racial discrimination in America. They had faced discrimination before Pearl Harbor and it worsened afterward. Japanese Americans were expected to prove their loyalty to America while, at the same time, their family members were interned by the U.S. government. Young Oak himself decided to give up his college education and wander around the country because his prospects of finding a good job were slim to none due to racial barriers. Since whites couldn't distinguish Korean Americans from Japanese Americans, Korean Americans were sometimes called "Japs" and had tomatoes thrown at them.

The typical American soldier fought against Nazi Germany or Japan. Japanese-American soldiers, however, waged war on two battlegrounds. Not only did they fight against the military enemy, but they also fought against racism and doubt concerning their patriotism. Young Oak had even a third battle to fight: he had to overcome the prejudice of being a Korean American officer leading Japanese American soldiers.

In the battalion, the officers and soldiers knew what they were fighting for and they discussed these issues openly. Sometimes they all got together and talked, but mostly the officers and soldiers met separately. They would begin discussions on Saturday afternoon and continue into the next day. Young Oak and the other officers always attended this weekly discussion. During breaks, they would play poker and sing songs. The main point of the meetings, however, was to discuss why they had to fight. They were not forced to attend meetings, but did anyhow because it helped them mentally prepare for the war.

One day, the 100th Battalion received the order to move: the destination was the port of Oran in North Africa. Finally, they were being sent to the frontline. Young Oak and the Japanese-American soldiers, who sweated together in training, were now to shed blood together on the battlefield. On August 21, 1943, Young Oak and his men boarded the James Parker, a cruise liner that had been converted into a military transportation ship. The James Parker slowly set sail out of New York. They watched the Statue of Liberty fade into the horizon.

Chapter 4
The First Battle

First Lieutenant Young Oak Kim suffered from severe seasickness and hated boarding ships. The Atlantic crossing was a nightmare. The weather was good and the voyage smooth, but he suffered nonetheless. He had to lie down for the entire voyage. During this time, he imagined himself in combat. Would he perform courageously or would he disgrace both himself and his family? The transport carrying the 100th Battalion arrived in North Africa two weeks after leaving New York. Since the 100th was an "orphan" unit, without a regiment or division, no military assignment had been issued.

The U.S. Army had no specific plans for them. Battalion Commander Farrant made several trips to Oran to negotiate an assignment for the unit. Finally, the 100th Battalion was assigned to patrol a railroad connecting Casablanca and Tunisia.

At that time, racial minorities were not sent to battlefields. When the Tuskegee Airmen were sent to Africa, white officers refused to assign black pilots to the front line. Both Asian Americans and African Americans were viewed as inferior soldiers. Lieutenant Colonel Turner rejected the idea of patrolling the rail line and demanded to be sent to the front. The battalion was eventually assigned to the 133rd Infantry Regiment, part of the 34th Division. The regiment was planning to land in Italy soon.

To end the war as quickly as possible, the United States had proposed to attack northwestern Europe. However, Winston Churchill, Prime Minister of Great Britain at the time, argued that the Allied Forces should attack Southern Europe and secure the Balkan Peninsula. Churchill distrusted the Soviet Union and feared a future clash with them over the Balkans. The Allies finally agreed to attack on both fronts. The Allied Forces had little time to prepare for the invasion of Italy.

Historically, invasions of Italy have come from the north, including Hannibal's famous crossing of the Alps to attack Rome. The only exception was the Byzantine General Belisarius, who crossed the Mediterranean, bypassed Sicily, and attacked Rome in the sixth century. The Allies plan was to follow Belisarius' route. Unfortunately, operational mistakes delayed the invasion. During this delay, the Germans withdrew 100,000 soldiers from Sicily, including three elite divisions, and reinforced their mainland defenses.

The main target of the initial landing was Naples, which had an airport, seaport and railroads. But it was logistically impossible to land on the beaches near Naples. The Allied Forces—Americans and British—landed at Salerno on September 9, 1943. This was the day after the King of Italy, Victor Emmanuel III, had surrendered to the Allies. The majority of the Italian forces had given up their weapons and returned home. The German forces in Italy, however, had no intention of giving in. They had anticipated the Allies' landing at Salerno and had added five additional divisions. The Germans launched a major attack against the Allied Forces at Salerno and a hard-fought battle ensued. In order to reinforce the landing troops, the 100th Battalion was sent to Italy sooner than expected. The ships arrived at Salerno on September 22 and were immediately attacked by a German submarine. One of the ships was destroyed, but no other severe damage was done. The soldiers boarded the landing craft and safely disembarked at Salerno. Young Oak almost had to crawl out of the craft due to his severe seasickness.

There were two major roads from Southern Italy to Rome. One was the "Via Appia," which followed the west coast to Rome. The other was the "Via Casilina," which ran south of Monte Cassino, through the Lili Valley and on to Rome. In the modern Italian highway system, Via Appia is Highway 7, and Via Casilina is Highway 6. The Allies chose Via Casilina. After the successful landing, the 100th Battalion boarded trucks and proceeded north. Although they had heard that the German troops had established a strong defense line along the Volturno River, they encountered no resistance. The next morning, after a night of heavy rain, thunder and lightning, the battalion moved toward Chiusano. All the bridges had been destroyed, forcing the battalion to abandon their trucks.

The 100th Battalion moved slowly north on foot in a driving rainstorm. The roads became muddy, slowing them down. The third platoon of B Company, headed by Second Lieutenant Paul Froning, led the march. Young Oak's second platoon followed from the rear. After several hours of marching they came to an area with low hills. As Young Oak's platoon went up the first hill, Froning's platoon left the hill and followed a curve to the right. Suddenly, the thunder of machinegun fire was heard all around. Germans had been waiting in a small clearing. Soldiers quickly hit the ground, some discarding packs of cigarettes to lower themselves further. From a distance, Young Oak saw Germans firing machine guns. It was the first time he saw the enemy. There was a valley between the German machinegun nests and his platoon. Young Oak realized his own platoon was the closest to the attackers. If he and his men were to cut across the valley, they could approach the Germans from the other side of the hill without being noticed. A platoon leader was supposed to wait for an order from the company commander, but the commander, Captain Taro Suzuki, could not be reached. Young Oak ordered his men to follow him and ran toward the valley. As he neared the Germans, a German soldier saw him and opened fire. Young Oak hit the ground, but continued to lead his men around behind the Germans. Realizing they were about to be cut off, the Germans withdrew. They were fighting only to gain time and didn't engage aggressively. Although B Company was no longer in danger, it had suffered its first casualty. Sergeant Shigeo Takata, a baseball star, became the first member of the 100th killed in action. Young Oak ordered his men to remain where the German machine guns had been. Shortly after, Captain Suzuki came up to him.

"Get up on the road and go down the road like we've been doing," Suzuki said.

"No sir, that's dumb," Young Oak said. "Why should I do that? Once you hit enemy resistance, you don't stay on the road. We go directly to the enemy. The enemy is right over there. I'd rather go down this deep gully and attack the enemy."

"We've got to be on the road."

"No," Young Oak insisted.

"That's an order that was given before you knew where the Germans were."

"Now that we know where they are, we should go after the Germans."

Captain Suzuki departed angrily. Soon he came back with the battalion commander and a whole bunch of staff officers. Lieutenant Colonel Turner ordered Young Oak, "Go by your company commander's orders."

"No sir, I'd rather just go up to the Germans over there."

They argued for a few more minutes until finally the battalion commander said, "If you're going to do it, I'll court martial you."

"Sir, you can court martial me, but if I get up on the road, I'm going to get men wounded and killed unnecessarily. We could go very safely down this gully and over the way. We may still lose men, but at least we'll do so while fighting the Germans."

Major James Lovell, who had come along with the battalion commander, also told Young Oak to follow the commander's orders, but Young Oak refused. Lieutenant Colonel Turner and his staff left angrily. Soon afterwards, Captain Kometani came running up to Young Oak. Breathing heavily, he tried to convince Young Oak to follow the orders of his superior officers:

"You know it would be terrible to have you court-martialed on the first day," Kometani said. "It would be really bad publicity. We don't want to have anything dishonorable like a court martial. Just for today, please, I am asking you."

"Yeah, but Doc, think about it," Young Oak said. "You can see the tanks there. If I get up on the road and go down there, they'll open fire on us and get our men killed."

"What you're saying is probably true, but it's better to get some men wounded than to have a court martial on the first day."

"I hate to go on this road when I know I should go another way. And I hate to lose men. I will go up there, for you personally and for the battalion's reputation, but what we're doing is wrong. I'm telling you right now that you, the battalion commander and the company commander have to be prepared to share the blame for anyone I lose here today. And I am going to lose men."

Young Oak might have refused this request from anyone else, but not from Captain Kometani. Kometani was a dentist by trade, but he functioned as an unofficial guardian of the men. Young Oak turned around and exchanged a quick glance with his platoon sergeant, Sergeant Masaharu Takeba, who had been standing behind him with a worried expression.

The platoon started marching on the road. As they came to a curve, a rumbling noise shook the ground as a shell exploded nearby. This was followed by the whistle of a shell and the sound of a gun firing a round. Looking toward the sound, he could see a German tank firing. In the same direction, he noticed a grove of chestnut trees in an advantageous position, difficult for the enemy tank to fire upon. Instinctively calculating the timing of the next round, he began running toward the enemy tank. As he ran, he raised his right hand over his shoulder, made two circles and pumped it up and down several times with a clenched fist. This was U.S. Army sign language for "Hurry up and follow me!" In war, there's very little talking due to noise. Without a second thought, the soldiers ran after him. As they reached the chestnut trees and hit the ground, fire flashed again from the enemy tank. As they looked back, they saw several of their buddies mowed down by the second round. The last squad had not followed Young Oak's order. Rather than running in the direction of the enemy tank, the squad leader made the decision to jump into a nearby shallow ditch. Seven men were wounded and one killed on the spot. Afterward, the squad leader came to Young Oak.

"If I had followed your order I wouldn't have lost any men, but I thought it was safe to jump in the ditch. I was wrong." Tearing off his corporal stripes, he continued. "I don't deserve to wear these. I don't want to be in a position with this amount of responsibility again."

Young Oak, a first lieutenant, nodded without saying anything. About an hour later, Jack Johnson, Battalion S3, came running down the road.

"Young, I apologize," Johnson said. "I was part of that group that came. You were right, we were wrong."

"You don't have to come here at great risk to tell me that."

"Yes, I do. I have to. I couldn't stay there and not apologize. I want you to know that we were wrong and you were right."

"How long are we going to be here?"

"Until nightfall. No one is going to come down that road."

Later that night, Division Commander Major General Charles Ryder visited the battalion. He gave orders to go across the valley like Young Oak wanted in the first place. Young Oak had experienced something mysterious during this battle. Although the situation was confusing and chaotic, he was able to see clearly what was going on. He felt as if he had been there before and he knew exactly how to resolve problems. He didn't feel any fear and remained calm all the time. He assured himself that the concerns he had had during the Atlantic crossing were unnecessary worries. He realized he was not a coward and would not bring shame to himself or his family. After that day, he never worried about his courage again.

This first battle fundamentally changed the relationship between him and the Japanese American soldiers. The soldiers began to trust his leadership. They had seen him risk court martial to save their lives. They realized that the hard training he had administered at Camp Shelby prepared them well for real battle. When his platoon lost several men during the battle and needed replacements, Private Irving Akahoshi was one of the first soldiers to volunteer to be transferred to the platoon. When he learned that Young Oak had immediately ordered his platoon to run toward the enemy tank, he knew that he was a trustworthy officer. Akahoshi's close friends, Sergeant Minami and Private Kubokawa, also volunteered to be transferred.

When Prime Minister Churchill had argued for an Allied attack on southern Europe, he often used the phrase "soft belly." The soldiers fighting in Italy, however, could not understand where he had gotten that idea. With the exception of the coastal plains, Italy is mostly mountainous, with many rivers, and the weather can be extremely cold. Heavy rain often posed major obstacles. Mud-covered roads made it difficult for tanks to maneuver and for trucks to transport supplies. The Allied air force could not be used effectively due to the often-cloudy skies. The German military took full advantage of these conditions in its defense of Italy. Although the Allies enjoyed superior military strength and supplies, Italy's natural conditions nullified these advantages. While the Germans had surrendered to the Soviet Union at Stalingrad several months earlier, and were losing the war in Africa, the German army in Europe was still very strong.

After the first battle, the 100th Battalion continued north, engaging in small battles along the way. In the beginning of November, they reached the Volturno River. The river flows from the northeast to the southwest across the Italian peninsula. It was located about 15 miles south of the Gustav Line. The German military was determined to delay the Allied crossing as long as possible in order to strengthen the Gustav Line. The Allies, on the other hand, wanted to cross the river as quickly as possible. A fierce battle over the crossing was inevitable. Previously the German's main objective was to gain time so they avoided aggressive battles. They would fight for a while and retreat. This tactic changed at the Volturno River, as they established their first major defense there. Before the attack, Captain Suzuki asked Young Oak to accompany him to a briefing at battalion headquarters.

"Why do you want me to go with you?" Young Oak asked him.

"Because I know you have a photographic memory of maps and we have only one map. B Company is going to lead the battalion across the river and you're going to lead company."

The fact that an entire infantry battalion had only one map was an indication of how unprepared the Allied Forces were upon entering the Italian front. Young Oak studied the map for more than 10 minutes, attempting to burn it into his brain. That night, the 100th Battalion began the river crossing. As planned, B Company led the way, headed by Young Oak's platoon. The water was icy cold and the current swift. The river was not wide, but it was between waist-deep and chest-deep. Soldiers made their way across in total darkness, at some places holding onto ropes stretched across the river, and, in other places with no help at all. It was extremely dangerous because, even in the shallow areas, there were slippery rocks underwater. The soldiers had to balance themselves while carrying weapons and equipment. Young Oak worried about his men; many were shorter than him and he was not that tall.

Suddenly the area was lit by exploding shells. Friendly artillery, misjudging the distance, fired into the river. Water and shrapnel were all around. The frightened faces of desperate soldiers appeared and disappeared with each flash. Soon after, artillery barrages came from the opposite shore. The German army had established its defensive line by placing its tanks and artillery in olive groves along the river. Casualties mounted and the river turned red. On the far shore, a minefield awaited them. In the 100th Battalion alone, about thirty soldiers were killed or wounded crossing the minefield.

After they had crossed the river, Young Oak moved his platoon along a small muddy path toward their target location. After they had advanced about a hundred yards, an order to stop came from the company commander. Captain Suzuki came up to Young Oak and said, "You're headed in the wrong direction."

"I'm headed in the right direction."

"You're headed in the wrong direction. I want you to go almost 5 degrees to your right."

"I'm not going to do that. The objective is this way. That's why you took me to the meeting. You said I could read and remember a map. Now you're telling me to go someplace else."

The company commander, remembering the argument with Young Oak on the first day of battle firmly said, "I'll take responsibility. We'll go this way."

Following Captain Suzuki's order, B Company marched in the direction he indicated. As they turned, Young Oak's platoon was now at the tail of the company. Suddenly sounds of explosion came from the front and the whole column came to a stop. The lead platoon had run into a minefield and suffered seven casualties. Captain Suzuki ordered all officers to report to him. They moved forward slowly, using mine detectors. One misstep could cost lives. Since Young Oak had been at the rear, he was the last to arrive. The other officers had already gathered. Suzuki, while sitting on the ground crying, asked, "Can anybody tell us how to get out of here?"

Suzuki and Young Oak were the only officers who had seen the map. No one spoke. Captain Suzuki turned to Young Oak and repeated the question.

"Sir, I don't know," Young Oak said. "You are the one who said we should go this way."

"No, no," Suzuki said. "Can you lead the way? I'll follow,"

"No, you lead the way. You're the company commander and you saw the map."

"No, you lead the way. I won't bother you anymore."

"Okay, I will lead. All of you are witnesses."

Young Oak again marched in the front, and led the company in the original direction. After moving forward for a while, an order to stop came from the rear. It was the company commander again.

"Now I know where we are," Suzuki said. "The objective is just down this road, a quarter mile away."

"No, this is the wrong road," Young Oak said. "We want the next road over. Come up, I'll show you."

There was a hedge and an embankment about the height of a room. Young Oak stood atop the embankment. He was angry that Suzuki had broken his pledge not to interfere.

"You said you weren't going to argue anymore," Young Oak said. "This is the way the objective is."

As he pointed, a German machine gun opened fire. He could see the traces coming from the embankment and passing underneath his arm. He instinctively jumped backwards and tumbled into a shallow ditch between the hedge and the embankment.

"Open fire!" someone shouted.

In the darkness, the soldiers began firing toward the embankment, although they could see nothing. The only person they had any chance of hitting was Young Oak, who pressed himself flat against the ground.

"Fix bayonets! Charge!"

This order was followed by the trampling feet of soldiers rushing forward. The soldiers charged in darkness, stabbing with their bayonets at the hedge. Some bayonets were caught in the thicket, while others became entangled with each other. At that moment, the sound of an explosion came from the direction of the German machine gun. It was Young Oak's grenade. When the soldiers had stopped firing, he had taken out two grenades, removed the pins and thrown them into the German machinegun nest. After the explosion, he went to check the site. He saw the soles of two boots. He gave them a hard kick and a German soldier jumped up with both hands held high. Another enemy soldier did the same.

Sergeant Takeba, assistant platoon leader, and Kenneth Kaneko, Young Oak's runner, came to see if he was all right. Soldiers thought that he had been killed or wounded by the German machine gun. They carefully searched the area and captured another German soldier. Five German soldiers had manned the machine gun nest. Two escaped and three were captured. These three soldiers were the first prisoners of war taken by the 100th Battalion in Europe.

Advancing through the olive groves, Young Oak finally led his platoon to its objective. They waited for the rest of the company, but no one came. Captain Suzuki had led the other platoons off in a different direction. His platoon was alone without enough men to secure the position. Young Oak knew that he couldn't leave his men and search for the others. He turned to Private "Kenny" Kaneko, who had been his shadow since Camp Shelby, and asked him if he could find the others.

"I can go back and find them," Kaneko said.

"You're sure you can come back?" Young Oak asked.

"Yes."

"Okay Kenny, go and get the captain."

Young Oak was not sure that Kaneko could successfully bring them back, but he had little choice. Kaneko disappeared into the darkness and, after a while, returned with the company commander and the rest of the men. Captain Suzuki was an ROTC from the University of Hawaii, and Young Oak had graduated from OCS. While they, at times, seemed to hate each other, in reality they respected each other and got along well. They often clashed because each possessed a strong personality.

The bayonet charge received much publicity in the United States. American newspapers ran long articles about the first "banzai attack" by Japanese-American soldiers. In actuality, they had only attacked a hedge, not German soldiers. It was a piece of comedy brought about by inexperienced soldiers in the midst of a chaotic battle. One thing, however, had become clear to Young Oak and the Japanese-American soldiers; it was meaningless to classify people based on skin or hair color. The white officers of the battalion learned this as well.

Chapter 5
Samurai Kim

Two days later, Young Oak's platoon climbed Hill 600 near Santa Maria Oliveto. Because the platoon had led the crossing of the Volturno River, this time they held the rear of the battalion. As specified in the army manual, Young Oak was immediately behind the lead squad with the remaining two squads behind him. Since the hill was heavily mined, the battalion was forced to climb in single file. The lead soldiers carefully marked each mine or trip wire with toilet paper for those who followed. As long as the soldiers avoided these markers, they were safe.

By the time Young Oak reached the top of the hill, it was getting dark. He was immediately summoned to the battalion commander, Major James Gillespie, who had replaced Lieutenant Colonel Turner a week earlier. Not knowing why he was being summoned, he stopped the two squads behind him, but allowed the lead squad to follow the rest of the company.

As Young Oak approached, Major Gillespie pointed to tracers being fired from a hill immediately to their east. This was clearly German machinegun fire. There appeared to be four to six guns on the hill, which should have been occupied by the U.S. 135th Regiment by that time.

"This is a terrible situation," Major Gillespie said. "Come daylight, if the Germans can see us on this hill, we will be in serious trouble. I want you to take your platoon and knock out as many of those guns as you can."

Young Oak was stunned. With two squads—maybe 20 soldiers—and no heavy weapons, he was to take on four to six machine guns.

"Yes, sir. Am I to report to my company commander and get the rest of my platoon?"

"No, if you lose too much time, you may get disoriented in the dark," Major Gillespie said.

"Am I supposed to report directly to you?"

"Yes."

This meant that Young Oak's new company commander, First Lieutenant Rocco Marzano, would be unaware that he was going on this patrol. Lieutenant Marzano had replaced Captain Suzuki, who had been wounded earlier in the afternoon. Young Oak returned to his two remaining squads. Since the Salerno landing, the number of soldiers per squad had shrunk by about 25 percent. Only 18 men remained from the two squads.

"We have no map," Young Oak explained to his men. "All we know is what we can see. We will cross the gully in front of us and try to get our orientation. We know the gully runs northeast, turns, and ends toward the German position."

They didn't have a map because the entire battalion only had one. Since he had only two squads, he couldn't use the traditional tactic of having a squad in front of him and two squads behind him. He decided to lead the patrol himself as first scout. The second scout was Takeba.

Takeba was a wonderful soldier. He was a black belt in judo, a star player on his high school football team, and one of the battalion's key baseball players. He was an all-around athlete, had good common sense, and was very bright.

They started across the gully to the east, Young Oak in the lead with Takeba close behind. Suddenly they heard German voices coming toward them. Guessing that there were 10 to 15 men in the German party, Young Oak quickly and quietly ordered his men:

"Stop, split up and lie along each side of the gully. Get out grenades and wait until the Germans pass below. On my command, everybody throw at least one grenade."

He did not feel he was in a position to take prisoners. His job was to eliminate the enemy machine guns. Since it was dark, Young Oak wanted his men sufficiently separated to avoid any chance of being wounded by their own grenades. They could not see into the gully, but when they heard the Germans below, he gave the signal. About 20 grenades were thrown. This was followed by much shouting and crying, and then silence. They appeared to have killed or badly wounded most of the Germans. The group appeared to be a one or two machine gun crew. Young Oak then had his men cross the gully and head up the hill. The ridge went in a northeasterly direction. By the time they reached the summit, he thought they were now about 500 yards into enemy territory.

The night was eerie. It was dark and windy, with low clouds almost touching the hill. The moon darted in and out from behind the clouds, casting ghostly silhouettes. Suddenly, he heard a strange noise and noticed a bush moving faster than the wind could shake it. A German soldier was walking toward them carrying metal boxes that appeared to contain ammunition. Young Oak took out his "good luck" pistol, which Captain Suzuki had given him before he was evacuated the previous day. Suzuki had won an ROTC shooting contest in Hawaii with that pistol. Young Oak stepped in front of the soldier and told him to stop. The soldier dropped the boxes and reached for the rifle on his back. Young Oak attempted to fire, but the pistol jammed. As the German soldier fired, Young Oak hit the ground and rolled to his right. Almost simultaneously, Takeba fired over Young Oak's left shoulder. It was dark and they could not find the German soldier. All they knew was that the German had fired one round and Takeba three.

At the top of the hill they had to cross a clearing. Young Oak told everyone to crawl. A standing man would have been visible in the intermittent moonlight. Young Oak and his men successfully crawled across the summit, but the last man—one of the squad leaders—decided to walk across. When he was halfway across, the moon came out. A German machine gun opened fire and hit him in the calf. He fell and crawled the rest of the way. The wound was not severe. They bandaged him and Young Oak asked, "What made you disobey my order? Why did you do such a damn thing?"

"I didn't want to crawl. I thought the rocky hilltop would hurt my hands and knees. When I saw that everyone in front had crossed, I thought it was safe."

"I can't afford to lose any more men. Can you get back on your own?"

"I think so."

Young Oak told him to crawl. After watching him for a bit, Young Oak decided the man could return on his own. They were now at the crest of a knoll that merged into another hill, where the German machine guns were. As he surveyed the terrain, Young Oak saw some nearby hills. He stopped his patrol.

"Right down there, where this knoll and that other knoll merge, there is a German machine gun," Young Oak told his men. "It's a good 150 feet away."

The soldiers were stunned.

"We can't see that far," someone asked. "How do you know a German machine gun is there?"

"If I were a German, I would put a machine gun there. Germans are very methodical and careful. We have to capture that German machine gun, otherwise we will not be able to move forward."

He split the patrol into two groups. He took one squad and sent the other in a circular direction to approach from the other side. At the bottom of the hill, they came to a bush. Young Oak lowered himself and moved toward the bush to look for the enemy. As he tried to peek through the bush, a face appeared right in front of him less than a foot away. The German soldier was also startled and uttered two words in German. Young Oak guessed that he had asked for the evening password. He pulled out his pistol, but again it jammed. As he twisted his body to the left this time, he heard a shot fired from behind. Again it was Takeba. This was followed by the sound of the German machine gun, less than 10 yards away, exactly where Young Oak had said it would be. The soldiers pressed themselves against the ground.

"Jesus, he's right!" one of the soldiers said. "There is a machine gun there."

"Didn't I tell you our platoon leader is a magician?" another soldier responded.

The gun fired only 100 rounds or so and fell silent. The other squad had come around and captured it and seven German soldiers. Young Oak had two of his men take the prisoners to the battalion headquarters. But they couldn't locate the German soldier Young Oak had encountered at the bush.

They continued up the hill where Major Gillespie had seen the German machine guns. This hill was about 10 yards higher than Hill 600, which the 100th Battalion was occupying. As they neared the top, they heard trampling boots.

"Everybody, back off from the trail," Young Oak said.

"Shoot them?" someone asked him.

"No. Wait," Young Oak said. "Our job is to get the machine guns off the hill."

Young Oak was calculating his odds: *We began the patrol with 19 men. One returned wounded, and two others took back prisoners, so we are 16. The German force is much larger. We are deep in enemy territory and not familiar with the terrain. My pistol is jammed. All we have are rifles. We are lying in a row and they will come upon us. If we attack the front, their rear will attack us. If we attack the rear, we will miss most of them. If we get involved in a firefight, I will lose men—maybe half of them. If the mission is accomplished, to lose that many men is unnecessary. The terrain is against us, the numbers are against us, and our deployment is against us. The Germans occupying that hill appear to be leaving. If they leave voluntarily, the mission will be accomplished.*

Young Oak decided not to engage. They lay there quietly and watched over 50 German soldiers march by. It looked like a five to seven machinegun crew. The Germans were talking loudly among themselves. Young Oak guessed they were asking each other what was going on. After the Germans had passed, Young Oak told his men, "We have finished our mission and are heading back."

They withdrew from the hill and returned to the knoll where the squad leader had been wounded. As they came down the hill, they captured a German soldier, the very one Young Oak had encountered at the bush. Then he turned to his men and said, "We have accomplished our mission, but the enemy will return. Wait here while I report to the battalion commander."

Major Gillespie suffered from ulcers and his pain had gotten worse after he took command of the battalion. When Young Oak came to see him, he was just getting over an ulcer attack. Bent over in pain, he was barely able to hear the report. He thanked Young Oak for successfully completing the mission.

"I knew something had happened when the German machine guns stopped firing," Major Gillespie said. "I can't believe it. Where are your men?"

"Still out there, sir," Young Oak replied. "You know, it will be extremely dangerous for the 100th come daylight. I think the Germans will try to retake the hill. That would put them directly behind us and in a position to fire."

"Well, what do you suggest?"

"I think I should stay out there."

"Okay, stay out there."

Young Oak returned to the knoll where his men were waiting. By now Young Oak had become more familiar with the terrain. Hill 600 was occupied by his battalion, lower than the hill where the German machine guns had been, and also lower than the German occupied hill to the north. His main concern was to figure out how they could avoid detection. On the knoll there were no trees, but there were rock piles four-and-a-half to five feet high around the edge of the hill. It looked like Italian farmers had put 10 of these piles there to farm.

"The Germans are higher than we are and they know what the hill looks like," Takeba said. "If we move the rocks and replace them with a man, they may not notice us."

Young Oak agreed. They removed the rocks and put one soldier in each location. The others remained on the south side of the hill. The night was cold and frost began to settle on the ground.

At first daylight the next morning, Young Oak climbed alone to the top of the hill where the German machine guns had been. Since the guns had been firing south, he guessed there must be American soldiers in that direction. As he reached the south end of the hill, an English-speaking voice ordered him to stop. The Caucasian soldier, seeing an Asian in a U.S. military uniform wearing the gold bars of a Second Lieutenant, asked Young Oak curiously if he was an American.

"Yes, I am Lieutenant Kim of the 100th Battalion, 133rd Regiment."

"Sir, I am going to take you to my company commander."

Young Oak followed him to the company commander, who then took him to the commander of the 1st Battalion, 135th Infantry Regiment who asked, "What the hell are you doing here?"

"Sir, I came from that hill," Young Oak said. "Earlier, I was on the adjacent lower hill."

"How can that be? The hill you say you came from is occupied by the Germans. Yesterday afternoon, we had the hill, but the Germans forced us off. We are trying to remain concealed on this side of the hill."

"Sir, the hill is vacant."

Young Oak told him about his night patrol and about the Germans abandoning the hill, but the commander would not believe it.

"It would be safer if your men go back up and occupy the hill," Young Oak said. "Your man saw me come right down the ridge. How could I come down the ridge if the Germans were there?"

"I don't know. I don't know who you are. I don't know where you came from. My men couldn't see you all the way down the ridge because they were hiding. They may have seen you the last 10 yards."

The soldier who had first stopped Young Oak was called back. He said he had only seen Young Oak the last 10 yards. Young Oak could not convince them that the hill was empty. He stayed about half an hour longer, then decided to return to his men.

"Why don't you and your men watch me? I'm going to go back up. If I walk up there safely, then won't you know what I'm saying is true? You can then occupy the hill."

"This may be a German trick, but we'll watch you."

As Young Oak left, he could see them watching him, but he didn't see any Americans come to occupy the hill. He was angry, but there was nothing he could do. The next battle could have been easy if they had cooperated. Now it was apt to be difficult.

Young Oak returned to his men. They were on top of the hill and the weather was bad. As Young Oak had anticipated, the Germans attacked soon after. The attack began with a smoke screen. The men of the 100th felt their fingers chilled by the metal triggers of their rifles as they waited for the Germans to emerge from the smoke. When First Lieutenant Sakae Takahashi of F Company saw about 90 to 100 German soldiers emerge, he asked himself: *Where is Young? Why is he not attacking them? Are they still asleep after getting back late last night? Something has happened to them.*

Takahashi was jittery as he watched the German soldiers move down the hill. The battalion commander, Major Gillespie, was also wondering about Young Oak, but couldn't contact him. In those days, a battalion commander could talk to the regimental commander or a company commander by radio, but not to a platoon leader. And Young Oak's company commander had no idea where Young Oak was. Major Gillespie thought that Young Oak and his men were still asleep and didn't know about the attack. But Young Oak and his men had spotted the Germans. Believing the Germans were about to attack them, he ordered his men to stay hidden.

"Don't open fire until they are all down the hill below us," he told his men.

Young Oak expected that the Germans would line up below and attack them. But when the Germans got directly below them, they turned their backs to Young Oak's platoon, and prepared to attack the hill they had occupied the night before. When this occurred, Young Oak had his men line up on the forward ridge facing the Germans. When the Germans began to move toward the vacant hill, Young Oak ordered his men to open fire. There were only 16 men in the platoon, but the Germans were caught completely by surprise. The Germans didn't even know where the bullets were coming from and scattered. Young Oak ordered his men to shoot in every direction but southeast. He allowed the Germans to escape to the southeast because he knew the 1st Battalion of the 135th Regiment was there. The battle was over in just about 15 minutes. The Germans who were not killed or wounded were standing with their hands up. Young Oak and some of his men walked down to capture the Germans. At that moment, a German soldier carrying a Schmeisser submachine gun began to escape to the southeast. Young Oak's men shot and hit him. As he fell backward, his finger clamped on the trigger, and the submachine gun started to fire. One of the bullets hit Young Oak in the right thigh, knocking him to the ground. At first he was not sure what had happened; it felt like someone had hit him with a baseball bat. Then he realized he was lying on the ground and his right leg was numb. He checked and determined that it was only a flesh wound, then got up and continued down the hill with his men, ordering them to round up the German prisoners. He had his men bring the wounded German soldiers to a flat area where they could lie down.

One German soldier was sobbing. Sergeant Takeba and several others gathered around him. Blood was spurting from his chest and stomach. They brushed his blond hair from his forehead. A few minutes earlier they had shot him; now they were trying to lessen his pain. They covered him with a blanket, which soaked red. The German was husky, but his face was that of a child. He seemed to be pointing to his chest. Young Oak pulled a leather wallet from his chest pocket. Inside was a photograph of the soldier's mother and father. Young Oak moved the photograph in front of the soldier's blue eyes, but they were now unseeing. Young Oak and his men stood still. The silence and the smell of gun smoke engraved the moment in their memory. It was very rare to see an enemy face on a battlefield. Usually all one saw were figures moving in the distance. In combat, it was better not to see the enemy as human beings suffering from the same inhumane conditions. This was the first time Young Oak had seen an enemy face in combat.

Young Oak rounded up the Germans, and came back up the hill. Once there, he cut off his trouser leg with his bayonet. He had a machine gun bullet in his right thigh. He applied sulfa and a bandage to stop infection and bleeding. About 40 minutes later, Lieutenant Candy arrived.

"I was sent to take your place," Candy said. "The battalion saw the Germans and thought you were sleeping. Why don't you go to the aid station?"

"No, I'll stay here until everything has settled down," Young Oak said.

At this point Captain Jack Mizuha, commander of the heavy weapons company arrived. He directed the soldiers to set up machine guns for defense, and then told Young Oak, "This is Major Gillespie's order: report to the aid station."

Lieutenant Candy saw blood coming from Young Oak's boot and ordered a stretcher. Young Oak refused it. But he was forced to go anyhow. Sergeant Takeba and runner Kaneko watched their platoon leader disappear in the distance.

The next morning, Young Oak woke up feeling cold. He was in a tent full of wounded men. He noticed that the furnace was extinguished. He got up, lit the fire and, dragging his leg, went outside. The hospital consisted of several tents and was capable of simple surgery. He vaguely remembered being brought there in an ambulance the night before. When he returned to his tent, Young Oak began caring for other wounded soldiers. A nurse came in and was startled to see him out of bed. She grabbed him and forced him to lie down.

"Don't leave the bed again," she said. After the nurse left, the fire went out again. Young Oak got up to put in more fuel when the nurse returned.

"I told you not to get up," she reprimanded. Then an ambulance arrived and Young Oak stood up again. "What are you doing getting up again?" she said.

She ordered a couple of aids to bring a stretcher and to strap him in, instructing them: "Put the straps where he can't reach them." While the aids were trying to strap him in, the nurse told Young Oak, "Whatever you do, leave those things alone. I don't want you to get up again. These are doctor's orders."

The ambulance took Young Oak to another hospital where he underwent surgery to remove the bullet. The bullet had not hit a bone, so the surgery was relatively simple. The second hospital was located on top of a hill in Naples, overlooking the Mediterranean Sea. It was a beautiful location, yet the supply situation was bad. Officers had to purchase their own toothbrushes, toothpaste and uniforms. Enlisted men received these items from the Red Cross, but not the officers. The surgeons had torn apart Young Oak's uniform during surgery and had cut away his boot with scissors. After the surgery, he received a pair of slippers and pajamas from the hospital, but he had to purchase everything else, including toothpaste, toothbrush, soap and boots, with his own money. Since he had been taken to the hospital, he didn't have his wallet or any money. He was unable to brush his teeth for two days. A nurse told him that if he walked down the hall to the Salvation Army, they would give him toiletries, but she added, "You can't walk, so you can't go." After she had left, Young Oak snuck out of the ward to the Salvation Army and they took pity on him and gave him a toothbrush, toothpaste and other toiletries.

During his hospital stay, he also learned that officers could receive 50 percent of their paycheck if their name and serial number were verified by the hospital administration. Enlisted men, on the other hand, could not receive any pay while in the hospital. Their only relief was the Red Cross or the Salvation Army. After learning this, he began giving one or two dollars to the hospitalized men of the 100th Battalion out of his own paycheck.

The situation in the hospital was tough for both officers and enlisted men. While in the hospital, Young Oak received his first Purple Heart. Young Oak healed much more quickly than the doctors anticipated, and he kept asking to be released. After about four weeks, he was allowed to return to his unit. Other returning soldiers from the 100th greeted him in the temporary assembly center and asked him for his clothing, shoe and hat size. Sometime later, they returned with six duffle bags full of uniforms, boots, hats, socks, field jackets, etc., enough to last him several years.

While in the assembly area, he met Battalion S-3 Jack Johnson. Several days had passed, but there were no orders for either of them. They learned that the wait for orders could take up to two months. Young Oak had an idea. He had studied the way the assembly center handled returning soldiers. After breakfast, they lined up the transportation trucks and assembled the soldiers. If a soldier's name and rank were called, he answered "yo" and got on the truck. Many were not present when their names were called. Early in the morning, the center checked and matched name and rank with a list, but, later in the morning, they didn't check carefully. Young Oak and Johnson waited for the end of the morning process, said "yo" to a second call when there was no response to the first, and quickly got on the truck.

While Young Oak was in the hospital, the 100th had gone into reserve. When he came back, the soldiers of the 2nd platoon broke into applause. The battalion staff, the other officers and soldiers informed him he was to be awarded a Silver Star. They angrily told him that the reason he would get only a silver star was because of First Lieutenant Marzano.

At the time, the regiment had ordered the battalion to submit a recommendation for Young Oak's decoration. Major Gillespie, who had given him the direct order, had been relieved due to his severe stomach ulcers. Lieutenant Marzano, who didn't know of Gillespie's order, was annoyed that Young Oak's platoon had not reported to him, so he wrote a lukewarm recommendation for a Silver Star. After reviewing the recommendation, regimental headquarters asked the battalion to revise it to a Distinguished Service Cross, but Lieutenant Marzano refused. Division headquarters, after reviewing the recommendation, also asked regimental headquarters to revise the recommendation to a DSC, but again Lieutenant Marzano refused. A recommendation had to be written by a superior officer in the chain of command. Since Major Gillespie had been evacuated, only Lieutenant Marzano could write the recommendation. Division headquarters had no alternative but to award a Silver Star. By the time Young Oak returned to the battalion, Lieutenant Marzano, notorious for his incompetence and insistence on his own authority, had been transferred to another unit.

The following year, February 1944, Young Oak received the Silver Star in an award ceremony presided over by Lieutenant General Mark Clark, Commander of the Fifth Army. A Silver Star is the third-highest military decoration of the United States Armed Forces. In the U.S., any soldier who receives a Silver Star is recognized for his bravery and service to the country in the face of the enemy.

Young Oak was quick in situation analysis and never sacrificed his soldiers for his own glory. His soldiers' safety always came first and at times, he disobeyed his superior officers to ensure the well-being of his men. Soldiers who put their lives on the front line instinctively knew this. War strips men of hypocrisy. Young Oak's character instilled respect and trust in the minds of his soldiers. When others, in the midst of extreme terror, could not make a decision, Young Oak always led his soldiers calmly and quietly. He never raised his voice to give orders. Not all the officers of the 100th were like this. Some Caucasian officers were unwilling to put their lives at stake for the Japanese-American soldiers. They were brave in training camp, but in actual combat they never wanted to be exposed to the enemy. The Japanese-American soldiers from Hawaii were straightforward. When Caucasian officers, who took care of themselves first, issued an order to attack, they would respond with, "You go first, we will follow." But when they trusted an officer, they fanatically followed him. Young Oak had also changed. On the battlefield, the soldiers wore dirty uniforms, marked by sweat, mud, rain, and wind. There was no laundry. Young Oak realized that ironed trousers and polished boots had nothing to do with discipline. They were meaningless formalities. After the 100th was put on the front line, officers and soldiers ate and slept together 24 hours a day. They ate the same rations and slept in the same mud. Some officers tried to maintain their privileges, but not Young Oak. As the relationship between Young Oak and the soldiers continued to evolve, he became one of the most respected officers in the battalion. Although Young Oak didn't learn of it until much later, the soldiers had begun to refer to him by the nickname, "Samurai Kim."

Chapter 6
Sniper

There were many changes in the 100th Battalion while Young Oak was hospitalized. The battalion had originally consisted of six companies: A, B, C, D, E and F. Since landing in Italy, the 100th had suffered many casualties, so headquarters decided to reorganize it into four companies, eliminating E and F, and reassigned their soldiers to the other companies. As a result, the F Company Commander was reassigned as the B Company Commander. Accordingly, many soldiers from F Company volunteered for B Company. Young Oak returned to his original B Company and became the company executive officer. He and the new company commander, First Lieutenant Sakae Takahashi, began to share a very special comradeship.

There were two changes in battalion commander. Major William Bright had taken command of the battalion after Lieutenant Marzano was dismissed for incompetence. During the Christmas season, Major Bright was reassigned and Major Casper Clough became the battalion commander. Major Clough, a native New Yorker, had graduated from West Point in 1939, only four years earlier. He was an experienced combat leader with a promising future. He had served as a battalion commander in North Africa, in the 1st Division, and was slated for promotion to lieutenant colonel. His military future seemed bright. However, he lost his command and promotion when another battalion in a different regiment of the same division participated in a civilian massacre. General Eisenhower, angered by the atrocity, relieved all the commanders of the division, regiments and battalions. Major Clough had been in the wrong place at the wrong time. So it was a gift that Major Clough was given command of the 100th. And the 100th had gained, for the first time, a truly competent battalion commander. But what awaited the 100th was the battle at Monte Cassino, destined to be the cruelest battle in the Italian campaign.

In the following year, 1944, the 133rd Infantry Regiment, 34th Division (of which the 100th Battalion was a part), was scheduled to relieve a Special Forces unit of the 36th Division in Monte Cassino. This unit was composed of Americans and Canadians who had been annihilated by the enemy, and it existed only in name. The day before the scheduled move to Monte Cassino, Takahashi asked Young Oak to bring money to the soldiers in the hospital in Naples. It would normally take two days to travel to Naples and back, but as the unit moved north, it would take longer to return. Takahashi wanted to take care of this matter before it became more difficult.

As Young Oak jumped into a jeep, Major Clough came outside waving and shouting into a radio. He was calling Takahashi. Knowing that Clough wanted to stop Young Oak from going to Naples, Takahashi picked up the radio with one hand while motioning to Young Oak with the other, saying, "Go, go, before I answer the radio." Young Oak took off quickly.

On his way to Naples, he stopped at C Company to meet company commander Captain Kenneth Eaton, who had been with C Company since Camp Shelby.

"Do you want me to visit your boys in the hospital and give them money?"

"I'd love for you to, but there are two problems. I don't have the money and you don't have the time. I just got a radio call from Major Clough to stop you, but I haven't seen you."

When Young Oak and his men arrived in Naples, they distributed the money, and then went drinking. They returned two days later and found that the battalion had left.

As Young Oak set out to rejoin his battalion, he was stopped by the maintenance officer, Paul Corbin.

"They left last night. You can't go tonight, it's too dangerous. You can't see, you're hungover, and the enemy is everywhere."

Early the next morning, Young Oak set out up the hill. He reached the battalion at about 5:00 p.m., just as they were ready to depart. The night was cold and there was a brisk wind. Snow fell for the first time since they had landed in Italy. They walked all night in the snow, unsure of their location. At daybreak, the snow stopped. Just as they were beginning to feel better, shots came from above. There were Germans on a ridge above them. Both sides exchanged fire, but at long range.

"What should we do?" Takahashi asked Young Oak.

"I don't think we should do a damn thing. They have the high ground. They are organized and dug in. An assault from here would be foolish. We're not equipped for winter. It would be difficult even without the snow, but with it, we'll be slipping and sliding. They'll kill us all."

"I agree. Let's lie here and snipe at the Germans."

As Young Oak was firing, he sensed someone lying down next to him. The new soldier said sarcastically, "You're a lousy shot. You can't hit anything. That German up there isn't worried, he's ignoring you."

Young Oak turned and realized it was the battalion commander, Major Clough.

"Lieutenant Kim, you went to Naples against my direct orders, didn't you?" Clough said.

"Sir, I never received any orders from you."

"That's a moot point, I can't argue one way or another, but I see you're back. I did give an order and you ignored it. So did Sakae Takahashi. Even Ken Eaton didn't stop you down the road. So, did you bring back anything important?"

"I don't know if it's important to you, but it's important to me."

Young Oak took off his pack and opened it. Instead of food or medicine, there were five bottles of alcohol.

"Glad to see you've got some sense," Clough said. "What is it?"

"I don't know. In Naples these days it could be anything, even colored water or gasoline."

"Probably."

"You can have your choice, any bottle you want. You're the first to choose."

Clough looked at the bottles and picked one. He opened it, took a shot and said, "I don't know what it is, but it's strong."

"That white one is supposed to be 110 or 120 proof."

"It feels like it. Have some."

As Young Oak drank from the bottle, the battalion commander said, "Not too much, it's my bottle now."

A moment later, he asked Young Oak, "By the way, where the hell are we?"

Young Oak was surprised by the question.

"Sir, I don't have the slightest idea. I don't have a map. I don't have anything."

"Well, I've got a map, but it doesn't do me any good. You look at it. The map has seven hills on it. I count nine."

Young Oak looked at the map and immediately realized that Major Clough had misread it.

"Give me five minutes," Young Oak said. "I'll tell you where we are."

"Hell, I've got all day."

"Can you call your artillery liaison officer for me?"

"Artillery liaison officer? He's down there. I'll get him."

When the artillery officer arrived, Young Oak gave him the coordinates he had located on the map. The artillery unit then fired a round, but no one could see where it landed. Sensing that the battalion commander and the artillery officer were waiting for him, Young Oak changed his request.

"The marker they fire is typically white phosphorous, so we can usually see it, but in the snow we can't," Young Oak said. "Fire a different round."

This time they could see where it exploded. Young Oak gave another set of coordinates and they fired another round. Young Oak turned to Major Clough and indicated on the map where the two rounds had landed and where they were.

"Son of a bitch," Major Clough said. "You did it in five minutes. How'd you do that?"

"I don't know," Young Oak said. "It just came to me."

"You're smart enough to bring the right stuff from Naples and you're insolent enough to disobey my orders. I'll tell you what, I want you to be the battalion two."

"I don't want to be two. I've always been with B Company and I want to stay there."

"Where did you get your commission?"

"I went to OCS."

"They didn't teach you military niceties there? If a commanding officer expresses a wish, that's an order."

"I was never taught that. You didn't give me an order. You said you wanted me to become two, but I don't want to."

"That's a wish. So that's a direct order. I'll let you stay with B Company because you're committed to this battle. But the moment we get down from this hill, you are to report to me to be the battalion two. Is that clear? This is a direct order in front of witnesses. You don't obey this, you go to Leavenworth."

"Yes, Sir."

Battalion two meant S-2, intelligence officer. Leavenworth was the site of the military prison. Although the reference to Leavenworth sounded like a threat, Major Clough was smiling when he said it. The skies darkened, and the battalion commander, giving up any thought of attack, withdrew his men.

The wind rose up and snow fell throughout the night. The soldiers could not tell whether the snow was coming from the sky or had been blown off the ground by the wind. Young Oak and his men tried to come down from the mountain, but did not know where they were. They wandered around all night in the snow and wind. At dawn, they realized they had moved to another mountain and still had no idea where they were. The map was inaccurate. It showed nine hills, but, in reality, there were more and they were all the same height and they all looked the same covered in snow. The men were also battling another enemy—a lack of winter clothing. The unit had not been adequately prepared for battle in Italy's cold, windy and snowy mountains. The men were suffering from frostbite and trench foot. After several more mishaps, the battalion made its way back to the base and waited for orders.

At that point, Major Clough issued an official order making Young Oak the battalion S-2. Only ten days earlier he had been promoted to first lieutenant, his first promotion since becoming an officer.

The 100th was specially designed to carry out operations independently. Its size was larger than average and its officer ranks were one level higher. In the 100th, the S-3 operations and planning officer was a major instead of a captain, and the S-2 was a captain rather than a first lieutenant. Major Clough had been closely monitoring Young Oak since becoming battalion commander. From the start of his search to fill the vacant S-2 position, many had suggested Young Oak. Jack Johnson, the Battalion XO (executive officer), had visited the intelligence section to ask around. Sergeant Minami, Private Kubokawa and Private Akahoshi had both transferred to the intelligence section while Young Oak was being hospitalized, not wanting to remain in the 2nd Platoon without him. They all recommended Young Oak as S-2.

The battalion began moving toward Cassino, a small town about 90 miles southeast of Rome, on Highway 6. Just north of the town is a steep mountain, Monte Cassino. Its summit offers 360 degrees of visibility. Tanks and artillery guns on the summit would control any passage on Highway 6. The Romans had built a castle on the mountain because of its strategic importance, and whenever there was war in Italy, Monte Cassino became the site of intense fighting. Monte Cassino was the center of the formidable "Gustav Line." But, before reaching Monte Cassino, the 100th had to pass Monte Majo first.

The snow had stopped, but the 100th suffered many casualties inflicted by the German machine guns on Monte Majo. The guns particularly targeted B Company, which had been trapped.

Young Oak, now Battalion S-2, was with B Company, which had a special affection for him. As usual, Sergeant Masaharu Takeba was lying next to him under the German machine gun fire. They were so close that they could feel each other's body heat despite the cold. C Company was positioned to the right of B Company, but was not under as strong an attack.

C Company Commander Eaton shouted over, "C Company will attack that machine gun. When I start to charge, you get out of here. In your position, you can't do anything but get killed."

As Young Oak and Takeba began discussing their escape, Young Oak suddenly felt Takeba's weight fall against him. Looking at Takeba's face, Young Oak could see his eyes were closed. A bullet had hit him directly between the eyes, but there was no sign of blood.

He had been with Young Oak from the beginning and had saved Young Oak's life twice at Santa Maria Olivetto. Takeba, whom Young Oak cherished like a brother, left this world without a sound at the age of twenty-five. He was one of the best soldiers Young Oak ever knew. He always kept his emotions under control, coolly assessed the situation and then took the appropriate action. In the midst of a deep sadness, and heedless of enemy fire, Young Oak stood up, walked to a nearby foxhole, and began giving orders in his usual calm voice.

C Company Commander Eaton and several other soldiers were also killed that night. It seemed to Young Oak that everyone he had talked to was killed or wounded. He felt jinxed. It was then that he promised himself, "If I survive this war, I will devote my life to the betterment of the community I belong to."

Ironically by then, an opposite superstition had been spread among the soldiers: enemy bullets would miss them if they were with him.

This was the beginning of the battle of Monte Cassino, a burning piece of hell on earth. It was a grueling and tragic battle for both sides. It was also a culturally barbarous act, as thousands of years of human civilization were destroyed.

Atop Monte Cassino was a famous and historic abbey, the Abbey of Montecassino. It was originally built by the Romans in the sixth century. It housed a priceless collection of European paintings, mosaics, books and manuscripts, and a critical collection of Christian cultural history that greatly influenced medieval European art.

As the Allies advanced toward Monte Cassino, the German command declared the area within a 300-meter radius from the abbey to be a neutral zone. This meant that both sides could not use the abbey for offense or defense. The Pope appealed to both sides to spare the abbey. The Allied command in Italy was split as to whether or not they should attack the abbey. Lieutenant General Mark Clark opposed an attack. General Bernard Frayburg, Commander of the New Zealand forces, favored an attack. Frayburg felt that even if the Germans didn't have artillery at the abbey, they might be using it as an observation post. The initial decision was to spare the abbey, so the initial attack involved Army units only. The first division sent was the U.S. Army 34th Division, which included the 100th Battalion. The battle continued for four months, requiring more than four additional divisions of U.S., British, French, Canadian, Indian, New Zealand, Polish and free Italian forces. It was no surprise that the 34th Division, which fought without air support, suffered heavy casualties.

After weeks of heavy casualties and no progress, an Allied air strike with 255 planes was ordered. Within three hours, a great repository of human cultural history was reduced to rubble. In addition, several hundred civilians who had sought shelter in the abbey were killed.

Young Oak witnessed the destruction of this cultural treasure. The air strike actually made the ground attack more difficult. The Germans, who had not positioned forces at the abbey, now quickly occupied the ruins and turned it into an ideal fortress.

During the first phase of the battle, the 100th suffered severe casualties. Its mission had been to capture a castle below the abbey. Though the Germans had declared the abbey a neutral area, they were unwilling to concede the castle. Three days after the air strike, the 100th was sent back to the front line. That battle lasted four days, resulting in about 200 casualties for the battalion. Four months after landing in Italy, it had lost 60 percent of its men, either killed or wounded. When the Battle of Monte Cassino began, the battalion had about 650 men, but lost 90 percent of them within two-and-a-half weeks. Now, only about 60 men of the 100th remained on the frontline. An average U.S. Army company consisted of 180 soldiers and six officers. In the 100th, which was specially formed, a company consisted of about 200 soldiers and 12 officers. Now only about 20 soldiers and one or two officers remained in each company.

The hell that surrounded Monte Cassino also followed Young Oak. He had been close to death several times, once on the embankment near the Volturno River and twice at Santa Maria Olivetto. The day Takeba was killed at Monte Majo, the bullet had missed Young Oak by the width of half a human face.

It was the last day for the 100th at Monte Cassino. Despite the heavy casualties, the 100th successfully advanced to a trail near the castle, but the trail was not wide enough to put 15 soldiers abreast. Attacking along the trail would be suicidal. The only road to the castle was blocked by two German tanks and an armored vehicle that had been destroyed earlier. Neither side could move along the road, so they began to exchange rifle fire.

Young Oak and Second Lieutenant Gary "Cloudy" Connor were in a small ditch near a protruding part of the castle. Conner had recently arrived at the front line. He was from Kansas. Young Oak, Connor, and their men could neither advance nor retreat from their position. A bullet flew so close they knew that they had been targeted by an enemy sniper. Sitting shoulder to shoulder, they couldn't move. The sniper seemed to be near the castle about 90 yards to their right. Young Oak was closer to the sniper than Connor.

The sniper fired at regular intervals, as if letting them know he was there. If they even slightly moved, he immediately fired. If they remained still, he fired every five minutes. Major Clough was about five yards to the left of Young Oak and Connor, also trying to avoid the sniper, but he was in a somewhat safer position. The men of B and C Companies, positioned on higher ground, were trying to bring down the sniper. The ground was covered with snow and a strong wind was blowing. Their uniforms were wet from rain. For more than four hours, Young Oak and Connor remained still in the freezing conditions. They thought they might freeze to death before the sniper got them. Then, the shooting stopped for 20 minutes. They thought their men might have finally killed the sniper. They waited another 10 minutes and nothing happened. They agreed the sniper had probably been killed and decided to get up. As they rose, Connor took out a cigarette and asked for a lighter and as Young Oak bent over to reach into his trouser pocket for one, the sharp sound of a gunshot rang. A bullet entered the right side of Connor's head, and completely passed through. Blood and brain spurted onto Young Oak. If Young Oak had not been reaching for his lighter, he would have also been hit.

The sniper again resumed firing every five minutes. Young Oak waited another two-and-a-half hours before finally deciding to escape while the sniper was reloading. He told Major Clough in a low voice, "I'm getting out of here."

"No, the sniper is still there. It's too dangerous. Even if you get out, you may fall down the cliff."

"No, I can't stand this anymore."

Young Oak couldn't stand listening to the moaning of his dying friend. He waited for the sniper to fire again, then sprang up and began rolling down the hill. If he couldn't stop in time, he would fall off a 150-foot cliff. But he was able to stop and he crawled another 30 to 40 yards down the hill and escaped. Sometime around then, Major Clough was wounded.

That afternoon, the Battalion was ordered to withdraw. With the few remaining soldiers, there was no hope of taking the castle. However, the task of retreating with their backs to the enemy on the ridge was not an easy one. Most of the officers, including Battalion Commander Clough, Mits Fukuda and Sakae Takahashi were wounded. First Lieutenant Samuel Sakamoto of A Company was the highest-ranking officer remaining, with Young Oak being the second-highest. While they were both First Lieutenants, Sakamoto had been at the rank for two years while Young Oak had only recently been promoted.

"Sam, you're the battalion commander now," Young Oak said. "Take command and withdraw the battalion."

"Are you out of your mind? I have to withdraw A Company, which has only 16 to 17 soldiers left. I don't even know where the other companies are. You're a battalion staff, so you take command. You're a better soldier than I am anyway. What's important now is not formalities, but survival."

Young Oak successfully led the withdrawal. The 100th went into reserve. It had lost so many men that it could no longer function as a combat unit. While in reserve, it received reinforcements from the 442nd Regiment, which consisted of Japanese American soldiers from the U.S. mainland.

The command post of the 133rd Regiment was behind a lower mountain facing Monte Cassino. One day Young Oak was ordered to report to the command post. As he arrived, the regimental commander said, "Our British friends will take over this attack. They want us to lead their officers to the castle to assist in formulating a plan of attack. I couldn't think of anyone better to lead them but you, Lieutenant Kim."

The order was to take the British officers to the castle and return. The British unit the regimental commander was referring to was an Indian unit known as the "Gurka Unit." The soldiers were actually from Nepal. It was a special unit with a rich tradition. Similar to the 100th Battalion, where most of the officers were white and the soldiers Japanese Americans, in the Gurka unit, the officers were British and the soldiers Nepalese.

They waited for dark and set out. There were more than 10 British officers commanded by a British lieutenant colonel. While they were studying the terrain, they were spotted by a platoon-sized German patrol. The group's formation had Young Oak and two lieutenants in the lead, followed by the lieutenant colonel, and then the rest. As soon as the Germans appeared, three lieutenants came from the rear to add to the protection of their commander. Young Oak could tell that this was truly an elite unit. The silence surrounding the castle was suddenly broken by German shouting and English whispers. In the darkness, running was not an option because of the nearby cliff. Unable to see anything but ready to pull the trigger of their rifles any moment, both sides had to go along feeling their way like blind men.

Having failed to capture Young Oak's group, the German patrol withdrew, and Young Oak's group returned to American headquarters. After they had returned, a British lieutenant colonel whispered into one of the other officer's ear. The officer hurriedly ran out and came back with something in his hand. It was a bottle of Scotch. The British officer handed the Scotch to Young Oak as a thank-you gesture.

After Young Oak returned to the 100th Battalion headquarters with the Scotch, soldiers all fought for a sip of it. As they enjoyed the moment, they forgot about Monte Cassino, Italy and the German soldiers.

While the 100th Battalion awaited replacements, Young Oak, First Lieutenant James Boodry, Communications Officer Frank De Maiolo, who was of Italian ancestry, and several enlisted men visited a small town near Apolino. The residents the town were initially puzzled by the Asian soldiers. When they learned they were Americans, they welcomed them like returning family members even though American artillery had destroyed many of their houses. An English-speaking resident took the men to his farm and organized a party. He served chicken and the best wine and cheese that he had.

"I lived in America for a while," the farmer said. "When I returned, I bought this farm with the money I made there. I haven't seen any Americans since I left and am very happy to see you."

With his wife, young daughter and neighbors standing by, he began to sing a beautiful Italian song.

The chicken on the table was his last brood hen. Upon learning this, Young Oak became upset.

"Why did you kill the chicken?" Young Oak asked.

"This is a special celebration. You have freed our farm, you have freed our town, and you have freed our country. We must celebrate."

"But this is your only chicken. You should have saved her to have more chickens."

"No. The Germans made our lives here miserable. Even though this is our last chicken, it is worth it."

At the end of the party, the Italians gave them wine, cheese and bread. In exchange, the soldiers gave them cigarettes, chocolate and other provisions they were carrying. The soldiers got the better of the exchange. The

Italians were poor and hungry, but they warmly and kindly welcomed these strange-looking liberators.

The Allies landed troops at Anzio in order to open a new front behind the Gustav Line. The operation was known as Operation Shingle. The name came from the image of peeling a shingle off a roof from both sides.

German resistance remained strong. The Gustav Line held, and the two sides entered into a long confrontation. The 100th was sent to reinforce the Anzio front. After the 100th withdrew, the Battle of Monte Cassino continued for two more months. The Allies launched another air attack on the monastery, where hundreds of planes dropped more than 200,000 bombs, but the Germans continued to hold. Finally, on the evening of May 16, German headquarters, fearing to be cut off from the rear, ordered a withdrawal. When Polish forces entered the monastery two days later, only a few dozen severely wounded German soldiers remained. The 100th Battalion became known as the "Purple Heart Battalion" because of the number of casualties it suffered at Monte Cassino.

Chapter 7
Beginning of a Legend

After the fall of Rome, the Allies pursued the Germans north. The 100th moved along the west coast. They marched day and night, finally arriving near Civitavecchia, about 40 miles north of Rome. Finally, the order came to stop marching and bivouac. It was about 11:00 p.m. and heavy rain was falling. Young Oak covered himself with his poncho and fell asleep immediately. Twenty minutes later, he was awakened by Battalion Commander, Lieutenant Colonel Singles.

"Go down to Civitavecchia and meet the 442nd," Singles ordered.

"You know the men. We have 25 officers. Can't you send someone else? I've had only five or six hours sleep in three days and I'm exhausted."

"No, you're the only one in the battalion who can find the road junction in Civitavecchia. It's almost demolished and the 442nd is arriving there at midnight. You have 40 minutes."

The 442nd Regiment had been formed before the 100th Battalion was sent to Africa. After the 100th had proven its loyalty to America, the 442nd was sent to Italy.

The driver didn't know the way, so Young Oak was unable to sleep on the way to Civitavecchia. They arrived at the location at about midnight and waited for the 442nd. After two hours, Young Oak told the driver to move the jeep out of the intersection and they fell asleep. Sometime later, someone shook him.

"Are you from the 100th?"

"Yes," Young Oak said.

"Are you the one who's supposed to meet us?"

"Yes."

"Then what are you doing sleeping in the jeep?"

"What time is it?"

"It's 0400."

"You were supposed to be here at midnight," Young Oak said.

"We got lost."

"Well, at midnight, I was out there. I was out there in the rain for two hours."

"If I hadn't seen your jeep and we had continued on, we could have been captured by the Germans."

Young Oak looked at him, and asked, "Who are you?"

"I'm Lieutenant Colonel Virgil Miller, Executive Officer of the 442nd."

"That's a lot of baloney about being captured."

"What do you mean?"

"There are two 34th Division regiments between you and the Germans," Young Oak said. "You would have run into them before you would have run into any Germans."

"You're a smartass, aren't you?"

"Is your whole unit here?"

"Yes."

"Well, let's go up to them and get going."

When they reached the regiment, Young Oak asked, "Is everyone ready to go?"

"We've been ready for a long time," one of the soldiers answered sarcastically. "We have more men than you and we've come to show you how to fight."

Young Oak stared at the face of the young officer. The 100th had been in combat for nine months, had proven itself to be one of the best units in all of Italy, and this brand new unit coming in was going to show them how to fight? He almost laughed in the man's face. He realized they had much to learn. Young Oak brought them to the bivouac area where foxholes had been dug and tents set up.

He was then sent to Battalion Commander. Lieutenant Colonel Singles, who welcomed him back. By then it was dawn.

"You made a tremendous first impression on the regimental executive officer and the regimental commander," Singles said, with a smile on his face,

"I don't want to hear about it," Young Oak said. "I'm tired and I need some sleep."

"Okay, get some sleep. Use that cot."

He fell asleep immediately. It was 10:00 a.m. when he awoke. He went to the battalion mess hall nearby. While he was eating his breakfast, a jeep pulled up in front of the mess hall. It was Colonel Charles Pence's jeep. Singles came out of his tent and saluted Colonel Pence. As they were talking, it appeared that Colonel Pence was trying to come to the mess hall while Lieutenant Colonel Singles was trying to take him somewhere else. He knew that Colonel Pence had heard about Young Oak's behavior the night before. Colonel Pence finally came into the mess hall while Young Oak was still eating breakfast. He did not get up to salute, but continued eating.

"Lieutenant Kim, what are you doing?" Colonel Pence asked.

"I'm eating breakfast, Sir," Young Oak said as he continued chewing.

"Isn't it late for breakfast?"

"I was up all night."

"So I heard. I think in the future you should eat breakfast at the right time."

After Colonel Pence left, Singles said to Young Oak, "Young, you should have stood up and saluted him."

"Sir, we're in combat and I'm dead tired. I've been running my butt off for nine months and I'm not going to do that for him."

"Young, you're a wonderful combat officer," Singles said smiling. "I'm a third-generation West Pointer, but if we think about talent as a soldier, you have more in one of your fingers than I have in my entire body. Still, you've got to learn something about the peacetime Army."

The 100th now became part of the 442nd Regiment. In the U.S. Army, an infantry regiment consisted of three infantry battalions. Since the 442nd had left its 1st Battalion in America, the 100th was supposed to be renamed the 1st Battalion. But the Fifth Army Commander Lieutenant General Clark, and Division Commander Major General Ryder, acknowledging the 100th's accomplishments and reputation, allowed it to continue using its name. Several days later, Lieutenant General Clark visited the 442nd to present the Distinguished Service Cross to Young Oak and Irving Akahoshi for their heroism in the liberation of Rome.

The 442nd Regiment fought its first battle at Belvedere, a small northern town south of the "Gothic Line." The Gothic Line was the other major defensive line established by the Germans. After the fall of Rome, they planned to defend the Gothic Line in the area north of Florence and spend the winter there. The Allied attack was planned for 8:00 a.m. Bolstered by his poor impression of Young Oak, Colonel Pence had developed a bad impression of the 100th. In addition, the 442nd wanted to win their first battle without the 100th. Colonel Pence ordered the 2nd and 3rd Battalions to take over the 100th's position and moved the 100th about four miles to the rear. From that position, the 100th couldn't know what was happening on the front. At noon, Singles became concerned.

"This is not good," Singles said. Four hours have passed, there is no news from the regimental headquarters, and we can't communicate with them. If they've been successful, we should join them. If they've been unsuccessful, we can't help them from here."

He gave the order to move forward. Led by Sakae Takahashi's B Company, the battalion began to move to the position they had turned over to the 2nd and 3rd Battalions. As they reached the high ground, Young Oak saw someone running down from above, followed by German soldiers. It was Division Commander Major General Ryder. As German soldiers, seeing the two stars on his helmet, tried to surround his jeep, Young Oak abandoned it and ran down the hill. It was clear that nothing good had happened to the 2nd and 3rd Battalions.

The day's attack was led by the 2nd, which was quickly surrounded by the Germans. All three rifle companies—E, F, and G—suffered major casualties. F Company suffered so much damage that it was unable to function as a rifle company for some time. Captain Ralph Ensminger, the well-liked former commander of E Company and now the battalion S-2, was killed. The Division Commander, wanting to witness the 442nd's first battle, entered an area that he had been told was secured, only to be surrounded by the enemy. The general's jeep and that of a colonel accompanying him were captured. The general's driver and the colonel's radio operator were both wounded. Major General Ryder lost his helmet, but managed to escape. With his face red with anger, he shouted to Singles, "Clean up the mess. Go around Belvedere and attack from behind."

The 100th marched eastward, then north. As they reached a mountain north of Belvedere, they could see Hitler's SS motorized battalion attacking the 2nd Battalion. The Germans had not noticed the 100th's arrival. Although Young Oak was the intelligence officer, he was in charge of operations because Operations Officer Oscar King had remained in the rear. Standing next to Singles, Young Oak began to issue orders as he watched the battle unfold. This was the beginning of his saga as a legendary operations and planning officer.

This was the first battle in which the 100th couldn't communicate with the other units involved in the battle. In those days, regimental headquarters could only establish radio contact with battalion commanders, operations officers and intelligence officers. But Singles and Young Oak couldn't contact the regimental headquarters. Also, since the 100th was not expected to be involved in the battle, it didn't have an artillery liaison officer. This meant they had to fight with no artillery support. The traditional plan of attack for a U.S. Army battalion was to send two rifle companies abreast with the third rifle company in reserve at the rear. Surveying the terrain, Young Oak decided that this approach was not appropriate and ordered all three companies to engage simultaneously. A and C companies were ordered to hide at the entrance of the town to cut off escape, while B Company attacked from the side. Young Oak explained this to Captain Takahashi. Takahashi, while a wonderful soldier, was not very talkative and didn't show much emotion, but when given a task, he completed it with the least casualties.

When B Company attacked, the Germans were so surprised that they began to retreat in disorder. As their chain of command collapsed, they retreated toward the entrance to the town. C Company began firing, driving the Germans toward the only remaining exit where A Company was waiting. In a short period of time, the Germans suffered major casualties and withdrew, leaving all their equipment behind. It was expected to take several days to capture Belvedere, but the 100th's surprise attack took the town in only three hours. While rescuing the 2nd and 3rd Battalions, the 100th killed 178 enemies and captured 73 prisoners, 2 tanks and 42 vehicles. The 100th emerged with only four dead and seven wounded.

The regiment's next objective was Sassetta, about four miles north of Belvedere. This time, Colonel Pence assigned the task to the 100th. The following day, although Singles was concerned that the enemy was too close, Young Oak took a patrol into the valley between Belvedere and Sassetta. He wanted to see the enemy positions with his own eyes. The battalion commander had already begun delegating the role of S-3 to Young Oak. The men in the battalion were fortunate. Summer had come and they were well hidden in the deep forest. The patrol included three artillery liaison officers. During the previous day's battle, he had been unable to coordinate with the 522nd Artillery Battalion, which was 442nd's artillery, so he decided to ask for direct support from the Army artillery and from the Corps artillery. Consequently, two of the artillery officers came from the Army and the Corps.

A U.S. Army infantry regiment was supported by one artillery battalion with 54, 105mm howitzers. Each artillery battalion consisted of three artillery batteries, each with 18 guns. Each battery supported one battalion, so an infantry battalion, in devising an attack plan, assumed the support of 18, 105mm howitzers. On the other hand, a Corps or an Army artillery battalion had 54, 155mm howitzers. When they gave fire support, the entire battalion fired. Using the two artillery battalions together meant the support of 108 guns, six times as many as one regimental artillery battery. And these guns were 155mm rather than 105mm, meaning longer range, more accuracy and more power. There was another factor as well. A regimental artillery unit often ran low on ammunition, as it was closer to the front lines and fired more frequently. Corps or Army units deployed further back from the front lines fired less and had a better supply of ammunition. This organization of artillery had developed in Europe where battles usually took place on a wide flat terrain. The larger guns were used solely to take out the larger guns of the enemy. Consequently, they held their fire until the enemy artillery had fired and could be located. Young Oak's decision to use the larger artillery in support of an infantry battalion, seemingly reasonable today, was a breakthrough at the time. No military school taught in this way. Both the Army and Corps willingly sent their artillery liaison officers to him. An hour before they set off, Captain Charles Feibelman of the 522nd Artillery Battalion came up to Young Oak. He was the artillery liaison officer for the 100th.

"I'm going to provide you with artillery support today," Feibelman said.

"I'm going forward, and you can come along, but I don't need you today," Young Oak said. "We needed you desperately yesterday. Where were you?"

"We should have been with you, but we weren't. We did something that never should have been done. We were moving A Battery—they're supposed to support you."

"That's 18 guns. In combat, you never move a battery that's going to be committed."

"We didn't know you were going to be committed."

"There's no excuse."

"You're right. There's no excuse."

Captain Feibelman kept apologizing as he joined the group. There were 14 soldiers in the group, three artillery liaison officers and their six radiomen, Sergeant Minami, Private First Class Akahoshi and two other members of the intelligence section. Radio batteries were so big and heavy that one artillery liaison officer needed two radiomen. Young Oak had determined that radio communications were adequate, so they didn't need wiremen. Once in the valley, he carefully examined the

German positions and began thinking about an operations plan. He was using a German scope captured the day before. German scopes had special heat filters and produced better images than American ones. At about 8:00 p.m., Young Oak picked up the radio and began describing his plans to the battalion commander.

"I can't see the things you're describing, but the plan you've outlined is wonderful," Singles said. "Go ahead and talk directly to the commanders."

Young Oak then contacted the company commanders and began issuing orders. As planned, he used the two artillery battalions from the Corps and the Army, but didn't use Captain Feibelman's 522nd. Feibelman became increasingly angry, but Young Oak saw no reason to use 18 guns of 105mm when he had 108 bigger guns with more ammunition. Young Oak and Feibelman eventually became close friends, but not that night.

The night operations plan was executed precisely. The artillery fire from the 108 guns of 155mm howitzers smashed the Germans and the 100th took Sasseta. Over 200 Germans were killed while the 100th suffered only two casualties. C Company commander Harold Ethridge was killed and one Non-commissioned officer (NCO) was badly wounded. After the battle, the only way for Young Oak's group to reach Sasseta was to return to the original location of the 100th and go the long way around.

It was getting dark when they finally reached Sassetta. As they passed through the ruins and entered the main road, Young Oak saw the regimental commander in the middle of the road. When Colonel Pence saw him, he raised his right hand, circled it around his head two or three times, and pumped it up and down repeatedly. It was the same hand signal Young Oak had used in the first battle. Pence was signaling him to come up to him quickly.

Instead of running, however, Young Oak slowed down. His previous encounters with Colonel Pence had been unpleasant. He was wondering what he might have done wrong this time. As he reached the commander, Pence put his arms around Young Oak's shoulders and said, "Young, from this day forward, you and I are going to be best friends."

Young Oak was stunned.

"Whether you're my friend or not, I don't know, but I'm going to be your best friend," Pence continued. "Can't you see me without my helmet? It's to copy you. Let's go in and toast today's victory."

With his arm around Young Oak, Pence led him into a bar filled with the men of the 100th. He ordered drinks for everyone, turned to the men, and proposed a toast.

"Today, I witnessed an almost perfect battle. I have witnessed hundreds of practices at Fort Benning. They were against a fake enemy on familiar terrain. Today, you attacked a real enemy on unfamiliar terrain. It's amazing what you did."

Then turning to Young Oak, he continued, "I want to propose a toast to Young Oak for planning and issuing the orders for today's victory. Cheers."

Everyone held his glass high and drank. After the toast, Young Oak asked the colonel, "What are you doing here, Sir?"

"I came to observe the 100th."

Young Oak was puzzled.

"Yesterday I had no communications with headquarters," Pence explained. "I still didn't have any this morning. The 100th was making the main attack, so I figured I should be with you."

"When are you leaving?" Young Oak asked.

"I'm not sure. When the 442nd gets communications, then I'll leave."

Colonel Pence had served in China for several years during the 1930s, when Japan was pushing into Manchuria and northern China. He had become known as an expert in Asian affairs, so he was made the commanding officer of the 442nd. The reason Colonel Pence said he was copying Young Oak, when he wore a neat cap instead of a helmet, was because Young Oak didn't wear a helmet in combat. At that time, the U.S. Army levied $50 fines for soldiers who didn't wear their helmets, regardless of rank, in order to protect them. Considering his wages were about $40, the fine was heavy. Nevertheless, Young Oak used a neat cap instead of a helmet because he couldn't think straight if he wore a helmet. Moreover, since he frequently gave orders through the radio, the helmet was an impediment. Members of his unit knew this, so when they would go looking for him, they would look for someone fighting without a helmet. As time went on, the commanding officers granted him the right, even though it was a violation of Army regulations.

In addition to not wearing a helmet, Young Oak possessed more quirks. He didn't use a foxhole. In the beginning, he used to sleep in a foxhole. But he grew to believe if he was destined to die, it wouldn't matter where he slept. American soldiers often said that if an enemy bullet had their serial numbers on it, they were going to die no matter what. Soldiers would dig a foxhole for him, but he didn't use it. He also frequently skipped meals. He wouldn't have three meals a day, since he felt he had to take care of lives in combat. Soldiers would set aside his meals, but more often than not he skipped them.

After spending a day in battle together, Captain Feibelman and Young Oak had grown closer. However, the next day, Captain Feibelman continued to complain.

"Young, are you going to keep doing this to me?"

"No, but you people screwed up the first time."

"I know we did, but we're ready to make amends," Feibelman said.

"Chuck, you saw yesterday that when I asked for support fire, a whole battalion kept firing five rounds per gun as fast as it could. Can you get the 522nd to fire five rounds per gun?"

"No, we don't have enough ammunition."

"Then why should I use your guns, which are smaller and less accurate, and able to fire only two or three rounds, when I can fire five rounds from over 100 guns, over 500 rounds, without question?"

"I can't argue with that."

"Besides, you people are too old-fashioned."

They were on the fourth floor of the beautiful house of a wealthy Italian. The walls were all glass, affording a clear view of the surrounding area.

"Do you want to play a game?" Young Oak asked.

"What?"

"See that church tower over there?"

"Yes."

"I bet I can get a round to hit near that tower more quickly than you can."

"No way."

"You start."

They pulled out a map and stopwatch and the contest was on. Captain Feibelman followed standard U.S. artillery practice—one round over, one round short, one to the right, one to the left and the fifth near the target. Then it was Young Oak's turn. As he spoke through the radio, one shell dropped to the right of the tower, one to the left, and then a third, closer to the target than Feibelman's fifth shell. Feibelman was surprised and asked, "How the hell did you do that?"

"You did it according to the book, like you've been taught," Young Oak said. "You people think your method is best because you have a closed mind."

"That was an accident."

"Then, let's try it again."

They repeated the experiment and the result was the same.

"Son of a bitch, you beat me again," Feibelman said. "You bracketed the target with two rounds, and hit it with a third. It took me four rounds to bracket it and my fifth round wasn't as close as your third. How the hell did you do it?"

"That's my secret. You're a graduate of Quartz Hill Artillery School. Tell me why your system's better."

"I've watched you twice now, so I can't say that my system's better, but this is the first time I've ever questioned Quartz Hill. Tell me how you do it. I want to adopt your method."

As Young Oak explained, Captain Feibelman applauded.

"You're right. We'd be crazy to use only our 522nd with only 18 guns. I'll go along with you. We'll get Corps and Army artillery battalions to support us."

From then on, Captain Feibelman gave total support to Young Oak's tactics, and the 100th always used its artillery as Young Oak dictated. It was in the battles at Belvedere and Sassetta that Young Oak's special talent as an operations officer began to shine. His special talent lay in quick analysis, precise judgment, creative thinking and bold decision-making.

Although Colonel Pence had not said anything at the time, there was another reason why he was enthusiastic about the battle at Sassetta. During the night of the battle, he had special guests with him at the 100th Battalion headquarters. They were the chief of staff of the 91st

Division and one of its regimental commanders. It was Fifth Army's policy that the key staff officers and regimental commanders of a division newly arrived in Italy witness a battle involving an experienced division, so the regimental commanders of the 91st Division had been sent to observe the 34th. As S-2, Young Oak's radio could communicate with the battalion commander and the company commanders. At the battalion headquarters, Pence and his guests could listen to the conversations between Young Oak and the company commanders. Young Oak learned of this much later when, on the orders of Lieutenant General Clark, the 100th was sent to occupy Leghorn, which had been captured by the 91st Division. The Chief of Staff of the 91st, Colonel Joseph Donovin, came up to him and said, "I was there the day you gave the orders for the attack on Sassetta. We were interested and very impressed."

Young Oak asked why he was there. After explaining the visit, Colonel Donovin continued, "You made a marvelous impression on me. I'll never forget it. If I have a vacancy, I am going to request you, and I hope you'll honor the request. I would like you to be a staff officer of the 91st. You're very junior, but I'll make you a Lieutenant Colonel."

Division intelligence officer was a position for a Lieutenant Colonel. It was unprecedented to offer such a position to a new captain, let alone one of Asian ancestry. Racial minorities couldn't aspire to a rank that high.

After the victories at Belvedere and Sassetta, the 100th received a U.S. Presidential Unit Citation, the highest honor for an individual unit. The 100th quickly became the core of the 442nd, making up for the inexperience of the 2nd and 3rd Battalions. This led to conflict within the unit. The 100th was composed mostly of Japanese Americans from Hawaii, while the 2nd and 3rd were composed of

Japanese Americans from the mainland, and this difference fueled a rivalry within the 442nd. With the 100th reaffirmed as the best unit in Italy, Lieutenant General Clark used them as an honor guard when Allied VIPs visited the front lines in Italy. Lieutenant Colonel Singles was to select a battalion staff officer or company commander to lead the honor guard. When the U.S. Undersecretary of War Robert Patterson visited Livorno in 1944, Young Oak led the honor guard. This was while the unit was enjoying an unusual reserve break in Vada.

Chapter 8
A Beauty and a Hero

With the 442nd in reserve, Lieutenant Colonel Singles gave Young Oak R&R.

"I should have sent you a long time ago, but I needed you badly," Singles said. "If I don't release you now, I don't know when I can later, so don't worry about the battalion and enjoy the break in Rome."

R&R (Rest and Recuperation) was a short leave for soldiers on the battlefield. Every Allied soldier in Italy wanted to go to Rome, so the Fifth Army established a quota for an individual unit. When a five-day R&R to Rome became available to the 100th, the battalion commander gave it to Young Oak. A unique feeling overcame Young Oak, as the jeep carrying him and another officer approached Rome. Young Oak had risked his life in Anzio to capture two German POWs to liberate Rome.

He checked into the Excelsior Hotel, the best hotel in Rome for officers on R & R. He went to his room and put away his luggage, just one duffle bag packed by his men. It was full of cigarettes, chocolates and other candies. There was a reason for this. The U.S. military paid its soldiers serving overseas in military scrip, not dollars. This scrip was worthless outside of military bases. Italy had undergone severe inflation, so the lira was also worthless. The Italian economy had gone into a barter system. Different items, of course, had different values. Chocolates like Hershey or Baby Ruth were popular, but they melted in the heat. Cans from C rations were also popular, but some people didn't like them. Cigarettes were the hottest item, because they were easy to keep and uniform in size. Five cigarettes could even buy a woman; a pack could buy anything. The U.S. military gave its soldiers the best cigarettes, such as Lucky Strike and Camel, and the soldiers always took them on leave. Cigarettes were plentiful on the front lines, even more so in a unit such as the 100th, which had suffered heavy casualties. Young Oak didn't take leave often, but when he did, his NCOs always filled a duffle bag with cigarettes and chocolates.

Captain Takahashi had arrived in Rome a few days earlier and he and Young Oak had agreed to meet at the hotel bar. The bar was packed with nearly 300 hundred soldiers and many young women. It was noisy and smoke-filled. Ordering a drink at the bar was almost impossible. Fortunately, Takahashi and a companion had procured a table. Young Oak joined them. It was Takahashi's last day of R & R and he was pleased to share a drink with them before his return. Takahashi was usually a quiet man, but tonight he wanted to share his experiences in Rome with Young Oak, who was listening to him carefully. Suddenly, the room became quiet. A beautiful blonde woman in her early twenties had entered the room and captured everyone's attention. Whistles and shouts rang through the room, as the soldiers tried to attract her attention. Young Oak turned back to Takahashi, but then felt a tap on his shoulder.

"May I speak with you briefly?" the woman asked.

Young Oak excused himself as Takahashi looked at him, stunned. When they reached a quiet place outside the bar, she asked, "Sir, when did you come to Rome?"

"Just today."

"Let me get to the point. If it's agreeable with you, I will stay with you for five days."

She knew his R&R would be for five days. Clearly, she had done this before, but Young Oak said nothing.

"This is the only way for my family not to starve. We are a noble family, so there will be conditions. Can you promise me to meet these conditions?"

"Conditions?"

"First, during these five days I will stay with you, I will see no other man. I expect the same; during these five days, you will see no other girl. Second, I can't sleep overnight. I will come here at 10:00 a.m. every day and leave at 10:00 p.m. Third, my mother will bring me each morning in a cart. You will wait for me at the entrance and escort me inside properly. Fourth, you will have three meals with me every day. I will take home all the leftovers. If we eat with other couples, I will share the leftovers with the other girls. Fifth, I will expect you to show a certain level of appreciation, but will leave that to you. Finally, other than my mother, no member of my family knows about this. I expect you to respect that."

"There are many other soldiers here and I am Asian. Why did you pick me?"

"They were all talking, you were listening. I saw you as a person of words."

It must have been very difficult for a young woman to speak in that way, but she didn't take a servile attitude. The way she spoke showed she was highly educated and from an honorable family. When Young Oak returned to the bar, Takahashi growled at him.

"For the last five days I tried to be with her. I promised her five cartons of cigarettes, but she wouldn't look at me. You just got here and she came up to you. What's going on?"

The four officers laughed in unison. That evening, Takahashi and his companion returned to the 100th.

The next morning at 10:00 a.m., the young woman appeared as promised. They entered a restaurant and the waiter seated them at an eight-person table with other women. Young Oak gave the waiter two packs of cigarettes, one for him and one for the manager. He instructed the waiter to replenish sugar, bread and anything else, as needed. He promised another pack if service was good. As the waiter kept bringing food to the table, the women at Young Oak's table couldn't stop laughing as they stuffed the food into their bags. It was evident that the Italian economy was ruined. Daily survival was the main goal. Even talking about having a job was a luxury.

They say war is hell. This is particularly true for women. Despite their sacrifice to feed their families during the war, they were ostracized afterward. As Young Oak was to learn, the situation was the same in France. On his fifth day, he gave the young woman his duffle bag, still full of chocolates and cigarettes. She was shocked, saying it was too much, and refused to accept it. Leaving the bag behind, he wished her good luck, and hopped in his jeep to return to the 100th.

After the liberation of Rome and the Normandy Landing, the Allies continued pressing the Germans. In Italy, the U.S. forces were responsible for the western front while the British fought on the eastern front. The Allies kept pushing northward, approaching the Arno River, which ran across the peninsula. Although the Germans had retreated from Rome, they had done so in an orderly fashion and were waiting for the Allies at the Gothic Line, their second major defense line. Ultimate victory in Italy required breaking the Gothic Line. For this, the Allies had to cross the Arno.

Chapter 9
The Leaning Tower of Pisa

The U.S. Fifth Army divided the western front in Italy into two parts and assigned the western half to the Fourth Corps. For the crossing of the Arno, the IV Corps established a special unit, "Task Force 45," and attached the 100th Battalion to it. Its operational area ran from the Adriatic Coast to the areas east of Pisa. The core of the task force was the transformed U.S. Army Anti-Aircraft Artillery Brigade. Since fewer and fewer German planes flew in the Italian sky, the anti-air units had little to do, while infantry casualties mounted. So, the 45th, AAA Brigade was suddenly converted to infantry. It was unrealistic, however, to expect an anti-air unit to be transformed into a reliable infantry brigade with only a few weeks of training. The 100th was assigned to the task force in an effort to compensate for this weakness. Also attached to the task force was the 370th Regiment of the 92nd Division. The 92nd, newly arrived in Italy, consisted mostly of African American soldiers. The high-ranking officers were white, but the junior officers and other soldiers were all African American. Brigadier General Paul W. Rutledge positioned the 100th between the 45th, AAA Brigade and the 370th Regiment, at a point where the Arno flowed just southeast of Pisa. Also attached to the task force were a light tank company, a heavy tank company, an artillery battalion and a chemical mortar company.

Claiming he knew nothing about infantry, General Rutledge left it to the 100th to handle these units. Thus, the 100th, sandwiched between two inexperienced units, became the core of the Arno River crossing. This meant that Young Oak, who had officially become S-3—operations officer—once again assumed heavy responsibilities. As he studied the map, he thought through a battle plan: *Our goal is to cross the Arno, secure a beachhead and liberate Pisa. But Pisa is like Rome in that there are historic cultural treasures. How can we possibly take Pisa without a direct attack on it? Enemy morale appears to be worsening. Psychology is very important in combat and I think they are becoming nervous. Before we came, they sent patrols several miles south of the river, but none since we've arrived. Now we're patrolling to the north of the river. We've been in Italy 11 months. They have learned to respect and fear us. Since Rome, they appear to be short of artillery—not just guns, but also ammunition. They fired much more before Rome than after. With the Normandy invasion, munitions are probably going to France rather than across the Alps into Italy. We know they are short of planes and other supplies. If anyone is going to be short of ammunition, it will be the German forces in Italy. So, how can we do this with minimum casualties?*

Two days later, he brought his plan to the battalion commander. He had decided to use a tactic never used before. He briefed Battalion Commander, Lieutenant Colonel Singles about his plan, along with Intelligence Officer James Boodry, Communications Officer Frank De Maiolo, and Artillery Liaison Officer Charles Feibelman. His plan was simple: launch two fake attacks, and then the real attack. When he finished the briefing, Singles slapped his knee and approved it. Devising the plan was the easy part; putting the details on paper was much harder. Young Oak asked the artillery liaison officer to plan their fire support. What guns would they fire, where and when? How would they move the barrages? Where would they put the smokescreen? He, in turn, would work with the chemical mortar company on their smoke round. The heavy weapons company commander had to make specific plans for machinegun fire and mortars. The tank commander had to plan the movement, order and timing. Each commander had to know everything. Young Oak held meetings with all these people.

The plan was to launch a fake attack at the time of day and location of the real one. This would be followed in two days by another fake attack, with the real attack being launched on the third day. The fake attacks were designed to lure the Germans into wasting ammunition. Even better, if they mistook the real attack for another fake, the river crossing would be much easier. The fake attacks would be mobilized exactly the same way as the real one—with artillery, tanks, machine guns, chemical mortars and trucks. The only difference would be the size of the infantry.

The location of the attack had been decided. The Arno looped up and down, forming several "U" shaped areas. Near the town of Taccini, the river formed a U with the bottom toward the south. There, the river was wider but shallow, no deeper than a man's chest. It had been a crossing point for centuries. There were also many rocks on the bottom, enabling the soldiers to cross on foot while keeping their weapons dry and also allowing tanks to cross. Lastly, since the Allies controlled the south bank of the river, they controlled both sides of the U, making it impossible for the Germans to mobilize a large force inside the U to the north of the river. There were no hills south of the river, but many hills to the north, so the Germans would have a clear view of everything the 100th did.

After all the documentation and plans were finished, Young Oak, the artillery liaison officer, the tank company commander, the heavy weapons company commander and the three rifle company commanders repeatedly simulated the attacks. General Rutledge and Battalion Commander Singles also attended the operations meetings with Young Oak in charge of the briefings. Though General Rutledge was silent at the meetings, he was curious as to how the 100th could communicate so effectively with its companies and other units. Task Force 45 couldn't even communicate between headquarters and the units directly under its command.

The first mock attack began at 7:00 a.m. with a barrage of 108 guns of 105mm howitzers. The barrage continued for more than 10 minutes, intensifying and moving north over time, as if supporting an attacking infantry. The artillery also attacked the hills, where the German observers were, in order to obscure their view. Mortars, machine guns and 50 caliber guns were also fired. About 30 Sherman tanks, the largest in the U.S. Army at the time, followed the artillery fire north, along with a company of light trucks. The dry weather helped the vehicles kick up a lot of dust, further obscuring visibility. The tanks had been instructed to stay relatively close to the rear, because the artillery fire was not going to last long. Very little infantry and no aircraft were involved. As expected, the Germans responded with heavy rounds of artillery shells designed to impede infantry that was not there. Two days later, during the second mock attack, the Germans did the same, but with a noticeable reduction in firepower. On September 1, when the actual attack was made, there was no artillery, nor small arms fire from the Germans. Young Oak was unsure as to whether they had run out of ammunition or simply thought this was another fake. By 7:30 a.m., 30 minutes after the attack had begun, the lead units of the 100th were across the river. By 8:00 a.m., the entire battalion was across, with no casualties at all. As it turned out, after the second fake attack, the Germans had withdrawn. During the crossing, the river became very colorful.

Prior to the crossing, the soldiers had discovered some abandoned factories filled with beautifully colored silk and linen shirts, which reminded them of Hawaiian aloha shirts. One out of four soldiers had picked some up, and put them on over their uniforms as the Arno River crossing began. Soldiers cheered that Hawaiian shirts brought luck as they crossed the river without casualties. Young Oak smiled as he watched the colorfully dressed soldiers cheering. He looked at Singles. Without saying a word, Singles smiled back and gestured his men to march on.

After the successful crossing of the Arno, the 100th marched to the north side of the town of Pisa, where they were ordered to hold until the other units had crossed the river. Young Oak and Singles stood looking into the city. Singles, who had traveled all over the world before the war, started talking about why the tower was leaning and the history of the city. They were just a few miles from the tower.

"Why don't we go down and take a look at it?" Young Oak suggested.

They had been ordered to wait until noon, so they had two-and-a-half hours to kill, and the tower was right in front of them. Everyone, including artillery liaison officer Captain Feibelman, wanted to go to see the famous tower, one of the Seven Wonders of the World. While it might have been dangerous for just a few soldiers to enter the city, which could still be occupied by the Germans, the men of the 100th had developed a strong superstitious belief that, with Young Oak, they would be safe. Singles, Young Oak, and five others took two jeeps into Pisa. It was a moving moment for Young Oak and the battalion commander, leading the Allied Forces into Pisa, home of one of the wonders of human civilization. In the early fall, with the heat of summer gone and winter having not yet arrived, northern Italy was beautiful. The day was perfect.

Even though German soldiers were positioned near the Arno River to defend against a river crossing, the city of Pisa was deserted: no Germans, no inhabitants. Residents had fled the city. Only fully ripe fruit trees, such as apricot, plum and peach, stood tall to defend the city.

Perhaps the Germans didn't want to put the treasures of Pisa at risk. Young Oak also had never considered launching a direct attack in the city. But, unlike Rome, the Germans had not declared Pisa an open city. Sitting beside the driver, who was on high alert for the enemy, Singles kept lecturing about art history. He was usually a man of few words, but not this time. He sounded like a tour guide as he described the history of the tower. As they approached, Young Oak's heart began to pound as well. The jeeps stopped right in front of the tower. They took each other's picture with the tower in the background, then climbed the 294-step spiral staircase to the top. They were literally the first Allied soldiers who climbed the historic tower. Young Oak tried to measure the angle of the tower's lean. It was a wonder that the tower, 14,500 tons of marble, had stood for 600 years at a 10-degree incline. Standing in the bell tower, Young Oak thought of Galileo and the famous experiment he was said to have conducted there, dropping two balls of different weights from the top. The tower is only about 60 yards high, so he was unable to see either the Adriatic Sea to the west or his men to the north.

Young Oak had accomplished his mission of crossing the Arno River and liberating Pisa without any bloodshed, and now he stood at the top of the famous Tower of Pisa. While Young Oak was enjoying the quiet of the tower, other units of Task Force 45 were still fighting with the Germans. German headquarters must have known that the 100th was already across, but not that they were right behind them. After their tour of the Tower of Pisa, they visited the Duomo of Pisa nearby, and returned to the 100th at about 10:30 a.m. Noon came, but the order to hold their position remained as some units still had not crossed the Arno. Some hours later, when the Germans learned that the 100th was across the river and positioned behind them, they withdrew from the area.

At about 4:00 p.m., the IV Corps ordered the 100th to move toward its next objective, the Serchio River. An hour and a half later, new orders arrived—to hold position. The AAA Brigade to the left and the African American regiment had not yet crossed the Arno and headquarters didn't want to create too much distance between the units. The units crossed during the next two hours. When the 100th arrived at the Serchio River, new orders were given. The unit was instructed to leave at midnight for a nearby port to be transported to Naples at 9:00 a.m. the day. General Rutledge visited battalion headquarters as the unit was preparing to leave. With tears in his eyes, he wrung his hands and expressed deep regret in releasing the 100th from his command.

"I don't know how we're going to do anything. I have a big brigade, but the only fighting unit I have is the 100th."

He was talking to the battalion commander and to Young Oak as well as a number of others. He turned to Young Oak and said, "What can I do to keep you? If you agree to be transferred to my brigade, I will make you a major immediately."

He said this in front of Singles, who didn't say a word. He then turned to Singles.

"Do you have any objections?" Rutledge asked.

"I have no objection," Singles replied. "It's entirely in the hands of Young Oak. If he doesn't want to stay with us, I will divest. If he wants to stay, of course I'll be delighted."

The general turned to Young Oak

"No sir, you don't have the authority to make me a major and, even if you did, I would still stay," Young Oak said. "My loyalty is to the 100th and to my men and I'll be going with them to Naples."

"I'm lost. I don't know what I'll do," General Rutledge said.

The 100th left the next morning for Naples. Leaving for Naples meant that their yearlong Italian campaign was behind them. Their next stop would be the battlefields of France.

Chapter 10
Smokescreen

On September 26, 1944, Young Oak left Naples onboard a ship headed for France. His unit belonged to the reinforcement troops. The Allies had already landed in the south of France over a month and a half earlier. In order to diffuse the German troops in France, the U.S. wanted to land simultaneously in Normandy and in southern France. However, the landing in southern France had been postponed due to British opposition. Initially, the southern France landing was to be led by Lieutenant General Clark. Instead, Clark had wanted to stay in Italy to finalize the victory there, so he agreed to send three divisions under his command over to France. The Allied command specifically requested the inclusion of the 442nd, so Young Oak was also being sent to France. As the reinforcement troops sailed the Mediterranean Sea, rumors spread quickly:

"The Allies are fighting bloody battles in the northern mountains of France."

"The German forces are going to collapse soon."

"The war will be over by mid-October."

"General Eisenhower has hinted that soldiers will be spending Christmas at home."

The fleet anchored in Marseilles three days after leaving Naples. Always vulnerable to seasickness, Young Oak had no time to worry about the battlefields, but was ultimately grateful that the trip had been relatively smooth. The quiet Mediterranean Sea was like a peaceful lake. Little did he know that it was the calm before the storm of the bloody battles to come.

Attached to the 36th Division, the 442nd moved to the north. The 36th Division had been nicknamed the "Texas Division" because it had been the National Guard unit of Texas. The division was moving north towards the Vosges Mountains. The further north the division moved, the stronger German resistance became. This was because just past the Vosges Mountains was Strasbourg and right after that was Germany. By the time the American troops had landed in northern France and approached Aachen, the historic gateway to Germany, the British were attacking through Belgium towards the heavy industrial region of Ruhr. But neither American nor British troops were able to make further progress due to increasingly strong German resistance. As the Allied Forces tried to push their way into Germany, the Germans concentrated their entire defense into the Rhine region. This was the last line of defense for the Germans. There were even rumors that Hitler had ordered death over surrender.

  The two largest cities in the Vosges region were Epinal and St. Die that were connected by rail through the small village of Bruyères. Thus, Bruyères was a vital tactical stronghold for the German forces. As the Allied Forces intensified attacks on Bruyères, German resistance intensified to the point of a stalemate. The German troops were strengthening their defenses and had just destroyed the railroad that ran through Bruyères when Young Oak's regiment landed in Marseilles. Two weeks later, Young Oak's regiment arrived at Bruyères.

  Bruyères is a small town surrounded by four mountains to its east, west and north with only flatlands to the south. The occupation of these mountains would naturally mean the taking of Bruyères. For ease of reference, the Americans referred to the four mountains as Hill A, B, C and D. Among the four, Hill A, over to the west, was the highest and thus, the key to victory. The 100th Battalion was ordered to take Hill A.

  As the operations officer, battle planning was Young Oak's mission. By that time, the battalion commander had so much faith in Young Oak that he would simply glance at Young Oak's general idea and approve it with a nod. In order to attack Hill A, Young Oak saw that the troops would have to pass through a forest to the west of the mountain. The regimental commander said that the division commander had reported no enemy in the forest and that the mission would be an easy task. However, after scrutinizing the terrain, Young Oak couldn't believe that the Germans wouldn't defend the forested region.

Taking First Lieutenant James Boodry, Young Oak went to the forest in order to make contact with the 45th Division, which was the unit to attack Bruyères from the north and to examine the forest. Boodry, the intelligence officer, succeeded Young Oak as S-2 in Italy; it was Boodry who would replace Young Oak if Young Oak were to be wounded or killed in action. Boodry was a brave and conscientious soldier; yet, he always had a smile for everyone. War is such a terrible and grim time; there is so much one could easily gripe and complain about. One couldn't do anything about the weather. One couldn't do anything about the casualties. One couldn't do anything about anything! The only thing one could do was stay organized, keep the men together and fight. Boodry was the kind of man who possessed an optimistic outlook on life, maintained his happy disposition and ultimately avoided ever being a toxic factor to the morale of the men.

As the two moved cautiously through the forest, Young Oak caught sight of an American second lieutenant lying in a foxhole. Just as Young Oak was about to call out to him, the soldier gestured and whispered, "Quiet, sir. The enemy is just ahead."

"Who are you?" Young Oak asked.

With his face covered with mud and showing extreme fatigue, he answered, "I'm G Company commander, 179 Battalion, 5th Division. My company got here only a week ago, but all the other officers are either dead or wounded. I'm the only one left. G Company has been reduced to a quarter of our original size."

Incredulously, Boodry intoned, "We had intelligence that the enemy had retreated."

"That's a complete lie. I haven't been able to move from this spot for a week," the soldier said weakly.

Young Oak's report of enemy presence in the forest moved quickly up the chain of command, from battalion commander to regimental commander on up to division commander. But the division commander didn't even blink an eye. The radio order that came back down from Regimental Commander Colonel Pence to Battalion Commander Singles was, "I want to believe Young's report, but we've got our orders to move 10 kilometers a day."

But Young Oak's report was accurate. The Germans were all dug in, waiting for the Americans to attack. They had set up machine guns everywhere and spread mines throughout the forest. Even their foxholes were so well camouflaged with leaves and branches that a soldier wouldn't have been able to see it without falling into it. Singles was furious, but had to issue attack orders nonetheless.

The battle that ensued in the depth of the Vosges Mountains was entirely different from any of the battles in Italy. The hills were densely covered with pine trees, and in a forest battle, the shattered branches of these trees were demons to the soldiers below. Exploding shells would splinter the pine trees into sharp shards that would rain down along with the shrapnel of the artillery in a cascade of death. The impact of German artillery rounds was thereby profoundly increased. Even the deepest of foxholes were defenseless without solid cover. Dusk quickly fell over the forest as early as 4:00 p.m. in the afternoon. It became pitch black and the wind whistled through the trees like a devil's flute. The soldiers could barely see their own rifles and the hairs stood on the backs of their necks at the mere sound of a pinecone dropping to the ground. Although it was only October, the chill in the Vosges Mountains was accompanied by a rain so bitterly cold that it was painful to the body upon contact. It rained incessantly and there was no shelter to be found. Foxholes filled with rain even before they were completely dug. Soldiers had to stay in foxholes regardless, and the cold penetrated their flesh down to the bone, every muscle of the body convulsing with hypothermia. Soldiers began to suffer from frostbite. Feet turned blue, then sometimes black as the dead flesh began to fall off. For soldiers of the 100th, from Hawaii, cold was altogether a different kind of hell. Somehow, the 100th managed to move through the forest despite considerable casualties, but Hill A was an impregnable fortress. B Company, led by Captain Takahashi, attempted two separate attacks, but couldn't even approach it. The 2nd Battalion suffered heavy casualties from intense artillery fire from the Germans on Hill B. The Germans had so many machine guns that the Americans couldn't even get within 10 yards from the edge of the trees. Without tanks, continuing the attack was a reckless gamble, so Young Oak finally put a stop to the attacks.

  At 6:30 a.m. the next morning, Young Oak radioed the regimental headquarters. Barely coherent because his face was so numb from the rain and cold, headquarters asked him to repeat himself multiple times. Finally, Young Oak succeeded in reporting the outline of his attack plan. Reading maps with a flashlight under a small poncho against the pouring rain, Young Oak and artillery liaison officer Captain Feibelman had stayed up all night to devise and prepare for this attack plan. Young Oak often stayed awake throughout the night before a battle to make detailed attack plans; even under conditions so harsh, he was able divide each unit by their tasks, and by the minute, including specific firing orders assigned to each artillery battery. Captain Feibelman called up every single artillery unit to confirm exactly which unit and which guns were assigned to shoot which particular target. Although Young Oak had devised a battalion attack plan, in reality, it was more a regiment attack plan, as it actually involved approximately 3,000 troops including the 100th, the artillery battalion, the engineering corps, etc., for the attack of Hill A.

H-Hour was scheduled for 10:00 a.m. Division headquarters had already repeatedly telephoned the regiment headquarters to verify whether the attack had begun. Another regiment had started the battle towards Bruyères 30 minutes earlier that morning. The key to Young Oak's plan was to mobilize tanks down the mountain. But due to the treacherous terrain, it was assumed that moving the tanks would be impossible. Naturally, the Germans also concluded that the Allied Forces could never mobilize tanks across the terrain. So it was all the more critical that the Allied tanks indeed be mobilized into battle. The Germans, with ample time to prepare for the attack, had positioned their tanks on both sides of Hill A. The Germans had dug deep foxholes and positioned machine guns all over the forest covering Hill A. Attacking against such well-fortified enemies without tanks would have been suicide for the foot soldiers. Young Oak could see that the terrain dictated that the only option was to move tanks to the position of the Americans facing Hill A and then send the tanks down the mountain.

As one tank platoon was attached to the 100th, Young Oak had access to five tanks and five tank destroyers. However, he decided he could only get three tanks and two tank destroyers down the mountain. Because a U.S. Sherman tank shell was unable to penetrate a German tank, the Wolverine, a M10 tank destroyer was hastily built by placing a three-inch naval gun on a caterpillar track. It was still no match against the German Tiger tank. Nevertheless, once Young Oak had found out that the Germans had tanks, he had no choice but to include tank destroyers. He would have to order his men to move the tanks and the destroyers down the mountain as early in the morning as possible. It was going to be an arduous task. A Sherman weighed over 30 tons and a Wolverine weighed almost 30 tons as well. It would require an exceptional tactical plan.

    Young Oak positioned two tanks on a relatively flat area of the hill, and between the two, positioned a third tank at a point where the steep slope began to sharply incline. This third tank was then tied to the two tanks with a thick cable about a thumb's width, creating a V-shape formation with the three tanks. When the third tank began its descent down the hill, it would naturally begin to tilt forward from its own momentum and gravitational pull. Thus the two tanks on the cable would prevent the tank from flipping over. This was why Young Oak had calculated that the most he could bring down the mountain was three tanks: two tanks were required for every one tank to descend the mountain. In addition, moving the two tanks behind the third at the exact same speed was crucial. If one tank was even slightly ahead of the other, the cable tying the other tank and the third tank would bear the entire weight of the third tank, and the cable would surely snap. A cable of that thickness breaking from that kind of weight would be able to slice down trees and kill anyone nearby. So to precisely coordinate the moving speed of the two tanks, Young Oak and the tank platoon leader stood behind each tank and exchanged signals. Although the thick forest made the job a bit difficult, it also blocked visual detection by the enemy. Once the first tank was brought down safely, Young Oak had a tank platoon sergeant help the platoon leader bring down two more tanks and two tank destroyers, then headed back to the battalion headquarters. On his way back, First Lieutenant Frank De Maiolo, the communications officer, called Young Oak with a message.

"Your friend wants to talk to you," De Maiolo said.

"My friend?" Young Oak asked.

"Guess who?" a different voice said.

Immediately recognizing the voice that replaced De Maiolo's, in one swift move, Young Oak yanked out the telephone wire. Young Oak had pulled out the only remaining live line. The other nine lines between the battalion headquarters and regimental headquarters had been hit by German fire. Startled, Singles, who had been standing next to Young Oak, stared at him.

"I guess the last line was hit by enemy artillery," Young Oak casually commented.

The voice on the line belonged to 36th Division Commander, Major General John E. Dahlquist. Before World War II, Major General Dahlquist had served in the Philippines. It was said he was one of General Eisenhower's favorites and was located at the general's headquarters in England. He had become the commander of the 36th Division only after it had landed in southern France. Until that point, he hadn't had any combat experience. Major General Dahlquist had a notorious reputation of being ignorant of infantry tactics; he had issued numerous reckless orders. He was the exact opposite of Major General Ryder, who had commanded Young Oak's division in Italy. Since early that morning, the division headquarters had called several times to order the immediate launch of an attack. When Dahlquist had finally gotten on the phone, Young Oak, knowing it would take another hour to get ready for the attack, pulled out the telephone line.

Once the three tanks and the two tank destroyers were taken down the mountain, Young Oak positioned the three tanks abreast of each other and the two tank destroyers between the tanks.

"Before the attack, do not allow the enemy to know that we have tanks," Young Oak warned the tank platoon leader. "As you know, the enemy tanks can shoot farther than ours. Don't engage them."

At 10:00 a.m., Young Oak began the attack with a heavy smoke screen above and on both sides of Hill A where the German tanks were positioned. Suddenly, the sky was thick with white smoke. Although the one major weakness in using a smoke screen was that it could be easily dispersed by strong winds, the morning was cold and windless. The smoke screen was sustained for a long time, completely blocking out German visibility. Once the smoke screen was complete, Young Oak mobilized the Corps artillery for the attack. For 20 minutes, 216 artillery guns fired at Hill A. Immediately following, Young Oak had the tanks and tank destroyers move as far as the smoke screen would keep them covered and opened fired for five minutes. The tanks and tank destroyers fired as fast as they could—about 100 rounds were fired as it took 15 to 20 seconds for a Sherman or Wolverine to fire a round. Due to the limited ammunition capacity, Young Oak had them fire after the artillery guns. He didn't want to use up all their rounds too early. So when the tanks and tank destroyers had used up about half their ammunition, Young Oak ordered them to stop. The tanks and tank destroyers played a vital role due to their unique firing capacity. Artillery shells were so sensitive that they easily exploded on contact with even a tree branch. Subsequently, artillery shells alone were not going to cause any real damage to the Germans unless the shells were directly hitting the German bunkers where German soldiers were sitting deep. On the other hand, tanks and tank destroyers were designed to fire shells at least a thousand yards ahead. These shells were also able to penetrate fairly heavy armor and then explode. Since the edge of the forest was only about 100 yards or less away, Young Oak sought to maximize the impact by combining both artillery and tank shells. In addition, he knew the tank fire would cause the ground to rumble and shake violently, thereby creating more psychological stress upon the German soldiers. The barrage of fire through the smoke screen was highly effective and even the American soldiers were shaken by the intense roar of the unrelenting explosions. As the Americans continued to fire at the Germans, Young Oak noticed that the Germans were not returning fire at all. Apparently the Germans had been taken by surprise and were stupefied by the immense firepower of the attack. Young Oak sensed they were losing the will to fight.

Instantly, Young Oak ordered the firing to stop. As soon as the firing ceased, Young Oak jumped up to his feet. Seeing him stand up, Captain Takahashi, who had been lying down beside him, also leapt up. Through the thick smoke, the two men emerged forward and began to wave their arms. It was clearly a gesture to invite the Germans to surrender. Miraculously, the Germans didn't fire at them. The forest grew silent. The Germans didn't surrender or return fire. Finally, Young Oak and Takahashi turned around and disappeared back into the smoke screen. Young Oak issued orders for another round of fire and the 216 artillery guns once again opened fire for more than five minutes. Then the tanks and the tank destroyers fired continuously, but this time for only about two minutes. Young Oak didn't want them to use up all their ammunition. The thunderous roar of the tank barrage was deafening. It seemed as if no enemy soldier could possibly have survived in the midst of so many exploding shells. Young Oak ceased fire once more. Again, Young Oak and Takahashi broke through the smoke screen as soon as their firing stopped. They completely exposed themselves to the enemy, so it looked like a mad suicide mission. Nonplussed, they waved their arms again and shouted, "Come out!" There was no sign of movement within the forest. After waving several more times, Young Oak and Takahashi turned around to go back, since there was nothing more to do but launch an all-out attack.

Suddenly, with hands raised high over his head, a German soldier rose to his feet, and staggered out of the forest. He was obviously petrified, and although he didn't know what was going to happen to him, he was not going to stay in the forest any longer. As soon as the German soldier came forward, Young Oak and Takahashi walked a good third of the way forward to greet him. The man was shaking from head to foot as he had been inculcated to believe all sorts of false atrocities that American soldiers supposedly inflicted upon their enemies. Young Oak reassured the man by lightly patting him on the back. Takahashi gave him a cigarette and Young Oak lit it with his lighter. During all of this, there was dead silence across the entire battlefield; if a pin were dropped, it would have been heard. Takahashi put his arm around the frightened soldier and walked him toward the American line. Young Oak motioned for someone to come take the German. Two more Germans surrendered and Young Oak could see about 10 more rising to their feet. The battle was over. Young Oak ordered B Company to take care of the ensuing prisoners of war. Soldier after soldier, the Germans approached the American line until there were more than 40 of them.

The Battle of Hill A ended without additional bloodshed on either side. The 100th eventually captured about 70 more German prisoners of war once they reached the summit. Perhaps the other German soldiers had retreated. The battle had lasted only five hours. Although it was crazy for Young Oak and Takahashi to have exposed themselves to enemy fire as they had, their dangerous gamble paid off Young Oak had decided to break through that smoke screen to minimize unnecessary casualties as soon as it became obvious how the battle would play out. Takahashi joined Young Oak as he instinctively knew what Young Oak was going to do and why; it was mental telepathy in combat. About 3,000 American soldiers were sent into the battle at Hill A and it was likely an equal number of German soldiers were defending. Without Young Oak and Takahashi disregarding their own lives to save many more—including enemy lives—both sides would have suffered great casualties. Upon capturing Hill A, they discovered that the Germans had over 100 machine guns in the forest. The Battle of Bruyères was over relatively easily upon the capture of Hill A by the 100th. For this successful assault on Hill A, the 100th received its second U.S. Presidential Unit Citation.

Chapter 11
Penicillin

After the battle at Bruyères the frontline moved steadily closer to the German border and the battles became more aggressive and chaotic. The initial orders for the 100th had been to immediately attack Hill C right after having captured Hill A. However, on the afternoon of the 18th, upon entering Bruyères, the order to attack Hill C was rescinded and instead the battalion was given three days of rest for the victory over Hill A. Since Young Oak had stayed up the whole night, he was dead asleep by 9:00 p.m., right after dinner. Unfortunately, around midnight, a messenger woke him up saying, "Colonel Pence is looking for you and the battalion commander."

When Young Oak and Singles went down to the regimental headquarters located south of Bruyères, Colonel Pence was very upset. Despite the fact they had a few days of rest left in Bruyères, the division commander gave the order for the 100th to capture Hill C by the next afternoon. Both regimental and battalion commanders expressed their aggravation and remarked how little common sense Major General Dahlquist had. But an order was an order. Once again, Young Oak stayed up all night planning for the next day. There was not enough time to integrate the tank company or get the artillery units together. Nevertheless, the 100th somehow managed to take Hill C around noon and captured 50 additional Germans. Just when the Germans were starting to prepare for a counterattack by rearranging and placing more soldiers at the bottom of the mountain, the Colonel Pence, the regimental commander called Young Oak over the radio.

"Young, can you do me a favor?" Pence asked. "Whatever I say, just answer with 'Yes sir.' Can you do that?"

"That's difficult for me to say."

"Just this once. Please just do what I tell you to."

The regimental commander was suspiciously gracious. He was clearly going to tell Young Oak something very difficult to hear.

"Sir, I can't do that unless I know what it is you're telling me to do. I'm going to ask you a question. Just answer 'yes' or 'no.' Is the division commander with you?"

"Yes."

"Okay. Go ahead and tell me."

"This is an order from the division commander. Retreat from Hill C right now."

Pence could have given these orders directly to the battalion commander instead of having the regimental commander relay it to Young Oak. However, the regimental commander knew that Young Oak, as the incisive operations officer that he was, would oppose it; he had to talk to Young Oak first.

"That's not possible, sir," Young Oak said. "We fought with our lives to take this hill and the Germans are readying for a counterattack. For the first time since our troops got to Europe, we're on higher ground and we have the advantage. We can easily defeat them now and you're telling me to just give up the hill?"

"Yes. Retreat. This is a direct order from the division commander. There is nothing I can do about this. You must retreat."

"Sir, my official answer is no. But I will confer with the battalion commander."

Young Oak then summarily reported the order to Singles, explaining: "If we retreat at this point, the Germans will regain the hill effortlessly. We will suffer many more casualties when we attempt to regain the summit. Regardless of who attacks, why suffer more casualties? If we retaliate now, we can completely crush them so they don't even attempt to come back."

Singles, who had been listening to Young Oak in silence, finally responded with resignation.

"Yes, you would want to ignore the order, but neither Colonel Pence nor I can do that," Singles said. "Think about it. This is a direct order from the division commander to the regiment commander and to me. How could I possibly sit here and just say I'm not going to follow the chain of command?"

"Then what should we do?" Young Oak asked.

"Listen, I agree with you entirely. But the order is to retreat. There's no way out."

"Give me some time to think about this," Young Oak replied.

He was waiting for the Germans to start the attack, but they were one-and-a-half miles away and hesitating to attack. Ten minutes passed. All was still calm.

"I don't want you to be court-martialed," Young Oak finally said to Singles. "However, what we're about to do is undeniably wrong."

"I know this and so does Colonel Pence" Singles said. "The problem is that the division commander does not," Singles.

The 100th retreated from Hill C. It was not easy for a battalion to retreat right after a battle when there was still the possibility of a counterattack from the enemy. Furthermore, if soldiers thought that the retreat was due to intimidation from the enemy, morale would plummet and the situation could easily get out of hand. Accordingly, the retreat process had to be executed carefully and conscientiously.

There were two reasons why Dahlquist had behaved so capriciously. The first reason was due to a simple "overlay." An overlay was a transparent sheet that was put over a map to mark out the positions of friendly and enemy forces, courses of attacks and retreats and the operational areas of each unit. According to the overlay that had been sent from the Corps to the Division just before the battle of Bruyères, Hill C had belonged to the 36th Division zone. Since capturing Hill A, Dahlquist promptly ordered the capture of Hill C. But the very next overlay showed Hill C in the 3rd Division zone, the zone next to the 36th, thereby causing the division commander to cancel the attack on Hill C. Insanely, the new overlay to arrive from the Corps after that, showed Hill C to once again belong to the 36th Division, which prompted Dahlquist to again order the 100th to capture Hill C. But then again, the Corps next overlay indicated that Hill C belonged to the 3rd again, to which Dahlquist unthinkingly gave yet another retreat order. The cause behind such madness was that the higher command, such as the Army or the Corps, made plans over vast areas. When drawing zoning lines, details such as to which division a small nameless mountain belonged was just not a pressing consideration. Of course for soldiers on the battlefield, such a line was life and death. In the process of all this chaos, the 100th suffered many casualties. After the 100th pulled out of Hill C, the Germans regained it without a single shot fired. The 3rd Division suffered 100 more casualties to retake it later.

  Another reason for Dahlquist's whimsy was petty rivalry among the Allied commanders. At this crucial time, these commanders were fiercely competing with each other over who was going to be the first to enter Germany. The U.S. division commanders were no exception. It would have been a significant advantage for the U.S. military to have kept the 100th on Hill C, but Major General Dahlquist didn't want to help another division with his own men.

  It was already dark when the 100th returned to the quiet farmhouses of Bruyères where they had spent the night before. The command group including Young Oak and Singles were able to arrive early in the evening, but the company, which retreated last in order, arrived past midnight. By then, the battalion was almost out of ammunition and supplies. Ominously, the supply officer, unaware that the battalion had been sent back to Bruyères, proceeded on to deliver Hill C with supplies. Around 9:00 a.m. the next morning, the assistant division commander suddenly rushed into the farmhouse that the 100th was using as its command post and shouted, "I want you all to move immediately! I want you to cross the line of departure in half an hour and take Biffontaine!"

Biffontaine was a small town located northeast of Bruyères and was surrounded by densely forested mountains. When the assistant division commander with a star on his helmet showed up out of nowhere and started screaming at everyone, the battalion command post erupted into chaos. When Young Oak picked up the phone to make a concurrent conference call to the company commanders, the general literally grabbed the phone out of Young Oak's hand and hung it up. "You don't have time for that! Get out now!" he shrieked. Because it was raining outside, Young Oak stretched out his arm to grab his overcoat when the general pushed him out the door and shouted, "Get out! Get out! Get out!" Standing in the rain with only his jacket and pistol and binoculars, Young Oak thought to himself, how stupid can this general be? It would save so much time just to call everyone at the same time instead of getting on the radio in the jeep to call each commander separately. Germans can intercept radios, but not land lines. People in the division headquarters must be the most asinine people on earth.

Furthermore, it would have taken over an hour for the assistant division commander to get from the division headquarters to the 100th command post. He could have at least radioed the regiment on the way to let them know, but he didn't. In the U.S. military, this kind of behavior was against regulations. If the assistant division commander had acted according to protocol, the situation would have turned out very differently. No properly trained army in the world would ever command battles in the manner that had been executed under Dahlquist's orders. Naturally, the assistant division commander had been sent by the division commander. It turned out that, for the moment, Hill C was designated in the 3rd Division's zone again. Assuming that the 3rd Division would intensify its attack on Hill C, Young Oak didn't want to fall behind the 3rd Division.

Without any time to eat, the soldiers were ordered to pack up their equipment and go. Getting into his jeep, Young Oak called Captain William S. Pye, C Company commander. C Company had led the assault the day before, but it was the only unit that could reach the line of departure in 30 minutes. Captain Pye suggested they capture the hill looking down on Biffontaine and Young Oak agreed. The 100th moved to that hill immediately. Oddly, there was almost no resistance from the Germans. It was as if they had already retreated. After a short while, the 100th settled on the hill and dug in. By then, the battalion was almost out of ammunition, food and water. Due to the incompetence of the assistant division commander, some of the soldiers didn't even have ponchos to wear as it rained all through the night. Young Oak had no coat—nothing but his pistol and binoculars. By some small stroke of luck, he had been wearing a tanker jacket. A tanker jacket was warm, as tanks usually get extremely cold in the winter when they aren't running. The jacket had been given to him during the battle of Bruyères, when a tanker noticed that Young Oak was outside almost all the time. Young Oak had decided to chop branches from a tree to help keep warm, unavoidably making a lot of noise.

"What're you trying to do?" asked Singles, who almost never got agitated. "Attract every single German to our location?"

"No, I'm trying to keep warm," Young Oak replied. "I'm going to chop some of these branches and lay them down on the ground, then chop some more to cover myself. I didn't have time to grab a coat."

"Well, keep that up, and you won't need any of those things."

Although winter had not officially arrived in the Vosges Mountains, it was already bitterly cold. It was said to have been the coldest winter in 40 years. Uniforms were soaked by the relentless rain, and the men's muscles ached and their hands trembled. Everyone had to fight the cold and hunger that long night while anxiously awaiting the arrival of friendly, support forces. However, those forces never arrived. In the meantime, the Germans had cut off the rear. If the Germans attacked, the situation would have been disastrous.

The next morning, Young Oak tried to contact the regimental headquarters by radio several times, but there was no answer. The battalion was beyond radio range. Young Oak then asked Captain Feibelman to call the artillery battalion since artillery radios could reach farther. Finally, Young Oak was able to communicate with the regimental headquarters via the 522nd Artillery Battalion.

"Capture Biffontaine," Colonel Pence seemed to order. But neither the battalion commander nor Young Oak could believe they had heard the order correctly. It was so unlikely for the colonel to issue an order that defied common sense. Something was wrong. Entirely surrounded by the enemy, the only advantage that the 100th had was that they were on higher ground.

"No sir, we're not going to go to Biffontaine," Young Oak said. "We don't have any ammunition or food.

We're already beyond radio range, so we can't effectively communicate with you if we go over that ridge. This is not going to work. Also, the moment we're over that ridge, we're also beyond artillery support. You're asking us to go into the next valley to take a worthless tactical objective at what cost? Yes, we could take it. There's no problem taking it, but for what? Why put us on the other side of the ridge? Why not attack the Germans from behind where they are unaware of our presence. The others can catch up with us in the meantime, up the hill, then we could all go down together tomorrow. No…"

The argument went on and on, but Young Oak wouldn't give in.

"You've got the boss next to you again?" Young Oak asked.

"Yeah," Pence said.

Colonel Pence was getting desperate. He didn't want the 100th to go either, but Major General Dahlquist was right there yelling into his other ear. Young Oak realized that if the division commander was standing right next to Pence, there was no use in arguing.

"Then can your friend promise me that the rest of the regiment or even another regiment, I don't care which, is going to be on this hill tonight?" Young Oak asked.

He figured, at the very least, if someone, anyone, could be on the hill by nightfall, the 100th might be able to afford getting off the hill to go down and take Biffontaine.

"Yes, I can make that promise," Pence said.

"Now you know that when we take off from the ridge, we'll no longer have communication," Young oak said. "I just want to state for the record that I am very much against this."

"I know, and I know where you're coming from, but I have no option."

Young Oak had B Company cover the rest of the battalion and sent the other companies to the village. As expected, they easily captured Biffontaine. It was a small village with just a few dozen farmhouses built around a church located in the middle of the town. All the villagers were gone and there were only about 50 German signal corps soldiers occupying the village. This could have been because the Germans had not expected the Americans to abandon the hill to take the village, or because the Germans didn't even know that their enemies were nearby. The men of the 100th satisfied their hunger with supplies taken from the captured Germans and many who were out of ammunition threw their American weapons aside and armed themselves with seized German ones. But by this time, the Germans outside the village had taken the hill, thereby completely surrounding the 100th Battalion.

Colonel Pence had advanced the other two battalions to keep his promise, but the German siege was like an iron net that could not be broken. The task force that had been promptly dispatched to deliver water and ammunition to the 100th was also stopped by the German forces occupying the hill. In the meantime, Young Oak fortified the defense positions of each company as the enemy could attack at any moment. On his way to inspect C Company, he stopped at the battalion command post. He wanted to interrogate the German signal corps commander who had just been captured. All of the German prisoners of war belonged to Hitler's Schutzstaffel. One, the signal corps commander, was a major, and another, a tank company commander, was a captain.

When Young Oak entered the farmhouse being used as the battalion Command Post, Singles, along with the other staff officers, were finishing the initial interrogation of the German major. Singles was sitting in the host chair across from the German major and the rest of the battalion officers and soldiers were watching him. But as soon as Young Oak entered, Singles got up, moved over to the next chair, and gave his seat to Young Oak. Then everyone focused on Young Oak, including the German major. The room hushed and tension filled the room. As he sat down, Young Oak took his pistol out of the holster, put it down on the table and said, "Everybody leave, except Singles and Jim."

Jim was First Lieutenant James Boodry, the intelligence officer. Everyone left the room except for Singles and Boodry. The German major straightened up in his chair as he felt the shift in the atmosphere of the room.

"Major, I'm going to ask you some very simple questions and I want you to answer these questions," Young Oak said. "But I want you to think carefully and answer carefully, but answer completely."

Young Oak didn't speak German, but communication was not a problem as the German major, appearing to be in his late thirties, sounded highly educated and spoke English well. Until then, the prisoner had been pompous and demanding. However, he was now quiet and observed Young Oak intently.

"Are you going to kill me?" he asked.

"I'm not going to say yes and I'm not going to say no," Young Oak said. "Just answer my questions and then you won't have to be afraid of me.".

"I'm not afraid of you."

"Just be careful. Understand that there is a pistol right here."

"I just want you to know that I'm a signal corps officer, not a combat officer. You're a combat officer. I'm sure you've seen much killing and I can tell you are very good with that pistol."

"Oh yes, I'm good."

"And you're quite sure of yourself. Who are you?"

"I'm the plans and operations officer."

"So everybody obeys you."

"Quit talking. Just answer my questions."

"Yes, Captain. I'll answer your questions."

Young Oak began by asking the prisoner his name and affiliation. The interrogation continued for about an hour. Singles interrupted only twice when questions he had already asked came up. Otherwise, Singles remained silent as he observed.

"Did you know we were on the hill?" Young Oak asked.

"No."

"How do you see the war?"

"We have already lost on the eastern front and we are struggling in the western front. It's not going to be easy."

The eastern front meant the Russo-German war. Although the German major had not explicitly stated Germany's defeat, he did acknowledge that Germany was on the brink of losing the war. Despite being a prisoner of war, he sustained his dignity by refusing to display any servile behavior. The German captain was no different. However, probably because he was very proud of being a Schutzstaffel officer, he demanded special treatment in a clearly elitist and arrogant manner. The captain was impatient and seemed unable to accept the fact that he had been taken as a prisoner of war. In contrast, the major didn't demand as much. Perhaps he, like the other German soldiers who had quickly and easily surrendered, was secretly happy that the war might be over for him.

After the interrogation, Young Oak left the battalion command post and headed over to C Company. C Company headquarters was also in a farmhouse located across a narrow road next to the town church. After he checked the defense formation and was getting ready to leave through the back door of the house, C Company commander Captain Pye called after him.

"Come here, I want to show you something," he said as he motioned Young Oak over to the window. Pye pointed over to the window into the night outside. Young Oak walked over and looked out while resting his hand on the windowsill. Standing near the door Pye said, "Can you see the tank down there? They're getting ready to bring another tank in. That's where they're going to launch their attack."

Young Oak could see the top of a tank and another one next to it. If there were more, he couldn't see them. Just then, gunshots rang through the night and Young Oak was on the floor with blood all over his body. A submachine gun fired from the basement trapdoor of a barn across the narrow street. The German soldier who had fired the shots had been hiding in the basement for several hours, ever since the battalion had taken the village. Once night fell, as soon as he emerged from the basement of the barn, he had spotted Captain Pye and fired at him. However, the bullets flew underneath Pye's outstretched arm and three bullets ended up hitting Young Oak.

A moment later, Germans were attacking from every direction. With tanks in the front, the Germans tightened their siege and approached the farmhouses where the soldiers of the 100th were hiding. An English announcement blared from an advancing German tank, "You are surrounded! Surrender!" In answer to the German's invitation, a grenade was thrown in the direction of the tank.

The men of the 100th Battalion fought valiantly with everything they had, but they were drastically outmatched before the battle had even started. Casualties mounted that night. The next day, the battalion soldiers realized they had to evacuate their wounded. Young Oak, who was bleeding profusely, was carried into the forest on a stretcher. The three bullets had extensively damaged his right hand.

Heading back toward where the 100th seemed to have come from, the soldiers moved as swiftly as possible in the darkness towards where the regiment headquarters was believed to be located. Dazed from numerous morphine shots, Young Oak vaguely sensed that First Lieutenant Samuel Sakamoto, also wounded, seemed to be running things.

"Sam, I think you're making a wrong turn," Young Oak called out to Sakamoto at the top of a hill. "You're turning right, you should be turning left."

"Young, for once, why don't you just let me run things for now," Sakamoto said. "You're full of morphine and lying flat on a stretcher and you're still trying to tell me which way to go? You don't even know whether it's day or night. Just let me take care of this, Young."

"Okay, Sam," Young Oak replied, too weak to argue. "You take care of it."

Sakamoto's rank had once been higher than Young Oak's, but with all of Young Oak's promotions, Young Oak was now the higher-ranking officer. Nevertheless, the two had become friends. After covering about 15 yards of the trail himself, Sakamoto returned to Young Oak.

"Young, we're surrounded by Germans," Sakamoto said. "What do you want us to do? I think we're going to have to surrender in all probability."

"Surrender? That's not for me, Sam. Besides, my wound is too serious and the Germans won't be able to help me. I don't think they have the antibiotics I need. I'll most likely die in a hospital somewhere in Germany."

"But Young, you can't escape in that condition! You'll get killed trying."

"Nah. I've got to try."

"Well, I've got to go back out there and talk this out with the Germans."

As Sam headed out toward the German officer, Young Oak whispered to Private Richard Chinen, the medic.

"Richard, I'm going to go. Will you join me? I need your help because I'm not steady on my own."

"Sure, but what should I do with this gun?" Chinen asked.

"What do you mean what should you do with the gun?"

"I don't know how to shoot it. I brought it along just in case because we had all those German POWs carrying the stretchers, but I have no idea how to shoot."

"Okay, give it to me. I'll probably do better with my left hand than you would with both your hands. Just stay with me, will you?"

The area was covered with heavy underbrush. Young Oak had rolled off his stretcher and had crawled into the foliage to hide. He continued his progress away from the patrol with Private Chinen and Sergeant George Hagiwara following right behind him. The Germans were so hasty to evacuate everyone out of the area that they didn't even look for escaping soldiers, thereby allowing the three to escape safely and easily. After hiding in the forest for a while, they accidentally ran into the rest of the 100th.

The next day, a wounded Takahashi was also rescued by friendly forces after he had deliriously wandered the forest. He had been wounded earlier on in the taking of Biffontaine and had retreated before Young Oak with the other wounded. Despite the tremendous pain the violently shaking jeep was inflicting on Takahashi as he was being transported to safety, he realized a conversation on the radio he was hearing was between Singles and Pence. He focused all the energy he had into catching their words.

"Is Kim hurt?" Pence asked Singles.

"Kim escaped, but yeah, he was wounded in the head."

Upon hearing the news, Takahashi was filled with grief. He recalled the battle at Bruyères when Young Oak and he walked through the smoke screen into enemy firing range. *Young, wounded in the head? He never did wear that helmet! How many times did I tell him...?* Fortunately, the battalion commander had actually reported that Young Oak had been wounded in the "hand." Captain Takahashi had misheard the radio exchange because of the delirium caused by his critical injury.

The 100th Battalion was on the brink of being wiped out at Biffontaine, so Colonel Pence intensified the attack. Slowly, the German blockade, which had been like an impenetrable iron curtain, began to melt. The 100th was finally able to reunite with the regiment.

Upon arriving, Young Oak was promptly carried to the aid station. However, his infection had gotten worse after four days of receiving improper care. One of the bullets had gone through the lower part of his right palm. The second bullet had hit the middle finger of the right hand, and the third bullet had entirely knocked out the last knuckle of the fourth finger of the same hand. He had been bleeding so heavily and the infection had gotten so bad that his right hand swelled out to twice its normal size, creating a gory mess of blood, puss and tangled constrictive bandages.

A medical officer on standby in the station took one look at Young Oak's hand and instantly shouted for scissors. There was no time to find a bed. Bracing himself against the right of Young Oak's stretcher, the doctor told the surrounding aides, "Hold him tight!" Checking the time of Young Oak's last morphine shot, he injected another. And although Young Oak had vomited from the first injection of morphine, his body had become accustomed to the drug after four days of repeated injections that this time there was no response at all. Taking Young Oak's wounded hand in his own, the doctor prepared to cut the bandages off. However, the bandages had stiffened and the doctor was not sure he would be able to cut through with scissors. Kometani, the dentist, was kneeling to Young Oak's right and Chaplain Israel Yost was kneeling to his left. Both were holding him down as firmly as they could. "Everything's going to be all right, Young," Chaplain Yost kept saying. Both men were openly weeping. Without even trying to wipe their tears, they focused hard on the tips of the scissors. The doctor started to cut through the hardened bandages. It seemed like he would never be able to cut through, but little by little, Young Oak's blood-blackened inflamed hand began to emerge. Finally, the doctor reached the tip of Young Oak's severed fourth finger. He almost cut through the last of it, paused, put down the scissors, and looked at Young Oak for a few seconds.

Taking a deep breath, he said, "Now this is the worst part, Captain. Up until now, even though I've been cutting through the bandages, they're still stuck to your hand. When I open this up and pull the bandages off, you're going to lose a lot more blood. Even though I gave you another shot of morphine, the pain's going to be intense and your body temperature's going to drop as well. Nobody knows what will happen, that's the most crucial part of this all. You've got to be prepared for the worse."

Young Oak nodded tersely. Then the doctor had Captain Kometani and Captain Yost grab one end of the bandage, which despite being cut into two halves remained tightly clenched around Young Oak's hand. As the doctor grabbed the other half and the men wrenched the bandages off of Young Oak's hand, blood indeed poured out of his truncated fingertip and the wound in his palm. And in spite of the warning, the pain was so great that Young Oak felt as though he was going to have a heart attack. The doctor was desperately trying to staunch the bleeding, to no avail. The moment the bandage had come off, Young Oak felt a terrifying shift in his body. His body temperature plummeted. Losing and then regaining consciousness, he felt as if all the blood in his body was pouring out of his fingertip. He could feel the tips of his toes becoming extremely cold, and soon the cold started to creep up his ankles, his calves and knees, and then his thighs. He was losing complete feeling in his entire lower body.

"I'm getting cold, and I can't feel my lower body," Young Oak said. It was a steady loss of sensation, and it was inexorable, simply coming and coming and coming. "My lower stomach is getting cold now."

Kometani and Yost were both vigorously rubbing his body, trying to keep it warm, and desperately shouting, "Fight! Fight! Don't give up, Young! Don't give up! We don't have any medicine. We don't have anything. If you give up now, there's no way to save you. You just have to set your mind on living. Only you can save yourself."

Young Oak figured that as the "thing" progressed up his body, it would get to about his navel, which would mean he didn't have much more time. He was sure he was dying. The sensation crawled up to his abdomen and he could feel his heart getting cold. "It's above the navel. Now my upper stomach is getting cold," he said faintly. Once it passed his stomach, he gave up hope.

Chaplain Yost, a Lutheran, whispered, "Young, be prepared." With a trembling hand, he picked up a Bible so he could administer last rites. Young Oak's mind was blank. The cold just kept creeping up and up, until it was just below his heart. Young Oak was a bit surprised however, because everyone said that in the last minutes before death, one's whole life supposedly passes before one's eyes, but no such thing happened. He knew he was dying and he knew it would soon be all over. Young Oak then heard the chaplain mumbling something in a quiet voice and realized that he was being given his last rites. Everything began to fade from his vision and the prayer diminished from his hearing.

Miraculously, after a while, Young Oak regained consciousness. He could sense that even though Kometani and Yost were still shedding tears, they were also rubbing his body. And then, something was different. The coldness stopped spreading. It didn't just slow down, it completely stopped. Calmly, Young Oak waited. His upper stomach warmed up and then the warmth moved down to his navel.

"I think it stopped," Young Oak said. "My upper stomach is warming up… And now it's below my bellybutton."

"You won, Captain!" the doctor shouted with joy. "You won!"

Everyone cheered and clapped their hands. Young Oak wasn't so sure though, so he figured he'd wait until the pain was entirely gone. It could just as well turn around and start back up again. However, from that point on, the pain gradually dissipated in the same way it had increased, slowly and steadily regressing. Warmth now passed over his lower stomach and spread into his lower body.

"I can feel my thighs now," he said.

The doctor sighed with relief and stated it was all over. He gave Young Oak another shot of morphine, which knocked him out.

Young Oak awoke inside an ambulance that was entering a general hospital near the French-Swiss border. He looked out the back window and could see the hospital on top of a hill. Then he passed out again. The next time he opened his eyes, he was surrounded by a doctor who was a major, and several nurses. The medical officer removed the old bandage on his hand, treated the wound, put a new bandage on, and then cautioned, "Captain Kim, it's too early to relax just yet. The gunshot wound may get worse. If anything comes up, immediately call me or a nurse."

That night, Young Oak, perspiring heavily and running a high temperature, started moaning. A nurse came in, opened his bandages, then shouted for the doctor. As if he had been anticipating something, the doctor was nearby. Racing down the hallway toward Young Oak's bed, the doctor loudly ordered for some alcohol. After quickly inspecting Young Oak's wound, the doctor held the bottle up for Young Oak to see and said, "Captain, we don't even have time to get to the cabinet and get the morphine for you. This is nothing but pure alcohol and it's going to be exceedingly painful. I'm telling you, we have only a few minutes here."

Ripping off the bandages, the doctor then took a pair of forceps, punctured the angry wound, exposing it wide open, and began pouring the bottle of alcohol directly into the wound. Forcing the forceps into the wound was excruciating enough, but Young Oak's entire body convulsed when the bottle of alcohol was poured into the wound. The pain was beyond description—even worse than when the hardened bandage had initially been removed from his hand at the aid station. The doctor finished pouring the entire bottle into Young Oak's wound.

"The wound is so bad that the infection could spread systemically and you will die very quickly because it will travel through your nerves," the doctor said. "If you are not dead in a few minutes, then we have won. We will have to wait."

Despite the doctor telling him that he could die, Young Oak still could not comprehend the situation. All he could do was bear the pain and wait. The doctor and the nurses stared silently and intently, both at the clock and the wound. The determining minutes of life or death passed quietly. In intense agony, Young Oak could not even think coherently. Finally, the doctor said with a smile, "Captain, you did good. I think we have won." Young Oak passed out again, just as the nurse injected yet another shot of morphine under the doctor's orders.

Penicillin was not recognized as an antibiotic miracle until it saved the life of British Prime Minister Winston Churchill, when he suffered from pneumonia during World War II. Nonetheless, it was rarely accessible to frontline soldiers. In 1929, Alexander Fleming, an English medical scientist, reported the discovery of penicillin to the academic community. In 1941, Australian pathologist Howard Florey and his team of researchers were able to extract pure penicillin and prove its exceptional medical effectiveness. But since the British government showed no interest, Florey went to the U.S. government to solicit funding for mass production of the antibiotic. Even with the financial support of the U.S. government, it was still a long time before penicillin was readily available on the frontlines. At the time, doctors only administered penicillin to key important individuals whose lives were threatened by fatal infections. When Young Oak awoke, the doctor was injecting him with penicillin.

"Even though we've been lucky enough to buy time, penicillin may be the only hope," the doctor said.

In those days, injecting penicillin was not only extremely painful, but required a heavy dose. It had to be injected in both arms and both buttocks, for a total of four shots per day. The repeated doses hardened the injection sites and by the time Young Oak received 20 shots, his arms had turned into rocks. They could hardly find a soft spot to put the needle in, as it would bend the metal tips. Somehow, the doctor administered penicillin for over 10 days, and thanks to the penicillin, which was indeed miraculous, he narrowly escaped death. As happy as if he himself had escaped, the doctor ecstatically observed, "Captain Kim, you're really lucky. If the penicillin hadn't arrived in time, you'd never have made it."

He was actually one of the very first Allied soldiers saved by penicillin during World War II. After the doctor confirmed that the critical time period had passed, Young Oak was transported to a general hospital north of Marseilles for recovery. There, he received his second Purple Heart. He was then told that after he recovered, he would be sent back to the U.S. However, the situation was to unfold quite differently because of "Hitler's Last Gamble"—the Battle of the Bulge.

Chapter 12
Ida

The Battle of the Bulge was Germany's last card; 250,000 soldiers were assembled in the forests of the Ardennes in France to launch a surprise attack on the Allied Forces on December 16, 1944. It was only two days after Young Oak had received his second Purple Heart and told that he would be sent back to America. Orders were given to all the hospitals to send back all the healthy soldiers to their unit. So Young Oak was returned to his unit instead of America. By then, the 442nd Regimental Combat Team had retreated from the Vosges Mountains in northeastern France to the French Riviera, a world-famous resort area in southeastern France.

Upon returning to his unit, Young Oak received a message from Captain Takahashi, who had been rescued in the forest after also being seriously wounded in Biffontaine, was in a general hospital in Nice awaiting his return to America. When he heard that Young Oak would be returning to the 442nd, he had immediately sent a message asking that Young Oak come visit him. The two had become more than just comrades-in-arms, they were like brothers. Although they didn't get a chance to get to know each other well at Camp Shelby because their ranks and units differed, they developed a friendship thicker than blood after facing life and death time and again on the frontlines of Italy and France. It was Takahashi who accompanied Young Oak into no-man's-land in the dead of night when Young Oak took the dangerous patrol for German prisoners in Cisterna near Anzio for the liberation of Rome. It was Takahashi who seemed to read Young Oak's mind when the two of them risked death as they pushed through the smokescreen for the sake of saving lives in the battle at Bruyères. When Takahashi had heard of Young Oak's whereabouts, he wanted to see his friend before returning to America. Young Oak felt the same.

Young Oak was able to take time off to visit Takahashi at the hospital in Nice. By this time, Takahashi had discovered that Young Oak had been wounded in the hand and not in the head. However, he greeted Young Oak without mentioning the traumatic incident. As the conversation continued, Takahashi became increasingly uneasy. He couldn't understand the order to send such a severely wounded soldier back to the war. However critical the Battle of the Bulge might have been, it was clear that victory was already around the corner for the Allies. Takahashi felt that it should have been left to the doctors to decide who should stay and who should leave. Both men had been wounded on the same day in battle. However, Takahashi was going home and Young Oak was staying. It was impossible to anticipate what lay ahead for Young Oak.

When Young Oak returned to the 442nd he received an urgent message. His wife Ida, a U.S. Army nurse stationed at a general hospital near London, was in critical condition. Ida was a nurse who had graduated from the University of Southern California. As soon as she had received a telegram from the U.S. War Department saying that Young Oak had been wounded on the Italian front and was being hospitalized, Ida had promptly volunteered to be an Army nurse. As a lieutenant of the Army Nurse Corps, she was stationed in the general hospital just south of London.

Ida had sent her husband to the war without even a honeymoon. When she had received the telegram informing her of her husband's wound, she didn't even hesitate in her decision to go to her husband on the frontlines as an Army nurse. One of the first Asian Americans to graduate from a four-year university nursing program in southern California, in an era of patent racial discrimination, Ida was a pioneer in her field. When Ida joined the European Theater of Operations, Young Oak and his wife became the first and only Korean American couple to fight together as Allied officers against Nazi Germany in World War II.

Although U.S. Army regulations prohibited soldiers from traveling beyond a certain distance, a high-ranking general granted Young Oak special permission to travel to England. He authorized his travel by any means available, but Young Oak had to make his own arrangements. Since no civilian aircraft connecting France to England was available in the middle of the war, the most expedient option was to go by military plane. Young Oak found that the quickest route to London was to fly from Marseilles to Paris and then to hop on another flight from Paris to London. With Kometani, who also happened to be headed to Paris, Young Oak took a transport plane to the city.

Once he got to Paris, he discovered that its airport was actually a misnomer as it was actually located nearly 40 miles south of the city. It looked more like a temporary hangar built on a big farm with a makeshift control tower and an inadequate runway. Unfortunately, there was no transport plane to London that day due to bad weather in northern France. Frantic, Young Oak explained his situation to the U.S. soldiers in the control tower.

"I am Captain Kim. My wife is an Army nurse in the general hospital in London and she's very sick. Is there any way I can get a seat on a plane to London today? I'm authorized to use a transport plane, but I hear that there's no plane due to bad weather."

"Yeah, there's no transport plane today. Well, there's a bomber going to London. But it's a combat plane, so we can't order them to take you. They might take you, if you ask."

Eyes fixed on the little twin-engine bomber idling on the runway, Young Oak ran hastily toward the plane. It was a B-25 Michel that the U.S. had used to raid Tokyo, four months after the Japanese attack on Pearl Harbor. It was being used, at the time, as a communication plane between the Allied Supreme Headquarters in London and the regional headquarters in Europe. Michel was the plane for Young Oak. It appeared that the plane was about to take off, as both the pilot and the copilot were sitting inside the cockpit. Young Oak dashed over to the plane and appealed to the all-white crew, since in those days, U.S. military pilots were nearly always white.

"I am Captain Kim. My wife is an Army nurse in the general hospital in London, and she's very sick. Can you take me to London?"

"Sure, if you're willing to ride this two-bit bomber, you can go," the pilots affably replied.

They did wonder how Young Oak had possibly obtained such special orders that allowed him to go to England. They were surprised to learn that he was allowed to leave southern France, which was part of the Mediterranean Theater of Operations, into northern France, which was part of the European Theater of Operations, then into England, and then all the way back again. Little did they know his fortune lay in the hands of the high-ranking officers, who were fond of Young Oak, in both the Fifth and Seventh Armies.

It turned out the plane would not be taking off for another several hours due to the inclement weather. The flight from Marseilles to Paris hadn't been that bad, but once in Paris, there was extreme wind and heavy rain. They were informed that the weather was even worse in London, and that the bomber wouldn't be able to land there. But the pilots didn't have much time because it would soon be dark. Finally, with the roar of each propeller on each wing, the bomber took off. It had been two days since he had received news about Ida. After a while, he could see the Strait of Dover from his window and memories of Ida flooded his thoughts.

When the plane flew over the airfield in London, the pilots were able to communicate by radio. They were circling the airfield, trying to decide whether or not to land. The flight was only two-and-a-half hours from Paris to London, but they spent over half an hour circling. The tower warned them that their plane could tip. If they went to another airfield, they'd be too far from London. So the crew took a vote. They all voted to land. Then they asked Young Oak how he felt.

"I want to land too," Young Oak said. "Let's land."

"Okay, let's do it."

The crew finally decided to touch ground. The bomber landed, jumped around, and almost didn't make it.

Young Oak and Ida's marriage was more than just a union. Ida was the granddaughter of an intellectual and high-ranking government official in the final days of the Chosun Dynasty. He was the first Korean to graduate from Princeton University with a master's degree in government administration. He returned to Korea to become a diplomat. When Japan's shadow fell upon Korea, he eventually sought political asylum in China, where he was appointed to be a high-ranking official of Chinese customs by the British. One of his sons married a Chinese woman. It was this couple that came to America and had a daughter named Ida. Likewise, Young Oak's father had sought political asylum in America around the same period. In a sense, both the births of Young Oak and Ida, as well as their courtship, could be said to be the fated consequences of modern Korea's tragic history of Japanese colonization.

Young Oak's parents owned a grocery store in downtown Los Angeles and Ida's parents owned a dry cleaning shop only three blocks away. Grocery stores and dry cleaning shops were two of the very few small businesses that colored people could start in those days. Because Ida's father had lived in Shanghai and Hong Kong for many years, he was fluent not only in Korean and English, but in Chinese as well. Young Oak's father was also fluent in English, which may be why both men were able to sustain relatively stable establishments. Politics among the Korean Americans living in Southern California were sensitive: a fine line was drawn between supporters of Syngman Rhee and those of Ahn Chang Ho . Sometimes, young, second-generation Korean American lovers were forced to break up because their parents supported different leaders. Fortunately, both fathers had joined the Dongjihoe, which supported Rhee's independence movement. Ida was two years older than Young Oak and they were close friends since early childhood. As a young girl, perhaps because of the patriarchal nature of Asian culture, Ida never mentioned that her mother was of Chinese heritage. In fact, Young Oak didn't even know this until the U.S. got involved in World War II. It was only after China had become an ally of the U.S. against Japan that Ida proudly revealed that her mother was of Chinese descent.

  During this time, the young bachelor Young Oak was serving as an enlisted man at Fort Ord just south of San Francisco. In the spring of 1942, he received a letter from Ida. After a day of strenuous training, as he sat on a hill under the radiant sunshine of California, Young Oak opened her letter. It was a marriage proposal from Ida. Although Young Oak's true character as a brave, bold and intelligent soldier later emerged on the battlefields, he was painfully shy around girls. So Ida had taken the initiative. However, because he had to stay in the barracks and live on a monthly paycheck of twenty dollars, he tried to persuade her to reconsider her proposal. Furthermore, he told her that he could be sent off to the frontlines at any moment. But Ida never wavered. As she was making four-hundred dollars a month as a registered nurse, she countered, "Money won't be an issue."

The wedding ceremony was held in April. As it was also the April just after the Japanese attack on Pearl Harbor and the U.S. declaration of war against Japan, Young Oak attended his wedding ceremony in the morning and returned to his unit that same afternoon. After several months of training, Young Oak was sent to officer candidate school, commissioned the next year, assigned to the 100th Battalion, and then sent to Italy.

When Young Oak finally got to the general hospital in London, Ida was being moved from surgery to a recovery room. Young Oak listened in pained silence as the surgeon explained her condition: "The critical point is over and she's okay now. But she won't be able to have a baby."

Twice seriously wounded, Young Oak was now hearing that his wife was suffering from a serious illness and they could never have a child. The war was brutal indeed. All Young Oak wanted at that moment, however, was for Ida to recover. Yet the only thing he could do was to move her to a quieter place and take care of her there. He moved her to a fancy hotel—one of the best in London—that the U.S. Army had taken over. With having been critically hospitalized as a patient only days earlier, in London he reunited with his wife who was a critical patient as well. Sadly, their reunion lasted only about four days as Young Oak had to report back to his unit. When he returned, rumors were circulating that the 442nd would be returning to the northeastern front of France.

Chapter 13
Champagne Campaign

Young Oak returned to the 442nd at the French Riviera, the world-famous resort in southeastern France that cradles the Mediterranean Sea. The official mission of the regiment was to stop German coastal infiltration and to secure the French-Italian border. But in reality, the Germans were busy defending their own land and lacked the military resources to attack southern France. The 442nd had become an occupation force. Once relocated to the idyllic French Riviera, Colonel Pence assigned the 100th to the area between Beau Soleil, located next to Monaco, and the French-Italian border. The assigned area also included Menton, another beautiful resort town. Perhaps it was Colonel Pence's way of recognizing and appreciating that the 100th was the longest-fighting battalion of the three under his command.

Upon arrival, Battalion Commander, Lieutenant Colonel Singles was the first to welcome Young Oak. After Singles inspected Young Oak's hands, arms and the rest of his body, he dryly remarked, "You look okay now. Nothing's wrong with your head and apparently you can walk. All right then."

The commander called for the Battalion Executive Officer Major Alex McKenzie, staff officers and the company commanders and announced, "From now on, what Captain Kim says is what I say. Captain Kim will command the battalion on my behalf."

Although this was quite humiliating for Major McKenzie, he could do nothing more than quietly listen. Singles then dismissed everyone but Young Oak.

"Young, I'm emotionally drained," Singles said. "I'm not being a good battalion commander. I haven't been doing what I'm supposed to be doing. Even though you're a captain, take over. I give you the power to do whatever you need to do. I'm going to sit here in this hotel room, sip cognac and try to recuperate. There's nothing wrong with me physically. It's all up here and I need time."

Singles had been deeply depressed over the heavy casualties his battalion had suffered during Young Oak's hospitalization. The 442nd had fought heroically for six days in October 1944 in the battle that later became known in U.S. military lore as the "Battle of the Lost Battalion." Due to the reckless and irresponsible orders from Division Commander Dahlquist, the 141st Regiment had gone too deep behind enemy lines. When the Germans surrounded one of its battalions and the remaining 211 men were in danger of being wiped out, Major General Dahlquist ordered the 442nd to rescue the battalion. Although the 442nd successfully accomplished the mission, it suffered heavy casualties with 54 killed and hundreds more wounded. From the very beginning, the mission was clearly too risky, with little possibility of success. Moreover, the 141st was a white unit and the 442nd was a colored unit; it was not hard to wonder if Dahlquist's order was racially biased. Singles was demoralized by the circumstances that had led to the great loss of so many soldiers of the 100th. During Young Oak's absence, Singles had three staff officers, including De Maiolo, take over Young Oak's tasks. Once Young Oak returned, Singles was ready to hand over the battalion entirely to him.

During wartime, whatever the commander of an occupation force said was law. So Young Oak ran the battalion as acting Battalion Commander for the next two months. From travel passes to permits for restaurants and bars, everything needed his signature. Proprietors of establishments in Beau Soleil and Menton would greet him with a glass of the best champagne. Upon hearing that he was the man in power, the police chief of Monaco invited him to a personal tour of the casinos in Monte Carlo and the other well-known attractions of Monaco. Monaco was neutral during World War II and had escaped the ravages of war. Yet, the police chief gave Young Oak the VIP treatment in exchange for military police protection along the French-Monaco so soldiers of the 100th couldn't cross into Monte Carlo at night and cause trouble.

The headquarters for the 100th was in Menton. It was a small beautiful beach town located on the French Riviera between Monaco and Italy. France is still proud of this lovely town, which is called the "Pearl of France" for its magnificent views, warm sunshine, wonderful pebble beach and gorgeous blue Mediterranean Sea. The city was virtually empty; all residents had been evacuated just as the city of Pisa had been prior to its liberation by the 100th. There were about 20 hotels in the city; Battalion Headquarters was located in one of them. Once, if it were not for Young Oak's assiduous nature to move headquarters to a different hotel every two weeks, it would have been bombed when the Germans had acquired intelligence of its former location. Overall though, other than the occasional artillery skirmish from the Germans, there wasn't much war-associated stress or anxiety in Menton.

As soon as Young Oak became the de facto battalion commander, Communications Officer De Maiolo reported to him some of the trouble the battalion was having.

"There's a brothel in Menton," De Maiolo said. "Our soldiers are getting in fights there at least twice a week. You need to decide whether to close it down or not."

Prostitution was legal in France in those days and Menton had one brothel, which was managed by a madam with five girls. The establishment itself was a kind of franchise where the madam remained in the city and girls were rotated in from Paris. The system was that whenever a new girl arrived from Paris, the girl who had been staying the longest in Menton would pack up and return to Paris. Although the soldiers were not supposed to use their pay of "U.S. Military Francs" anywhere off base, the brothel accepted it illegally. Sometimes the soldiers were able to pay with French francs that were dubiously obtained. France, like Italy, was impoverished during the war. And as was the case in Italy, the real currency was cigarettes. Chocolates and candies were popular as well. Soldiers would sell these items on the black market in exchange for francs and then spend them in the brothel.

Young Oak had an appointment scheduled with the madam and went to the brothel with his staff officers. The brothel was well-maintained and orderly, equipped with a grand piano and two hefty security guards. A blonde woman, the madam, apparently in her early 30s, greeted Young Oak.

"I hear that you are the new commander," she said. "I am aware that you have the power to close down this house?"

"You can keep it open on one condition," Young Oak said.

"And that is?"

"You will not allow my men to fight in this establishment again."

"But that is not fair! The people who are fighting here are not my girls but the soldiers. I cannot control your soldiers."

"It might be unfair. But if there is a single report of soldiers fighting here, you will have to close down."

"That is simply unfair."

"Madam, do you not have everything? Wine, girls, and this elegantly decorated house...You have more power than you think you have. If you were to make it clearly known that one more fight meant no more wine and no more girls, you will not have anything to worry about."

"I still think that this is unfair."

"This is my decision. To accept the judgment is not your choice."

"I have five beautiful girls here," the madam said after a long pause. "Would you like to meet them?"

Young Oak politely turned down her offer and stood up. She then continued to lament the injustice of his decision and added, "What if you come to inspect my house... I'm pretty sure you are supposed to do this anyways, once or twice a week."

"No. This is the first and hopefully last time I will be visiting this house. The next time I come here, it will be to close this establishment down."

Young Oak then walked out of the brothel with his staff officers. However, even before he visited the brothel, he had already informed his officers and commanders of the policy he had given her. Even an officer who was rather close to Young Oak complained.

"What! I, myself, am a good customer of that house," the officer said. "If you're going to announce that, you'd better mean it!"

"Have I ever been known to break my word?" Young Oak said. "If I say something, you know that means I will do it."

The officer most certainly knew Young Oak was true to his word, as he had served under Young Oak and gotten a battlefield commission after the 100th had suffered too many casualties and needed men.

"You're dismissed," Young Oak continued. "Go tell your men about the new policy and tell them I said so. If I hear one more word, that's it. No more girls. Alcohol is okay. Getting drunk is fine, but no fighting."

Young Oak's new policy spread quickly among the soldiers. Consequently, the MPs no longer rushed to the brothel every few days.

The soldiers were genuinely appreciating some peacetime relaxation for the first time during the war. The soldiers nicknamed the French Riviera operation the "Champagne Campaign," associating this frontline with women and alcohol. Meanwhile, the war waged on. And although stress relief was just fine, too much relaxation was a problem. Therefore, Young Oak would meet with each and every one of his soldiers in order to know exactly who was in line. More importantly, he wanted the soldiers to recognize that every soldier must execute his individual missions in order to achieve victory as a whole.

If a company commander or platoon leader wants his men to spend the night in a foxhole covered with snow, he must be ready and willing to do so right alongside them. Spending time with the soldiers was essential as the men who fought on the battlefields only believed in what they saw with their eyes. And a sense of unity was the lifeline to high morale. Without that, soldiers would not courageously risk their lives in combat. In this sense, the 100th Battalion and the 442nd Regiment were particularly privileged in that many soldiers not only knew each other, but also their families back home. Such conditions helped forge strong bonds. Young Oak inspected the frontlines every single week he served in the French Riviera. He focused his primary efforts on training the soldiers. The regiment had received about 1,200 new officers and enlisted men due to the mounting casualties on the French battlefields; training was a fundamental function of the 100th Battalion. It was practically an entirely new unit because the regiment received so many replacements.

One day, Singles called for Young Oak. Rumors were going around that the battalion would be returning to the frontline in northern France.

"Young, this is between you and me, I'm being reassigned and I'm going up to command a regiment up in the north of France," Singles said. "Colonel Pence has been ordered to England, which means you have a new regimental commander, Virgil Miller, who doesn't like you. The ranking officer next to me in the 100th is Alex McKinsey, who can't stand you. So I'm going to suggest you take leave now. It's going to take at least six months for you to get home and come back. Spend your 30 days of leave now."

"Yes sir," Young Oak replied.

The reason it took soldiers so long to travel from France to the U.S. was because soldiers on leave had the lowest priority. Trucks, trains, warships and planes were always first filled with soldiers being dispatched to the frontlines and military supplies.

As soon as the regimental commander found out that Young Oak was going on leave, he called him in.

"Young, you're leaving? If you want, you can stay here. If you stay, I'll make you a major."

But Young Oak decided to take leave as Singles had advised. A few days later, Colonel Pence left for England and Lieutenant Colonel Miller became the regimental commander. Despite the apprehension, Miller actually became a very competent commander. Sometimes, an individual has an entirely different persona when he is thrust into a high position with major responsibilities, as opposed to when he is in the second-highest position without as much accountability. Miller was such an individual. In fact, Miller had been planning on promoting Young Oak to a major and making him a battalion commander. Young Oak didn't know this until many years later when Miller visited him in the Presidio of San Francisco, and told him over dinner.

On February 22, 1945 Young Oak left the French Riviera. He had to wait several days to board a truck going to Paris. In Paris, he waited several more days to get to Le Havre. Unlike the previous journey he had taken to see his sick wife, this time the wait for an airplane took forever. Aboard a warship from Le Havre, France to Portsmouth, England, memories of the bloody battles in Italy and France crowded his thoughts. Young Oak's sea route was a reverse of the Allies' Normandy Landing. Allied Forces left Portsmouth and crossed the Strait of Dover to invade Normandy. Young Oak had spent a year and five months fighting in Europe since he stepped ashore in Italy. Allied victory was only a matter of time.

He had almost died on numerous occasions. He had witnessed countless comrades dying on the front. He especially couldn't forget the moment when Takeba and Cloudy passed away. Takahashi, more than a blood brother to him, had been wounded and sent home. At last, he was on his first long vacation, going home to see his mother. The naval ship from Liverpool to America was interminably slow. Nevertheless, at long last, the Statue of Liberty greeted him, standing tall and proud in the same place she was one-and-a-half years before, when she saw him off to the war.

As soon as he arrived, the Korean community in Los Angeles warmly welcomed him with several ceremonies. After his leave was over, Young Oak reported back to Camp Bill, located in central California, in order to catch a train to New York to go back to France. But one day, while still at Camp Bill, he heard loud whooping and yelling. Soldiers were hugging and joyously celebrating. Germany had finally surrendered. It was May 8, 1945. With the invasion of Poland, World War II had erupted and raged for five years and eight months, but it appeared that it had finally ended, at least in Europe.

The U.S. military immediately stopped returning soldiers on leave in America from being sent back to Europe. Six years prior, recruiting soldiers was a priority, but now reducing the troops was an issue. Although Camp Bill had received the order to stop the return process, they didn't know what to do with the soldiers. So, Young Oak was issued another 50-day leave pass. After 50 more days of leave, he returned to Camp Bill. A few more days passed and he was told to report to a base in San Antonio, Texas. The place was full of soldiers like him, who had spent their leave in America and had been put on provisional hold. While others were getting reassigned within three to four days, he was put on standby for another three weeks. Finally, a lieutenant colonel came to him.

"Captain, I have an unusual opportunity to offer you," the officer said. "We want you to join the regular Army. We want you to go to Princeton University. We'll pay for your tuition as long as you're on active duty. Forget all the schooling you've had; we want you to get the degree that we want."

"That sounds great, sir. But why the fuss and what am I waiting for?" Young Oak replied.

"Well, we want you to be an intelligence officer."

"No. I'm not an intelligence officer. I'm an operations officer. I'm not particularly good at that kind of work, and furthermore, I don't like that kind of work. I'd rather be up at the front where I can speak what I feel, do what I think I can, and do some real good. I don't want to sneak around and I don't want to be spying and all that soft stuff. If you let me go to Princeton, I'll go to Princeton. But I don't want to be tied down to being an intelligence officer by signing an agreement for the rest of my military career, whatever that may be. Is it for two or three years?"

"No. We're talking long term. You've got to go to college for four years. We're not going to let you get away with two years."

"No. I don't want it."

"Think about it."

"No, I don't even want to think about it."

"You're going to stay here for at least another two or three weeks. I'm going back to Washington. Here's my phone number. Think about it for two or three weeks because you're not going anywhere."

When the lieutenant colonel called back weeks later, Young Oak said he hadn't changed his mind.

"The offer stands even if you get reassigned. I just want you to know we want you badly enough that we're going to allow this."

"You mean the intelligence service wants me, not the Army, Sir?" Young Oak asked.

"Yes."

Young Oak ultimately turned down the offer. He was then ordered to report to Camp Robert, California, as an operations and planning officer. A few days after arriving at Camp Robert, he received a call from Colonel Joseph Donovan, the 91st Division Chief of Staff. Young Oak had completely forgotten about him.

"We're being deployed to the Pacific, Captain Kim. Join us as our G-2."

G-2 referred to the division's intelligence officer. Although he had forgotten the offer Colonel Donovan had made in Italy, the offer was serious.

"You know that's a lieutenant colonel position and I'm not even a major," Young Oak said.

"That doesn't matter. The moment you join us, we'll make you a major. Take the job and in a few months, we'll make you a lieutenant colonel. That's all. It's that simple."

"Yes, I'll join you," Young Oak said.

His father had long yearned for Korea's independence. Now Young Oak could fight Japan and help liberate Korea. Colonel Donovan officially requested for a transfer to his division and a promotion to major. But while the first dispatch of the 91st Division from Europe arrived in the U.S. to go to the Pacific, Japan surrendered. World War II was over in Asia as well. Young Oak's transfer and promotion were cancelled and he remained at Camp Robert.

At Camp Robert, Young Oak noticed that none of the officers at the training camp possessed any combat experience. Despite their best efforts to train the recruits, they understood nothing. Perhaps tragedies for the U.S. Army during the impending Korean War were already germinating at Camp Robert. About a month later, Frank De Maiolo, Communications Officer of the 100th Battalion, arrived at Camp Robert. The acting commander had admitted that he and the instructors had no combat experience, so Young Oak and De Maiolo were allowed to take over training the recruits. Yet, the pervading mood of the military during peacetime changed from that of wartime. During the war, everyone had to unite for survival and victory. Prejudice and racism had to be put away. Unfortunately, after the victory, these ailments emerged once again. Although minor improvements in the military could be detected here and there, the overall atmosphere of inequity remained unchanged. So Young Oak decided to leave the military and was honorably discharged as a captain in 1946.

Captain Kim is greeted by his mom Nora Koh at the Union Station in Los Angeles upon his return from the European Theater of Operation during World War II in 1945

Biffontaine, France cathedral plaque reads:
To the left of the entrance of this church, Captain Young Oak Kim, a hero of the 100th Battalion, was wounded on Oct.23, 1944. Being captured he successfully escaped with Mr.Chinen.

Captain Young Oak Kim commands the honor guard for U.S. Undersecretary of War Henry Stimpson in Italy 1944. Lieutenant General Mark Clark, behind Kim, chose the 100th as the honor as a token of appreciation for the battalion's sacrifice and valor.

Battalion Comm. Kim hands over a Sherman tank shell and encourages a private in Moondeung Valley in the winter of 1952 during the Korean War.

Young Oak Kim with President of Korea Roh Mo-Hyun and First Lady Kwon Yang-Soo at the Blue House in March 2003.

Young Oak Kim and two-time Olympic gold medalist, Dr. Sammy Lee rode in a Rose Parade float in Pasadena in January 2003. They were recognized as Korean American heroes. The float was also created to commemorate the centennial of Korean immigration to America.

Kim, second from the right in the back is with other officers of the US Army 31st Infantry Regiment during the Korean War in 1952.

Young Oak Kim as a Lieutenant Colonel in 1965.

Young Oak Kim at the Moran Medal of Korea Ceremony
Los Angles 2003

Part II
The Korean War

Chapter 14
Back in Uniform

After being discharged from the Army, Young Oak had no specific plans. War was over now. Though only a few years had passed, it felt like more than twenty. Having witnessed so much death, Young Oak had aged beyond his years. His father had passed away during the war, never having seen the independence of Korea he had so fervently desired. Now his mother operated the grocery store alone to support his younger siblings. A devoted Christian, she urged him to attend church with the rest of the family. Yet despite the fact that he regularly attended church in his youth before the war, religion was a terrain of contested thoughts and emotions for him after the war. He just couldn't understand how Americans and Germans prayed to the same God for victory and kill each other at the same time. After the Battle of Monte Cassino, his weekly worship attendance had decreased to just once a month. His relationship with his wife changed as well. While serving at the field hospital in London, Ida also witnessed the cruelties of war. Having had to battle her own near-death illness during the war, she was physically and psychologically overwhelmed. In the end, she sought refuge by accepting an overseas assignment in Germany, where she was quickly promoted to the rank of captain.

One thing that did not change and persisted was the racial prejudice against minorities in America. Without the contributions of minority soldiers, it would have been impossible to defeat Germany and Japan. However, once the war was over, America easily forgot the heroic contributions of its many minority soldiers and quietly slipped back to its prewar mindset of prevalent racism. Of course, it could be claimed that racial discrimination improved a little, but in truth, discrimination against ethnic minorities was still a judicially sanctioned institution in the United States.

Along with his photograph, the Los Angeles Times had printed a valorizing war story on the return of the young hero, Young Oak Kim. But that was it. The war was now over and no one really cared about war heroes anymore. Unfortunately for Young Oak, there were few financial options available. He thought about going back to school, but decided against it. As long as racial prejudice persisted, a college degree was nothing more than a piece of paper that wouldn't change his situation. He was convinced that the best way for a minority individual to succeed in a capitalist society was to earn a large amount of money. Although he later realized this reasoning was perhaps misguided, at that moment it was what he firmly believed.

Once he decided upon becoming a businessman, Young Oak knew he wanted guaranteed success for whatever his new venture would be. He figured business acumen couldn't be so different from the military strategic planning he had been so adept at during the war. Both required careful planning in order to achieve optimal results by effectively and efficiently utilizing human and material resources. The responsibility of a military strategic planner was to accomplish given martial objectives with the least amount of friendly casualties. In order to attain this objective, one had to assess the strengths and weaknesses of friendly and enemy forces and then devise a creative plan accordingly. Although Young Oak had no formal training in business administration, he was confident that the cognitive demands of his business venture would be similar to those of his military strategic planning experience. In essence, he was quite familiar with the deduction of maximizing profits under limited human and material resources within particular market conditions.

Briefly, Young Oak did consider helping out his mother at the grocery store, but as his brothers and sisters were already helping, he knew his contribution was not needed. In the end, entering the business world was the clearest choice to make. Moreover, Young Oak wanted to use his creative talents.

Since Young Oak always fought on the front line during the war, he never had time to spend money. In fact, the only time he had ever spent any of his pay was while he had been hospitalized and had distributed his salary among his fellow soldiers. He was able to send money to his mother every month and she saved it all. Subsequently, more than $3,000 was in his savings account, which was sufficient to start a small business at the time. Young Oak thought long and hard about where to invest his savings. The majority of his Asian American contemporaries were engaged in labor-intensive businesses, such as garment laundering, mini-markets, fruit stands and restaurants, which white Americans were not pursuing. However, starting yet another business that catered to the already small Korean American community was not practical, as it would have been difficult to yield sufficient profits. He concluded that the garment laundering business was his best option.

It was a time in American history when it was important to the conservative American to maintain a clean and acceptable appearance. And since the ordinary American didn't own a laundry machine, he had to spend a little money for clean clothes if he wanted to keep up respectability. On the other hand, Young Oak felt that the traditional hand-laundering business were besought with problems. Not only did it cost too much to start up such a business, but one also had to obtain numerous permits from the government, which was not always easy for a minority business owner. Because it was a labor-intensive business, work was arduous for both owners and employees alike. Furthermore, if problems were ever to arise, the owner was the one solely relegated to assume the fiscal burdens of accountability. Finally, the customer was always obligated to wait several days for his or her garments. Young Oak decided to pursue a new garment laundering enterprise that would solve the problems of a traditional hand-laundering business.

Eventually, his new business venture came to be what we now know as a coin laundry. Family and friends alike advised him not to do it. It sounded impossible and risky; it was too novel and untested an idea. Not to be deterred, he was convinced he was right. He also knew that he could take the safer road by opening a traditional hand-laundering business, but he only foresaw a bleak future of low profit margins on this path. A major deterrent to opening a coin laundry business at the time was high repair costs. Machines broke down frequently and it would cost a great deal of money to hire a repairman to fix them. But he had attained training in mechanics for eight months in the Army and was confident he would be able to fix the machines himself. In addition, a coin laundry relinquished him from obtaining the kind of strict business permits required from an owner who was directly accountable for the handling and care of customer garments.

Young Oak proposed his coin laundry business to Bendix. The company found the idea brilliant and decided to give exclusive rights to him to start up such a venture. Just as he had always tried to secure sufficient artillery support prior to a battle, he assiduously secured operational funds in preparation for his new business. Bank of America was also enthralled with his idea and readily loaned him several thousand dollars. But where would he open it? He decided upon the corner of 6th Street and Bixel in downtown Los Angeles, where he fortuitously found a vacated building ideal for a coin laundry. This was an area of apartment complexes predominantly inhabited by white residents. Once he decided upon the location, there was no reason to delay. Upon signing the lease agreement, he immediately installed 30 washers and three dryers. Then he hired two Japanese American women to manage the business. Many of them were returning to Los Angeles from the internment camps that the U.S. government had compulsorily enforced during World War II, and he had pointedly resolved to hire these disenfranchised Japanese Americans. To justify the forced internment, Japanese Americans had been labeled "enemy aliens" and subsequently faced many difficulties finding employment due to the persistent overt discrimination against them. In addition to the two female employees, he hired a man to lift heavy loads. He was now ready for business.

Although it was not large, as soon as the coin laundry opened, customers quickly filled the modest establishment. As few people ventured into the coin laundry business at the time, Young Oak's shop literally dominated the market. Every day, he opened for business at 7:00 a.m. and closed at 10:00 p.m. The shop was always filled with customers; his business prospered. For people who didn't have the time to wait, an express service was even offered for an extra charge. Because his two Japanese American employees were honest and diligent, business ran smoothly. He trusted his workers. He not only entrusted them to run the day-to-day operations on their own, but he also gave them full charge of the financial management as well. The business began generating an average profit of $1,500 a month—not an insubstantial amount at the time. One of the distinct advantages of this business was that the proprietor didn't have to be present all the time. This meant he could turn it into an extensive franchise. Indeed, with all the extra time he had to focus on matters outside of the business, he could expand to five or six more coin laundries, ultimately turning a much larger profit.

Young Oak's foremost problem in the business world was his compassion. To be a prosperous businessman, one ought to be somewhat calculating and cold-hearted. A business must generate profits or else it will be forced to close. Thus, a businessman must always focus on money and profits. For him, the life of a businessman was onerous. He desired something other than money. Around this time, he received a letter from Colonel Singles, who had become the chief of staff at the Officer Candidate School in Fort Benning. With the letter, Colonel Singles sent an application form for the "regular" U.S. Army. Excited, Young Oak met with his landlord and requested the termination of the lease agreement. The landlord refused. Young Oak was not only the anchor tenant of the building, but he had also never been late paying rent. At the time, he couldn't pay the penalty for violating the lease agreement, so he couldn't accept Colonel Singles' offer.

Then, one day in the summer of 1950, Young Oak was surprised to hear that war had broken out in Korea. He kept up with international news and already anticipated that something would happen, especially after U.S. Secretary of State Dean Acheson announced that the final line of defense for the U.S. would run along the Aleutians Islands, Japan, Taiwan and the Philippines notably not protecting South Korea. He was nonetheless surprised, since he had not anticipated war to break out so quickly. It didn't take long for him to decide to rejoin the Army.

He had already witnessed how the extremist views of Nazism and Fascism had victimized the innocent people of Europe during World War II. He was sure that Communism was wrong when it ruthlessly sacrificed human lives in the name of ideology. As he saw it, the

Acheson line was an invitation for the Communists to wage war on the Korean peninsula. Because the United States failed to the Korean peninsula, Young Oak felt that America owed a considerable debt to Korea. As an American citizen, he felt an obligation to pay back this debt to Korea. And as a son of a Korean independence movement fighter, he felt even more compelled to go and fight for Korea. The coin laundry no longer needed him to run it, as his employees managed it very well. He decided to sell it. If he had to pay a fine for early termination of the lease agreement, he was now able to pay. Immediately, he went to see his mother.

"Mother, war has broken out in Korea," he said. "I will join the Army again."

"There is one thing you must promise me," his mother replied. "When you get to Korea, you must visit President Syngman Rhee and pay proper respect to him. When your father was alive, he sincerely supported him. President Rhee will also be glad to see you."

"Yes mother, I will go meet him."

Young Oak volunteered for the Army again. Separately, the U.S. Army took measures to contact him. As the U.S. military was facing a desperate shortage of Korean-speaking soldiers, its top priority was to call up every Korean American veteran. Whether these Korean Americans spoke Korean fluently or not didn't matter. He received the order to report to an Army base near San Francisco on September 25, 1950.

In September, he had a visitor—Sakae Takahashi. He had been wounded during the battle of Biffontaine and had returned to the United States earlier than Young Oak. After returning from the war, Takahashi graduated from a law school. On the way to Honolulu to start his law career, he went to Los Angeles to see Young Oak.

"Sakae, I guess you heard the news; war broke out in Korea," Young Oak said. "I've decided to wear the uniform again."

"You're crazy! Why would you want to go to war again? You might get killed. There's no guarantee you can come back alive!"

"I know. But Korea is my parents' country and it's also because of the U.S. that war has begun in Korea."

"I will take you to San Francisco," Takahashi said after a long pause.

Both knew each other very well. Takahashi knew that once Young Oak made up his mind, he wouldn't change it. He also knew that Young Oak would volunteer to go to the front line. He wanted to see him off.

On September 25, 1950, Young Oak reported to the Army base. Since the Korean War began on June 25, 1950, it was exactly three months after the breakout of the war.

Chapter 15
To Father's Country

The Army had called upon Captain Young Oak's service not because he was a decorated World War II hero, but because he was a Korean American. Consequently, Young Oak was sent to the U.S. Naval Intelligence Language Center instead of Korea. Along with approximately 10 other Korean American officers, he was required to undergo intensive Korean language training: listening, writing, reading, speaking, translating and interpreting. As a boy, he had attended Korean language school, so his scores were good. And yet, he was unsure of his Korean language abilities. More importantly, he had joined the Army again in order to fight on the front line, not to serve as an intelligence officer. He complained about this every day.

Although he didn't know it at the time, the instructors training the Korean American officers were members of the Army Security Agency, later to be consolidated with the National Security Agency. His daily complaints paid off. By December, ASA came to the conclusion that he might be harmful to the unit in the long run and assigned him to Fort Lawton in Washington. Since the majority of the soldiers reporting to Fort Lawton were ultimately sent to the Korean War, the assignment indicated that he would eventually go to Korea. Soldiers were to be shipped out from there to Japan. Once they arrived in Japan, it would be up to the General Headquarters, Far East Command to decide whether a particular soldier would be sent to Korea or would remain in Japan.

As was the case in San Antonio during World War II, Young Oak's orders at Fort Lawton were to wait despite the other soldiers being deployed to Japan only days after their arrival. Fort Lawton was waiting for the arrival of a group of Army nurses who were to be sent to the Korean War. According to U.S. Army regulations, nurses couldn't command regardless of their rank, and only officers of certain categories, including infantry and artillery, could command. Young Oak was required to take those nurses with him on his way to Japan. Since they were arriving from all corners of the United States, he had to wait for everyone to arrive. Even after their arrival, the nurses couldn't believe that he, a colored officer, was a World War II hero with all those decorations. They wanted confirmation, so the delay was extended. Young Oak knew that having understanding nurses were essential in war, so he patiently waited for the departure order.

  Finally, Young Oak and the nurses boarded a Canadian Airlines plane in Vancouver, B.C. Probably because the nurses were women, the Army had chartered a civilian airline instead of simply utilizing military transportation. He was happy that he didn't have to sail all the way to Japan. The Army and Canadian Airlines treated them with extra special care. Whenever they boarded or disembarked from buses or trains, red carpets were ready.

  Since he was the commanding officer, he had to approve everything. Whenever the nurses were to go anywhere, they needed his approval. Not only did he have to sign all their paperwork, but all documents such as airplane tickets were also required to be in his personal possession at all times. But he exercised his authority only in formality and delegated the real authority to the most senior nurse. There were three majors among the nurses, and he designated the most senior major to be practically in charge of command. He simply granted and signed everything she requested. Everything went smoothly.

  Airplanes carrying soldiers being sent to the Korean War were to land first at Haneda Airport in Japan. From there, the soldiers would be taken to Camp Drake, and then finally to Korea. However, the nurses' airplane directly landed at a small military airport near Camp Drake. As they deplaned, attributing the successful trip to his magnanimity, the major graciously thanked him for not undermining her authority over her nurses and said, "Captain Kim, I've seen several officers lose their cool in front of these beautiful young nurses. I was told not to worry about you at Fort Lawton and I realize why they said so."

"I just tried my best to do what I was supposed to do, major," Young Oak said. "So long."

After he handed the command over to another officer awaiting the nurses at the airport, he was again alone. He headed to the bus terminal to go to Camp Drake.

Located about 20 miles south of Tokyo, Camp Drake was the single largest U.S. military base in Japan. Both replacements going to Korea and wounded soldiers returning to Korea after recovering in Japan first came to Camp Drake. Upon arrival, Young Oak couldn't believe his eyes when he saw the commanding officer's name on the front gate: Colonel Gordon Singles. Since the letter Singles sent him at Fort Benning years ago, Young Oak hadn't heard anything about him.

"Can you connect me to the commander?" Young Oak asked a sentry.

"Soldiers are forbidden to talk directly to the commander."

"Then can I see your superior officer?"

A lieutenant came outside, but his answer was the same. Young Oak again asked to see the lieutenant's superior officer. A captain then came out, but again Young Oak received the same answer.

"There are strict orders not to connect anyone to the commander due to these cases trying to get out of going to Korea," the captain said.

"Colonel Singles was my commander in Italy and France during World War II," Young Oak said. "I'll leave tomorrow, but if he finds out that I couldn't call him because of you, I assure you, it will cause some headaches for you."

The captain hesitated for a while, looked at his watch and said, "It's already 10:30…he might be sleeping. But I don't think you're lying."

The captain went inside to call and immediately, he returned.

"The commander himself is coming here right now to pick you up. You aren't allowed to leave, as he has ordered me to hold you here. It'll take about 30 minutes by car, so please stay put."

About 25 minutes later, Colonel Singles arrived, driving not a military jeep, but a GM civilian jeep. Young Oak wondered why it had taken so long, but once they got in the jeep, Singles explained that he didn't live on the post. He was living quite far away, in a big beautiful Japanese mansion on a hill overlooking the camp. Mrs. Gratcher Singles' hospitably greeted Young Oak. Born to a rich miner from Denver, Colorado, she inherited a big fortune from her parents, allowing Colonel Singles to live quite an affluent life when not on the front lines. Over a bountiful meal prepared by Mrs. Singles, the men tried to make up for six years of missed communication. It was apparent that Colonel Singles was still a chain smoker. Young Oak had never seen anybody who smoked like him. He would light up a cigarette before even finishing the one he was still smoking. People often said that he didn't need to carry a lighter. As they talked, amidst the steady puffs of smoke, Young Oak related how this was his first night in Asia. In a frank discussion, he explained to Colonel Singles why he had decided to wear the uniform again and why he wanted to go to Korea. At the end of the long conversation,

Singles looked at his watch and said, "You know, you could stay with me, but I think if you do that, then it would just mess up the system down there. They need to process you and they probably have already assigned you a room. Maybe I'd better take you back and let them finish processing you. Tomorrow morning, after breakfast, you come back and visit me in my office at around 9:30 or 10:00 a.m. In the meantime, I'll tell them just to process you and give you a place to stay."

The next morning, after breakfast, Young Oak went to visit Singles at his office. When he got there, a number of officers who used to be in the 100th were there to greet him. Colonel Singles had a lot of them at Camp Drake; they were all happy to see Young Oak. They were not on their way to Korea, but they were assigned at Camp Drake. Singles gathered them there on purpose.

"You know everybody in the room. How about joining us?" Singles said. "Stay here."

The night before, when Young Oak told him he wanted to go to Korea, Singles suggested he think about staying at the camp.

"Your friends are here and you have a lot of friends in Tokyo," Singles said. "You've got a lot of friends all over. It's not as if you're going to be among strangers."

They had lunch together and then the others left. Singles continued trying to convince Young Oak.

"Stay here at Drake," Singles said. "I'll give you any job you want. I'll make you a major faster than if you go to Korea."

"You know the military better than anybody else," Young Oak answered. "If you make military your career, if you don't fight in a war at the time the war's going on in the position your rank calls for, then all of your future assignments are going to reflect that, and it's going to hurt your career. I'm a minority and if I don't do what the rules call for, I'll be lucky to make lieutenant colonel. You could make me a major, and that's probably how I'll end up…as a major."

"Okay, so Camp Drake is a training camp and doesn't have much of a future. What if you go to Tokyo, be in the GHQ, and you could be in the G-3. Purcell is there and he'd be happy to have you. Why don't you think about it?"

Alfred Purcell was a battalion commander of the 442nd in Europe.

"I've got to go to work, Singles continued. "Go see some of our other friends here and let them show you around Camp Drake."

Some of the people Young Oak met that morning took him around the camp and they had a good time. The next morning, he got a call from Singles to come down to his office.

"Let's go for a ride," Singles said.

"Where are we going?" Young Oak asked.

"Let's go to Tokyo."

It was the first time Young Oak saw Tokyo. They went to the big GHQ building near the Imperial Hotel and the Emperor's Palace downtown. They went upstairs and met Alfred Purcell. By then, Purcell had been promoted to colonel. They went to have lunch. Purcell and Singles had already talked the night before.

Over lunch, Purcell said to Young Oak, "So, you don't want to stay at Camp Drake? I got a wonderful job for you here. Come here and stay with me. You can be in Tokyo. You'd be right in this building. I'll show you the desk."

Purcell and Singles didn't want to send Young Oak to Korea. They felt that his chance of getting killed was too great.

"You're an officer with wonderful abilities and talents," Purcell continued. "Why not just stay here, enjoy life, and have a good time with us?"

Young Oak refused. After Purcell left, Singles took him to a bar. There they had a long discussion again over Scotch, because Singles was still trying to talk him into not going to Korea.

"Don't go, it's dangerous," Singles said. "You fought in World War II and got a bunch of decorations. You don't have to go to the front line again. More importantly, you'll be the only Korean officer in the GHQ. I'll give you any position you want."

But Young Oak remained steadfast in his decision. That night, when they were talking, Singles said, "Young, you can't go to Korea. They got all kinds of rules and regulations stating that if anybody can speak any Korean at all, even a couple of words, you can't go to Korea. You either stay in the G-2 here, or you're going to get caught by the Eighth Army. You're not going to the frontline."

"Gordon, you're smart enough, and you know how to do things in the military. If anybody can get me to the frontlines, it's you. Now that you know how strongly I want to go, instead of fighting me, why don't you help me?"

Young Oak could see that Singles was beginning to give up.

"Well, I was afraid you were going to ask me that," Singles said. "Yes, there is a way. If you are badly wounded in Korea, you end up at hospitals in Japan. If you end up in Japan, there is a certain code that takes you back to your unit. And nobody stops you in between. So, once you leave Japan, you go directly to the unit. You won't get stopped by the Eighth Army or the Corps or anybody else. Where do you want to go?"

"I'd like to go to the 7th Division," Young Oak replied.

"Why?"

"Well, that's where I started my military career."

"Which regiment?"

"Seventeenth Infantry, it's where I started."

"I'll cut orders, but before I can cut you loose, you've got to clear out of Tokyo."

"What do you mean?"

"Well, by Army regulations and orders, you've got to go to the GHQ here, before I can cut you loose. I have to have their okay. Your record shows that you've been attending the Korean language school at the Naval Intelligence School in Washington, D.C. for five months. How can I say you don't speak one word of Korean?"

"Again Gordon, if anybody could do it, you could do it. You know how."

"Tomorrow morning, let me make a couple of phone calls and we will see."

The next day Singles called him.

"I didn't want to tell you before, but my classmate heads the organization that screens all the people that come into Japan and go to Korea, to see if they have language capability. I asked him as a personal favor whether he would bend and he agreed. So, you have to go to Tokyo and fail this test. Now, when you get there, remember, don't say one word of Korean, even though your record says you know the language. Don't say one word. If they speak to you in Korean, tell them you don't understand. Not one word. If they know you understand one word, you're not going to go to Korea. You're going to be here in the GHQ, and at the G-2, not at the G-3."

A couple of days later an arrangement was made. Young Oak returned to Tokyo, and went into the basement of the same building where he met Colonel Purcell. A Korean civilian welcomed him and introduced himself.

"Welcome," he said in Korean. "My name is Cho. How are you?"

Mr. Cho was very short and stout, about five feet and two inches. What he said was easy Korean, but Young Oak pretended not to understand. Cho wanted to shake hands, but Young Oak didn't take his hands. Cho finally took him by the arm into a room. They sat and began to talk. Cho kept speaking in Korean and Young Oak kept acting like he didn't understand. Soon, Cho began to mix Korean words with English. But Young Oak still pretended not to understand anything.

Finally, Cho asked in English, "You don't understand any Korean?"

"No, I don't," Young Oak said. "I was born in America."

"You must be aware of a simple thing like, 'How are you?'"

"No."

"You must know at least one or two words. Didn't your parents speak Korean?"

"No."

"Captain Kim, didn't you attended the Navy school to learn Korean? We know everything."

Young Oak didn't answer because he couldn't say no to this question because it was on his personnel records. It wasn't easy pretending not to know anything when he in fact, understood everything. The conversation lasted for about 15 to 20 minutes. Then, he had to take a written test. Mr. Cho was getting the papers ready when a colonel walked in. Cho jumped up to greet him. From the way Cho was talking to him, Young Oak could see that the colonel was not his direct boss, but someone even more senior.

The colonel said to Cho, "You know, Captain Kim just flunked the test."

"Sir, he hasn't even taken the test yet."

"Well, he flunked it," the colonel said.

"No, no, he speaks Korean. He knows Korean. He is just pretending that he doesn't know Korean. He is a Korean."

"Whether he's a Korean or not, understands Korean or not, it doesn't matter. What matters is whether you understand English or not. Do you understand English?"

"Yes, of course, I understand English," Cho said.

"I just told you he flunked the test."

"He didn't."

"Mr. Cho, don't you like your job at the GHQ?"

"Of course I like it, sir."

"Then he flunked the test. You sign the paper and give it to your boss and have them bring it up to me and I will sign it. Make sure everybody signs the paper first. Forget about Captain Kim."

The colonel turned around and left. Cho didn't say a word. Young Oak gathered that the man was Colonel Singles' West Point classmate. When the door was closed, Mr. Cho was so angry that Young Oak thought he was going to burst. Young Oak felt sorry for him, but couldn't say anything to ask for forgiveness.

Colonel Singles cut the orders, as if Young Oak was a returnee to the 17th Infantry following medical treatment in Japan. Then he called Regimental Commander Colonel William Quinn to ask him to take good care of Young Oak. Colonel Quinn was another one of his classmates from West Point. As the order was issued for Young Oak to report to the unit one week later, he had some time to enjoy Japan.

When Singles, Purcell and Young Oak had lunch together in Tokyo several days later, Purcell said, "You know, General Clark is coming over and we're having this big reception. Young, you should stay and go to that reception."

Singles agreed. They both thought it was a great idea. The General Clark who Purcell was talking about was the very same Lieutenant General Mark Clark, who had promoted Young Oak to captain on the spot during the Distinguished Service Cross award ceremony in Italy. Since then, Clark had gotten one more star on his shoulder. There was already a rumor that he would be coming to replace General MacArthur, whose relationship with President Truman was said to have crossed the bridge of no return. Colonel Purcell explained GHQ would hold a big reception for General Clark at the Imperial Hotel.

"Who is going to that thing?" Young Oak asked. "I'm not invited."

"There's no trouble getting you invited," Purcell said. "Just stay in Japan a little longer and say hello to him."

Purcell then picked up the phone to call someone. From the conversation, Young Oak and Singles could see he was talking to the people who were organizing the reception.

"This is Colonel Purcell at G-3. Add two more names to the reception list: Colonel Gordon Singles and Captain Young Oak Kim."

At the mention of Young Oak's rank, Purcell must have received a negative response from the other end because he started to shout.

"It's not Captain Kim who wants to see General Clark!" Purcell yelled. "It's General Clark who wants to see Captain Kim. Captain Kim is a personal friend of General Clark. You just have to add the names I am giving."

Firmly setting the phone back down in its cradle, Purcell looked up, smiled at the other two men and smugly stated, "Even though there's going to be a lot of people there, and all of them are famous and all that, the odds are General Clark will remember you and not even remember anybody else."

On the day of the reception, Colonel Singles and Young Oak went to the hotel together. The main ballroom was reserved for the invitation-only affair. It looked like most of the American generals and colonels in Korea and Japan were there for the function, with the exception of General MacArthur. Naturally, Young Oak was the lowest-ranking officer.

Before delivering the speech, General Clark was to shake hands with everyone attending the reception. General Clark was standing with his aide, who helped him greet more than 1,000 high-ranking officers. As each officer lined up and stopped in front of the general, his staff officer would whisper the person's name to him. Clark greeted and shook hands with each officer for no more than 10 seconds a piece. Singles was right in front of Young Oak and Purcell was right behind Young Oak. When it came to Young Oak's turn, before the aide could even whisper to the general, Clark exclaimed, "Young! You're Young, aren't you? I'm so happy to see you again."

Vigorously pumping Young Oak's hand the entire time, General Clark enthusiastically began recalling battles in Italy. Young Oak could sense all eyes focused on him as a hush fell over the room. He began to feel uncomfortable as he became aware of so many high-ranking officers lined up waiting to meet with the general staring at him. The staff officer whispered to General Clark that others were waiting, urging him to end the conversation.

When Young Oak started to leave, Clark said, "No, no, no, no. I want to talk more to this young man. Young, you wait here. I want to apologize. I used your name and quoted you in my book without getting your permission. I hope it's okay?"

The person who wrote Clark's memoirs had put some quotes in Young Oak's mouth. Clark was a little embarrassed and wanted to ask for Young Oak's understanding.

"Sure it's okay, General," Young Oak said.

General Clark unreservedly continued to converse with Young Oak for a good five more minutes and then finally released him. Young Oak was embarrassed, as military protocol dictated that talking was kept to a minimum when going through the reception line. Young Oak, Singles and Purcell had a good laugh about what happened when they finally left the reception. Young Oak told them that he was a little embarrassed to which they replied, "Don't worry, don't worry. These people are just jealous. They wish General Clark would spend five minutes talking to them too, you know."

Colonel Singles added, "You know, Young, you have a unique place in military history. You should take advantage of the fact that you're the only captain in the whole room. You're the only one General Clark knows by name without having to be introduced. I'm a full colonel, but he didn't know me. Alfred is a full colonel, but he didn't know him. But he knew you."

However, that was the last time Young Oak had contact with General Clark. One year and three months later, Clark became Commander of the United Nations Forces and Young Oak was commanding a U.S. battalion in Korea.

Singles, devoted to Young Oak like a brother, decided to personally accompany him to Korea. The night was pitch black as the ship from Sassebo, Japan approached the southeastern port city of Pusan, Korea. Young Oak hated boarding ships. Now, dead tired and nauseous, he glimpsed the outline of his fatherland in the darkness for the first time in his life. Many thoughts filled his mind as the chilling oceanic winds blew around him. He sensed someone cautiously touching his shoulder, it was Singles. Neither man uttered a word. Upon disembarking, they went straight to the American military barracks and fell asleep.

The next morning, keeping his promise to his mother, Young Oak went to see President Syngman Rhee in a U.S. Army VIP sedan. Colonel Singles, who had arranged for the car before leaving Japan, drove. In the reception area, when Young Oak requested to meet with the President, the expression on the secretary's face clearly mirrored his own thoughts: *How dare a mere captain expect to meet with the President of Korea?*

"Please tell the President that Young Oak Kim, a U.S. Army captain who is a son of Mr. Soon Kwon Kim, is here to see him," Young Oak said. "I will wait here for exactly five minutes. If there is no response by then, I will leave quietly."

About four minutes later, a profusely apologetic secretary emerged from the President's chambers and requested that Young Oak wait for just 20 more minutes because the President was presiding over an emergency cabinet meeting. Twenty minutes later, President Rhee entered the room and led both Young Oak and Singles into his reception room. Remembering all of Young Oak's family's names, the President genially inquired about Young Oak's mother, sisters and brothers. He recalled Young Oak's father and spoke about the Korean War. Half an hour later, the President personally escorted the two to the front gate. Putting his hand on Young Oak's shoulder,

President Rhee said paternally, "Be sure to let me know how you are doing, even if you are sent to the frontlines."

However, that was the last time Young Oak saw President Rhee. During his 18 months of fighting in Korea, he never contacted the President again. He thought a line officer on the frontlines had no business contacting the President of Korea. Young Oak had personal "hotlines" with two of the most powerful men in Korea, President Syngman Rhee and General Mark Clark, but he never contacted them again while in Korea.

After meeting with President Rhee, Young Oak headed to the Pusan train station to go to the 7th Division. The division was in reserve to get replacements and equipment, since it had suffered major losses in the Battle of Chosin Reservoir, also known as the Changjin Lake Campaign, in North Korea the previous year. It was this day at the Pusan train station that he would never forget.

It wasn't snowing, but there was snow and ice on the streets and on the ground in slippery patches. It was very cold. It was one of the coldest winters in Korea in many years. Children were roaming all around the snow-covered station. More than 1,000 boys and girls between the ages of five and 10 were begging for food, desperately grabbing at things. Although the winter was bitterly cold, most of them didn't have any pants and were barefoot. They were only clothed in torn tee-shirts. They were undersized from malnutrition. They stretched their arms to beg for food, or crawled underneath the steam train cars to find a scrap of coal to warm their homes. It was very dangerous because some trains were moving. Whenever there was an American soldier entering the station, they followed him in groups, begging. They were dirty: black and blue, and green and yellow.

After a final farewell to Colonel Singles, Young Oak tried to suppress his sad feelings as he made his way to the train through the milling children. One of the train cabins was reserved for officers. He went in and saw many boxes of C-rations piled up in a corner. Each officer was given a whole box and it had about eight C-rations—enough for three days or more. He thought they weren't going to be on the train long and that they had a surplus of food. Assuming one of the boxes was his, he took it to the doorway and opened it. As he began distributing the contents, multitudes of children suddenly rushed over to him, pushing and shoving to grab a bit of whatever they could catch. The single box of C-rations was gone in an instant. When they were still yelling and screaming, he went back to the cabin. There were about 25 to 30 officers in the cabin waiting for the train to depart. From the hallway of the cabin, Young Oak shouted, "I am Captain Kim going to the 7th Division. We are United States Army officers and the Army isn't going to let us starve. All of us could do without eating one or two meals. We're not going to be on this train more than one or two days and before too long, I'm sure we'll get more food. These rations are yours. How about just holding out one or two cans for yourselves and give me the rest to give to the kids?"

"Sure, sure," many officers immediately answered. But two or three officers complained.

"Oh, come on you bastards," someone shouted. "Give us your food."

The officers began to stand up and line up in front of the pile. They opened their boxes, took a can, left the rest in the corner and went back to their seats. Opened C-ration boxes were piled up one after another. One officer volunteered to help Young Oak. The two of them carried rations to the entrance near the platform and began to give them to the children. It looked like all the children in the station were coming to them. In order to prevent the children from closing in on them, they had to throw the rations farther and farther away. They couldn't think about anything else but worrying about children getting hurt in the mad rush. Just as he finished distributing the C-rations, the train began to move. When Young Oak took a seat in the cabin, he could see through the window the happy faces of the children holding the rations. Moved, he couldn't look at them anymore.

War is cruel to civilians, especially to women and children. In Italy, Young Oak had witnessed a woman sell herself for five cigarettes and a soldier who had just lost his arms and legs crying out for his mother. In France, he had seen a soldier's head and chest blown off his body by a bomb, yet his torso-less body still ran forward for a good 20 to 30 yards. But of all his memories of World War II and the Korean War, it would be the faces of those children at the Pusan train station that he would remember as the cruelest experience of war. He shed hot tears. Young Oak was a man who rarely showed his emotions, but at that moment there was nothing he could do. He couldn't see or think about anything else. It was the first and last time that he ever cried so deep and hard in his life.

Chapter 16
Horse Trading

When Young Oak reported to the 7th Division, he encountered the problem Singles had warned him of back in Japan. The division headquarters wanted to keep him there for his Korean language abilities, so they put him into the intelligence section. Upset, Young Oak complained.

"Sir, I could have stayed in Tokyo if I wanted to become an interpreter," Young Oak said to the Division Intelligence Officer, Major Hazard. "I came to Korea to fight on the frontline."

After listening to him, Major Hazard became angry. The two came to exchange rather harsh words with one another and Young Oak left the G-2 tent without resolving the issue. Right outside of the tent he met with Captain Walter Johnson, who also fought in the 100th Battalion during World War II. They had not seen each other since they were at the French Riviera.

"Young!" Johnson said delightedly. "You're alive!"

After Young Oak related his predicament and his conversation with Major Hazard, Johnson grabbed his hand in earnest appeal.

"Come let me show you around," Johnson said. "Don't go up to the frontline. You'll get killed. Stay here. I will take care of you."

Johnson took Young Oak over to another tent, which was the main tent for G-3, the operations section. Johnson was a staff officer of the G-3. The division headquarters consisted of about 20 tents and they had two big tents pulled together for the G-2 and G-3. The G-3 tent had big maps and everything else needed for combat. Johnson began to explain the current situations on the maps that Young Oak had started to read. About 30 minutes later, a lieutenant colonel walked in and began to yell.

"Goddamn, you son of a bitch, what the hell are you doing with a Korean?"

Johnson tried to explain that Young Oak was an American officer, but the lieutenant colonel wouldn't listen to it. He was G-3, Division Operations Officer Mel Houston.

"You two get out of this tent," Houston said. "And don't ever come back here again."

Upset, Johnson argued with Houston. Still angry with Captain Johnson, Houston turned his tirade on him. Johnson was a senior captain, soon to be a major. He was very upset and kept arguing.

At that moment Young Oak said, "Don't, let's just go."

He took Johnson outside, went straight back to the G-2 tent, and said to Major Hazard, "Sir, it does you no good to keep me here anyway. I just got orders from the G-3 never to step foot in the operations tent again."

"He can't do that," Hazard said.

"Well, he just gave me the order and I'm not going to go in that tent again."

"I want to go talk to him."

"No use because I'm not going in there again; he already gave me a direct order and I'm not going to disobey."

"Well, I'll tell you what. The 'Benedae' group has been requested to go on a long-range patrol with the 31st Infantry. And the commanding officer has to go back for a medical checkup because he was just awarded a regular army commission. So he's going to be gone for five days and the patrol has to go out tomorrow. If you take this patrol out for me, then when you come back, I'll transfer you to the 17th Regiment, 7th Division. Deal?"

"Deal!" Young Oak said.

"Meet the intelligence officer of the 31st Infantry and get briefed. The Benedae group went there already."

"Yes sir."

The 31st Infantry Regiment CP was located south of Odae Mountain, in the town of Soksari. He arrived there on the evening of March 27. The regimental headquarters consisted of around 15 to 20 tents. He saw a tent with the sign of S-3, the regimental intelligence section, and went in. As the daily briefing had just ended, the tent was filled with officers. He didn't know whom to address, so he simply stood and waited until finally, a lieutenant colonel came to him.

"Who are you?" the lieutenant colonel asked. "What are you doing here?"

"I am Captain Young Oak Kim, sir. I came here to lead the patrol."

"The Benedae group?"

"I'm not sure, but it looks like it. I just arrived here and received an order to lead the patrol."

"You are an infantry officer. Did you serve during World War II?"

"Yes sir!"

"Which unit?"

"The 100th Infantry Battalion."

"What was your position?"

"Battalion S-3, sir."

"When was that?"

"1944."

"Since you've just arrived, I'll ask you just one more question. Are you interested in being my S-3?"

Young Oak was very surprised. A regimental intelligence officer was a slot for a major. In addition, it was unimaginable to offer such a position to a colored captain in those days.

"Thank you sir, but I am not. I don't know who you are. We just met and never served together. More importantly, I am already committed to the 17th Regiment."

"I am the 31st Regiment Commander William McCaffrey. Although we just met, don't think I'm joking."

"How can you suggest this without knowing me?"

"Well, I won't take no for an answer. You're going to patrol, so let's talk afterwards."

The Benedae group was an anti-communist guerilla unit consisting of about 100 Korean civilians. They were evacuated with the 7th Division, when it withdrew from North Korea the prior year. Their primary duty was to gather enemy intelligence at the request its division or its regiments. The Korean military referred to such a unit as "Pyon Eui Dae," meaning a unit in plain civilian clothes. Somehow, the lingual transference from the Korean usage to the U.S. troops evolved into the word "Benedae." Lieutenant Smock was in charge of providing supplies and training for them. He was a responsible and competent officer, wholly dedicated to training them. When he discovered that division headquarters had decided to send the group to gather enemy intelligence, he was furious. They had never been under live fire and he thought they were not ready.

Meanwhile, at a planning meeting for the upcoming operation, Young Oak took a seat at a table with the intelligence officer of the 31st Regiment. Young Oak opened up a map and began to scrutinize it.

"According to South Korean military intelligence, a North Korean guerrilla unit is in the mountain area north of Bangtae Chon," the intelligence officer informed Young Oak. "Korean civilians also reported that North Korean soldiers have dug in there."

Quickly absorbing the map, Young Oak mentally drew three-dimensional images of the area. With a mental camera, he photographed the U.S. 7th Division, located south of Bangtae Mountain, flanked by a Korean division to the west and to the east. After discussing with the intelligence officer how to proceed, he picked up the map and left.

The next morning, Young Oak met with the members of the Benedae group. One of the first things Young Oak wanted to assess was the extent to which they could communicate. Both their leader and deputy leader could speak a certain level of English. They were very delighted to see an American officer of Korean ancestry come to command them. As he was curious about their English fluency, they wanted to know his Korean-speaking skills. They were glad to know that his Korean was better than they expected, and that there would be no language problem. Yet, he mixed Korean and English, and when he spoke in English, he tried to speak clearly and slowly. Apparently the leaders were also adept at reading maps and were fully cognizant of their mission. He also wanted to test each man's physical condition. They were relatively older, as the youngest person was in his early 30s. On average, they seemed to be about 10 years older than a regular U.S. soldier. Young Oak himself was 32 years old at the time and wasn't in the best shape because he hadn't exercised in two months. However, their physical condition was even worse. Finally, he conducted an inventory check of clothing and weapons. Although it was late March, the eastern front was still bitterly cold and the ground was covered with snow. Naturally, the cold weather was a major concern. Furthermore, the group possessed outdated weapons that wouldn't effectively facilitate their mission. Since the order was not to engage in any combat, the group had to move fast. Young Oak told the men not to carry heavy weapons.

Leading the guerilla unit, Young Oak left the regimental CP at 8:00 a.m. They marched for an hour in combat formation and then rested a few minutes. They repeated this several times as they moved north. During the first rest, Young Oak explained the situation to the unit leaders. After that, he tried to communicate with as many other members as possible. Although he couldn't remember their names, he got to know who was responsible for what specific roles. From his experiences during World War II, Young Oak knew that a commanding officer should lead the unit right behind the lead group. He always positioned himself right behind 10 men, and the rest followed him from behind.

When they first entered enemy territory, the men didn't see any enemies. To pull off the mission, they would have to get to their final destination, Hill 736. But just as they were nearing the hill, gunshots rang through the air. A member instinctively fired his gun upon sighting enemy troops. Their direct orders were not to exchange fire, but it was too late. Young Oak immediately ordered them to engage. Most escaped, but they were able to capture two enemy soldiers. One was a nurse and the other was an enlisted man who was severely wounded. Once they stopped, Young Oak anticipated a possible counterattack during the night, so he had the men take a defensive formation.

That night, he had to attend to a major problem: a severely wounded prisoner of war. The soldier presented complications for the mission. To complete the reconnaissance mission successfully, the group had to move swiftly, but the wounded soldier was slowing them down. They had two choices: give up the mission and return or continue the mission after killing the wounded soldier. The enemy soldier begged for his life. Members were torn by the decision. Their argument lasted throughout the evening. In case they concluded that they should kill the man, the leaders selected a member to carry out the difficult job. As the night wore on, with much heated debate, Young Oak learned a great deal about his unit. They came from different backgrounds—teachers, doctors, lawyers and policemen. Most of them were highly-educated intellectuals who had escaped the Communist regime. As the morning approached, a tough call had to be made and such a decision was always a commander's responsibility. From Young Oak's mouth, a heartbreaking command spilled out.

"Let's continue the mission."

As they marched east toward Hill 736, they could see enemy movement becoming more active. Although their artillery battalion surveillance airplane flew over them several times as planned, they couldn't communicate with the pilot. Young Oak realized that the heavy radio equipment they carried was useless.

Perhaps the radio was broken or the battery was bad. Or Young Oak's radio operator was unable to coordinate a radio frequency with the airplane. And yet, he thought regimental headquarters must have gained valuable information on enemy positions as the group of about 100 men was able to penetrate certain locations without resistance. Soon they arrived at the top of Hill 736, located about 37 miles from regimental headquarters. From the mountaintop, they were able to see the North Korean unit's headquarters to the northeast. Young Oak decided to stay there overnight to watch enemy movements and then return the next day. They already accomplished the mission. The weather was cold and many of his men were running out of water. Young Oak allowed his men to light fires at the opposite side of the mountain where the enemy wouldn't be able to see them. It was a dangerous gamble, but some of his men would have frozen to death without the fires that night.

Early the next morning, the enemy headquarters suddenly bustled with activity. For some reason, several hundred enemy soldiers began to gather. Initially, Young Oak thought that they were preparing to attack his group. He repositioned his men and weapons to bolster a defensive position, and at the same time ordered them to be prepared to retreat quickly. Strangely, however, the North Koreans didn't position their troops in a location where they could have launched an attack against the group. The company-sized enemy lead unit was preparing to hide in a mountain overlooking the road along a narrow river in the area. It meant that they were not planning to attack his group. Young Oak thought it was a strange move as he looked around. All of a sudden, American soldiers appeared from around the curve from the south. Looking at the marching formation, it was obvious that the company commander had very little combat experience. Although he was behind a lead group, the distance between the lead group and main unit was too close. If the enemy ambushed them, they might be annihilated. Since it became obvious why the enemy soldiers busied themselves, Young Oak called for the group leader.

"I have to go to the American soldiers down below and come back," Young Oak said. "Since the enemy doesn't know we are here, position the weapons in place in order to attack if something happens. If the enemy attacks the Americans, immediately launch an attack. At the same time, be prepared to retreat anytime. If the situation is bad, retreat immediately even if I don't come back. When you retreat, you must use the same road we came from. If I come back, let's retreat together right away."

Young Oak gave his map to the leader and ran toward the American soldiers down below. He planned his actions carefully so he wouldn't get shot by them. The American soldiers did not know his group had penetrated into this position. More importantly, Young Oak looked Korean but was wearing an American military uniform. In many instances, North Korean and Chinese forces wore American military uniforms to disguise themselves. Therefore, American soldiers could have perceived him as a disguised Chinese or North Korean soldier. It felt so far to run the half mile toward the Americans. As he approached near the lead unit, he shouted, "Don't shoot. I am an American officer. I have something to say."

As expected, American soldiers pointed their guns at him. They asked a few more questions to check his identity. Finally, they shouted back, "Have your pistol in the holster, raise both hands above your head and come out."

With guns pointed at him, he was taken to the company commander. In the beginning, the company commander didn't believe him. As he described the facial characteristics of Lieutenant Colonel McCaffrey, the company commander began to believe him and identified themselves as part of the 31st Regiment. They were G Company.

Surprisingly, they were coming to attack his group. They got wrong information that the group was a North Korean guerrilla unit. Young Oak suggested the company commander abandon the road and climb the mountain to retreat together. The company commander accepted the suggestion. From the way the American soldiers climbed the mountain, Young Oak knew that they were not trained well for mountain combat. It wasn't difficult to avoid the North Koreans who were busy preparing themselves to ambush the American soldiers. After he safely returned to his group, he had his men retreat immediately.

Although the members were tired, they followed his orders well. Since they were all exhausted, they couldn't help carry other soldiers' equipment. But the captured North Korean nurse was willing to help carry Young Oak's equipment. In the beginning, after being captured, she couldn't relax. However, she changed when she saw Young Oak try to protect her from possible misconduct by his men. When he allowed her to carry his equipment, she offered to carry his weapon as well. He didn't let her carry it, but thought that it was fortunate the war had ended for her.

G Company, who had mistakenly come to attack Young Oak's group, escaped from a possible disaster. Since G Company was armed with heavy equipment, they were slower than Young Oak's group but possessed superior fire power. Young Oak and his men were happy to have G Company between them and the enemy.

Young Oak told his men to rest when they were just about to enter the 31st Regiment headquarters. A jeep approached and came to a sudden stop. It was Lieutenant Colonel McCaffrey.

"I heard about it," McCaffrey said. "You accomplished the mission very successfully. So did you think about it?"

"Yes sir. But I still think I've got to go to the 17th..."

Before he could finish his sentence, McCaffrey interrupted.

"No, no. Let's think about this more seriously. How about this? I know the regimental commander of the 17th very well. Tell him straightforwardly that I offered the regimental intelligence officer. If he comes up with a match or better, you stay there. If not, come back to me. You have nothing to lose."

"Yes sir," Young Oak said. "That doesn't sound bad."

"You must be tired. Why don't you take a shower and rest? Tomorrow morning I will send a jeep to take you there. Don't worry about anything and sleep well."

The next morning, Young Oak headed over to the 17th Regiment. While reporting to Colonel William Quinn later that afternoon, Young Oak explained everything.

"I see. Is that what happened?" Quinn asked. "If you stay here for a month, I probably can give you a position requiring a major. However, the position may not be as good as the regimental three. If I were you, I would accept his offer."

"Thank you, sir. I know you and Colonel Singles are West Point classmates. So I wanted to stay here and serve you well. But since you're letting me go comfortably, I'll go there."

"Good luck!"

Young Oak returned to the 31st Regiment and became the intelligence officer. About one month later, he asked McCaffrey why he had offered such an important position to a captain he met for the first time in his life.

"Do you remember that the 442nd Regiment in France was assigned to the 92nd Division in Italy at the request of the Fifth Army and came back to Italy to break through the Gothic Line?" McCaffery said. "Well, it was me who was the Division Chief of Staff. On top of that, because I was the military advisor to the U.S. Reserve Army in Hawaii after World War II, I know the 100th Battalion better than anybody else. If you were the operations officer of the 100th in 1944, it means you're better than any officer of this regiment under my command now. There was no reason to hesitate. So, it might seem like I made a silly offer, less than five minutes after we met, but based upon my experience, it wasn't silly at all."

McCaffrey didn't say anymore that day, but later he was more honest with Young Oak. During World War II, the 100th Battalion and the 442nd Regiment enjoyed a stellar reputation among U.S. soldiers, particularly among those in Italy. In addition, both Casper Clough and Gordon Singles were McCaffrey's West Point classmates.

Naturally, McCaffrey came to know more about the 100th and about Young Oak. When McCaffrey saw his name on the 7th Division reinforcement list, he went to the 17th Regiment and met the regimental commander, Colonel Quinn.

"There is one Asian captain coming to your regiment," McCaffrey said to Quinn. "If you give him to me, I'll give you two majors under my command."

Quinn agreed.

McCaffrey, Singles, Clough, Quinn and the colonel who took care of Young Oak's Korean language test in Tokyo were all part of West Point's class of 1939. In this sense, Young Oak had a unique destiny with this class.

They graduated and were commissioned in the very year that World War II began and by this time most were promoted to colonels and commanding regiments. This kind of personnel exchange was commonly called "horse trading." In those days, racial discrimination was prevalent in American civilian society and there was no difference in the U.S. military. Considering this, McCaffrey's exchange of two Caucasian majors for one Asian captain was far beyond imagination. McCaffrey was such a creative and decisive person and it was rare luck for Young Oak to be able to meet such a person and boss.

Chapter 17
Soyang River

Early in April 1951, Young Oak joined the 31st Infantry Regiment as the intelligence officer. The regiment, under McCaffrey's command, had been in reserve to reinforce itself while getting replacements. The regiment had advanced near the Sino-Korean border after the Incheon Landing and was almost annihilated by the Chinese army at the Battle of Chosin Reservoir. Its regimental commander was killed in action.

After Young Oak joined the 31st, McCaffrey invited him to his tent for card games every night. Occasionally, he would invite other officers: Executive Officer Lieutenant Colonel Frank Smith, Operations Officer Major William Clark or other staff officers like Captain Joe Conmy. But it was most often McCaffrey and Young Oak by themselves. They played cribbage or Gin Rummy for two to three hours every night. Young Oak would win almost every time. One night, McCaffrey said with a smile on his face, "Now I know why you were such a brilliant operations officer. You're a professional Gin Rummy player. I have never lost a game so fast to anybody. Losing in Gin Rummy is okay, but I can't believe that I lost in cribbage as well because I consider myself a good cribbage player."

McCaffrey offered card games every night so he could get to know Young Oak better. One evening, McCaffrey told him, "During World War II, I was in Italy as the 92nd Division Chief of Staff, but I wasn't on the frontlines like you."

McCaffrey wanted to discuss the Italian and French fronts. He asked many questions: how and why Young Oak devised and implemented particular tactics during battles and what Young Oak would do in case of similar circumstances in Korea. The regimental commander was particularly interested in the battle at Pisa, where Young Oak liberated the city without a single drop of blood. Their discussion continued almost endlessly, covering operation plans for a hypothetical combat situation to general management of the regiment. During these talks, McCaffrey considered the best way to utilize Young Oak's talents, while Young Oak was seeking to understand the commander and his expectations. Young Oak's conclusion was that McCaffrey wanted him to devise an overall strategy for the regiment.

At 1:00 p.m. on April 18, while the division band was playing, Major General Edward Almond's helicopter landed at the 31st Regiment for inspection. The Corps Commander began the inspection with a briefing at regimental headquarters, and Young Oak knew there was going to be a Corps inspection personally led by the Corps commander. One week prior to the visit, Regimental Commander McCaffrey gathered all the regimental staff officers.

"Everybody must make a presentation three minutes long," McCaffrey explained. "But you must say everything you need to say in those three minutes. I want you to do it very quickly, very precisely and make your key point. I don't want more than three minutes. So each of you write what you're going to say and come talk to me."

Young Oak wrote exactly what he was going to say in three minutes and submitted it. After reviewing it, McCaffrey said, "I like this, but I don't like this. I like this, but I don't like this...Put in something else here. Make your points quickly enough, sharp enough, and complete enough. Always think about what questions General Almond will ask, as if you were General Almond."

Young Oak rewrote the presentation and gave it to McCaffrey a second time. "Now you're beginning to understand what I'm talking about," the regimental commander said. "Good, it's okay. Now, number one, I may be General Almond's fair-haired boy, but you're not. General Almond is a very, very bright man. He's got a lightning-fast brain. That's why he's the Chief of Staff of the GHQ in Tokyo. Never underestimate. From now on, you have to approach every three-star general as if they are Almond. They're very, very bright people. Otherwise they wouldn't be a three star. Now, I'll be General Almond. You're up there. You talk to me."

So Young Oak gave a mock presentation. McCaffrey was actually timing with a stopwatch and said, "You got 10 seconds."

When the practice briefing was over, McCaffrey said, "It's over three minutes. You've got to learn to talk fast so that there is no time for him to think and ask a question. If he asks a question, you're going to give him a prompt, complete, immediate answer. If you don't, it's too late. By that time, his mind already thought of five more questions, and he will devastate you. You do one thing with General Almond, you please him, or you displease him. If you please him, that's fine. If you displease him, he's never going to forgive you or forget you either, and he's never going to let anybody underneath him forgive you or forget you. Practice more and come back."

Back at his own tent, Young Oak practiced repeatedly in order to complete the briefing within three minutes. Young Oak presented the briefing to McCaffrey again, who corrected it again. The same process was repeated several times. Never before had Young Oak had so strenuous a practice for one briefing. McCaffrey was very demanding. Even though McCaffrey liked Young

Oak very much, he demanded perfection when it came to business.

Finally, after about six practice briefings, he said for the first time, "That's enough." Then he added, "Now, I want to tell you this. You may be just as bright as a three star is, but you're a lot younger and they have a lot more experience than you. Don't forget that they get briefed everyday by all kinds of people. Finally, when you're finished, get out. Don't hesitate for one-tenth of a second. That one-tenth of a second is all the time he needs to ask you a question you can't answer. It's a game he's playing. Don't ask him if he's got any questions, because he's going to. You can't fool him. And don't let his brain get ahead of your briefing. Because if he's bored, he's going to ask you questions you can't answer. He enjoys his power and he'll keep you up there for 10 minutes, just playing with you."

On the morning of the inspection day, Lieutenant Colonel McCaffrey assembled all the staff officers of the regiment and said, "Final time. Give me a rehearsal of what you're going to say."

When every officer finished his briefing within three minutes, the commander said, "Fine. Do it that way. Don't deviate."

When Major General Almond arrived that afternoon, the briefing began with McCaffrey, the regimental commander. His brief was very impressive. He began with a short welcoming statement and gave an overall picture of the regiment in a gentle, yet firm and steady way. Then he handed over the podium to his staff. He was to be followed by S-1, S-2, S-3 and S-4. The S-1, who was the personnel officer, went first, and did very well. Boom, boom, boom, and finished. But like McCaffrey said, the Corps commander wasn't that much interested in S-1 and S-4. It was S-2 and S-3 he was going to zero in on. As S-2, Young Oak was the second on the platform. So he got up there and gave his presentation. He did exactly as McCaffrey said.

He got up there, delivered his report and boom, boom, boom, he finished and got out. The next person, Major William Clark, S-3, went up. Everybody said he had a good personality and was a wonderful and very polished speaker, almost like an actor. But that was the problem. He was so proud of himself that, instead of following his script, he decided to use some of his charm, and it didn't work. He took a little too long to end the briefing and he paused. At that moment Major General Almond asked him a question and he couldn't answer right away. From then on, Almond just kept asking him questions. He kept him up there for about 10 minutes. Each question got harder and harder, and Clark couldn't answer. Before he was through, he was almost devastated psychologically. Finally, Almond told him in front of all the officers, "Young man, I think you need to do some work. You're not prepared. I don't have any more time to spend with you, but that was a terrible briefing. You're dismissed."

After the briefing, it was no secret to the regiment's officers that McCaffrey's attitude toward Major Clark changed. McCaffrey had a high opinion of him once and so gave Clark the job of S-3. But after Young Oak came to the regiment, McCaffrey was waiting for the right opportunity to make him S-3 instead. The briefing helped McCaffrey make up his mind. Like anywhere else, it's the same in the U.S. military, an important briefing could either be an opportunity or a disaster.

After the briefing, Almond commenced an intensive inspection of the 3rd Battalion for an interminable two hours. Due to weather problems, the next day he resumed the inspection of the tank company and the reconnaissance platoon for another two-and-a-half hours. For the second day inspection, General James Van Fleet, Commander of the Eighth Army, was slated to attend, but it was suddenly cancelled on the day of the inspection. The fact that General Van Fleet was going to attend a regiment inspection was clear evidence of how great of an interest the U.S. Army had in the resurrection of the 31st Infantry. When Almond inspected the 2nd Battalion the next day, he questioned every officer. The inspection continued into the 22nd of the month, a Sunday. Almond's inspection of the 1st Battalion lasted for four hours and 20 minutes. Finally, at the close of the inspection, the Corps commander announced to the Division commander, Major General Claude Ferenbaugh, that the regiment was ready to fight again. Ferenbaugh then turned to McCaffrey and delivered the attack orders right then and there.

Throughout the inspection period, as S-2, Young Oak received a steady stream of intelligence. On the 18th, the first day of inspection, there were no major battles on the front, although small skirmishes continued. There was a stalemate on the frontline, but the quiet was a prelude predicting the typhoon that was to come. Around 10:00 p.m., three Korean soldiers infiltrated the 1st Battalion zone. They claimed that they belonged to the 35th Regiment of the South Korean Army and that they were the only survivors of their regiment; the rest had been killed by the enemy. Major Dudley, the 1st Battalion operations officer, inquired with the 5th Division of the South Korean Army. Oddly, the South Korean 5th Division answered they were not attacked. The three soldiers had lied. Although the South Korean 35th Regiment had indeed been attacked, the enemy had retreated without causing much damage. The three soldiers had either fled their unit upon enemy attack or deserted before the attack had commenced. They were handed over to the South Korean military the next day.

On the 19th, the South Korean III Corps sent out an interrogation report about three North Korean soldiers that had been captured the previous day. The report said the three soldiers belonged to the North Korean 32nd Division. The primary mission of this enemy division was to secure high mountain areas in the vicinity to help the Chinese army in the back regroup and launch an attack. They also said that one-third of the North Korean division was actually made out of confiscated South Koreans.

On the 20th, the South Korean 5th Division commander and his staff visited Young Oak's regiment to see a shooting demonstration of one of its heavy weapon companies. On the 21st, a patrol discovered three dead Koreans in a remote area: a policeman, a male civilian and a female civilian. Their bodies were still warm.

Civilian interrogations had also been going on throughout the inspection period. One of the most serious problems for American soldiers during the Korean War was that it wasn't easy to tell friends from foes. The war was between one and the same people, and all Koreans wore white. It was hard for Americans to distinguish refugees from enemy soldiers in civilian clothes. The only action American soldiers could take was to check whether there were young Korean men of military age in their area. Sometimes enemy soldiers wearing white clothes over their military uniforms or just white clothes, approached Americans, and attacked them. At other times, enemy guerrillas in white civilian clothes, mixed with civilian refugees, penetrated friendly lines and attacked from the rear. For these reasons, the 31st had to interrogate hundreds of civilians every day. The Counterintelligence Corps (CIC) was in charge of this matter and relied heavily on the South Korean police.

The 31st Regiment's first mission after the inspection was to cross the Soyang River, relieve the 17th Regiment and advance further north. The 17th, which had been in contact with the Chinese for a while, was scheduled to pull back a little to the south to get some rest, but stay north of the river. The 31st began to cross the river the night of April 22, 1951. The next morning, when most of the regiment had crossed the river, the situation had changed drastically. The previous night, Communist forces began an all-out attack on all Korean fronts. This was the attack that was to become famous in the Korean War; the First Spring Offensive of the Chinese forces. On the western and central fronts, Chinese were the primary forces, while North Koreans were the primary forces on the eastern front.

As the massive assault by the Communist forces were confirmed, the 31st Regiment's mission quickly changed from offensive to defensive. Now the regiment had to take a temporarily defensive position around the river to allow both American and South Korean troops to retreat south of the river and regroup for a counterattack. Unfortunately, there was only one bridge— a floating bridge built by the Americans—that the friendly troops could use to cross back. For everyone to safely cross, it was very important to secure a different bridge over a very narrow and deep valley about four miles north of the floating bridge. This valley is still called "Crematory Valley," because it was where dead Korean soldier bodies were cremated during the Korean War. Because of the terrain, if a large number of troops had to move south, they would inevitably have to pass this small bridge. From the viewpoint of retreating troops, they would have to keep the enemies to the north side of this bridge, if they wanted to use the floating bridge and cross the river safely. This small bridge had been built during the Japanese colonial era.

The previous night when the regiment began crossing the river, Lieutenant Colonel McCaffrey called up Young Oak before the operation began.

"A friend of mine is coming down tomorrow and he needs an airplane," McCaffrey said. "Take him to the airstrip tomorrow morning."

McCaffrey's friend was a colonel and an American advisor to the South Korean III Corps. The airstrip that McCaffrey mentioned was just a small, hastily-built runway where only one reconnaissance plane could land or take off. It was just north of the city of Inje, which the South Korean Army 5th Division was defending.

The next morning, Young Oak left the regiment without knowing the massive Chinese attack had begun. The jeep moved further north towards the airstrip, and the sound of artillery fires increased. Young Oak and the colonel sensed that something was happening. They were not sure whether they were going in the right direction. Six miles to the north from Inje, they could see the airstrip and soon an L-19 showed up in the sky. The colonel, who had been riding on the passenger side, got out and went around the front to the driver's side to shake hands. All of a sudden, Young Oak shouted, "Enemies!"

They were company-sized North Koreans. They were slowly descending from the mountain, as if to avoid being noticed by the aircraft. With eyes on both the enemy soldiers and the aircraft, the colonel said quickly, "Whatever happens, as soon as that plane lands, I'm going to run for the airplane and you get the hell out of here as fast as you can, because you might get cut up by those enemies coming down."

When the airplane touched ground, the colonel got out of the jeep and ran towards it. As the airplane landed without reducing its speed, it immediately turned south and shook violently. The L-19 picked up the colonel and went back up in the air. At the same time, the driver pressed the accelerator hard, heading full speed towards the mountain, straight to where the North Korean soldiers were approaching. They had to beat the North Koreans to the pass. It felt like racing towards the edge of a cliff. Enemy soldiers, who had just missed the airplane, saw Young Oak's jeep and began running along the ridge toward it. The jeep had to whip around curves on the winding mountain road. The enemy soldiers were running in a straight line, but they had to run on the mountainside. It was a race of life and death. The distance between the jeep and the enemies repeatedly narrowed and widened, depending on the variegating terrain. Even when the distance fell within shooting range, the enemies just yelled and shouted, but they didn't open fire. It was obvious that they were trying to capture Young Oak alive. The race continued this way for about three miles. As they approached a place called Nojeonpyong, a sharp curve lay ahead. This curve was the last obstacle. The distance between the jeep and its pursuers narrowed to only 50 yards. At that moment, giving up the idea of capturing him alive, the enemies began shooting like crazy. Moving at full speed, the jeep had to slow down to make the curve. It was truly a punctuated moment of life or death. Just as the jeep made the turn, the driver accelerated as hard as he could. The jeep almost flipped over, but that day, again, the goddess of luck took Young Oak's side.

Around 11:00 a.m., when he got to the other side of the hill, McCaffrey contacted Young Oak by radio. The regimental commander had tried earlier, but the radio couldn't reach him on the opposite side of the hill.

"I've been trying to get hold of you. What happened?" McCaffrey asked.

"He left safely," Young Oak said.

"Good. But the situation here is really serious."

"What's the matter? I just escaped from the enemy myself."

"I see. It looks like the enemy launched a major attack on all fronts. It is really serious for us now that the Koreans collapsed and retreated in total disorder. You must have passed through a small bridge on your way to the airstrip. Don't come back to the headquarters. Just come to the bridge. When you arrive at the bridge, cross it and wait there. One tank platoon will come up that road. Use them to secure the bridge. You must hold the bridge for at least several hours to let the 17th safely retreat south of the river."

As the jeep turned the final curve before Gaeundong, Young Oak caught sight of the bridge. From the other side of the bridge, they could see a column of tanks coming over the hill toward the bridge. Since they were five M4 Sherman tanks, it was obvious that they were the tank platoon McCaffrey said he'd sent. Young Oak crossed the bridge and stopped the jeep to wait for the tanks. Suddenly, with the sound of loud propellers cutting through the air, a helicopter landed and someone jumped off. His helmet showed one star. It was Brigadier General Robert Sink, Assistant Commander of the 7th Division. He was the legendary regimental commander of the famous U.S. 101st Airborne Division during World War II. He saw the tanks and the jeep and came straight to Young Oak. As regimental intelligence officer, Young Oak had met him several times, and the general recognized him immediately.

"Aren't you Captain Kim?" Sink said. "Good."

As if the general had already anticipated his arrival, he continued without waiting for Young Oak's reply.

"South Korean soldiers are retreating in disorder," Sink said. "They will come down this road. Stop them."

"How sir?"

Young Oak believed he didn't have any authority over Korean soldiers.

"I don't care how, just stop them. Stop them and commandeer them. And form a line here. How you do it, that's your responsibility. I want you to block this bridge. I want you to make sure that nobody gets across this ravine. And get South Korean soldiers along this ravine. Stop the South Koreans to help stop the enemy. You can use these tanks."

After surveying the ground situation from the air, the general probably concluded that securing the bridge was the key to successful retreat. Because the assistant division commander didn't know that one of his regimental commanders had sent the tank platoon, it was clear that the division and the regiment didn't properly communicate, proving that the Americans were also in great turmoil. Sink didn't know whose tanks they were either, but as if he didn't care about such things, he told the tank platoon leader, "Lieutenant, are you the platoon leader? Take orders from Captain Kim."

General Sink made sure Young Oak had the five tanks and took off. At the southern end of the bridge, Young Oak looked around the area, thought for a moment and ordered the tank platoon leader, "Line up all five tanks abreast, right here."

The tanks took formation on a small flat area in front of the bridge. With them at his back, Young Oak took several steps toward the bridge and stopped. The small old bridge could determine the fate of thousands of lives. Brigadier General Sink's helicopter had disappeared into the sky. As soon as the tanks stopped their motors, there was absolute silence. Only the sounds of artillery barrages in the distance sporadically broke the calm. The soldiers in the tanks, Young Oak's jeep driver, and the war orphan Choi quietly stared at Young Oak, who was standing in front of the bridge like a statue.

Choi was about 15 years old. The Korean War cost him both parents. He performed household duties at regimental headquarters. When Young Oak came to the regiment as S-2, Choi was so proud that there was an American officer who shared a face like his. During the Korean War, American units were one of the most popular shelters for war orphans. They could at least eat and sleep there. Regardless of being on the frontline or in the rear, war orphans came to American units. Americans soldiers, in turn, needed help with domestic tasks. They saw that the orphans would do anything to survive, so they quietly took them in. There were thousands of war orphans in the regimental headquarters; it looked like every American officer had one war orphan. American soldiers called them "houseboys." Some houseboys were not war orphans, but residents of the area where American troops were stationed, who worked to provide food for their family. As Young Oak cared for Choi like a family member, the boy called himself his bodyguard and slept inside Young Oak's tent. He shadowed Young Oak everywhere. The morning when Young Oak took the colonel to the airstrip, Choi had volunteered to accompany him.

The silence was broken by the sound of the military boots of the retreating South Koreans. Roughly 600 hundred of them were running from the same area Young Oak had just come from. They were in a complete panic. Their uniforms looked terrible. About one-third of them didn't carry weapons and over half didn't wear helmets. Many of those who were carrying weapons were not wearing ammunition belts. They must have gotten rid of them, because they were too heavy to run with. Soldiers running in front passed Young Oak, but he didn't stop them. Stopping a few enlisted men wouldn't solve anything. After letting about 150 of them pass, he spotted three officers. The highest-ranking officer was a major.

Although his face was filled with fear, he was at least wearing a helmet and carrying a pistol. Holding his gun pointed down, Young Oak stopped the major. Then Young Oak aimed the weapon at his face and the major stopped. Young Oak said, "Major, I am an American officer. You've got to regroup your soldiers to stop the enemy here."

"I don't have to."

"We have no time to discuss. I just received a direct order from the assistant division commander to stop retreating Korean soldiers right here. You do what I tell you so that everybody here can get out and then we can get out."'

Young Oak was speaking half Korean, half English. The major didn't want to listen. Young Oak then pointed at the tanks and said, "As you can see, those are our tanks. Even if the enemy comes here, they won't be able to attack us, because they will clearly see those tanks. You shouldn't be afraid of them anymore."

The major looked over at the tanks without any words.

"What I am asking you to do is to stop retreating Korean soldiers, go a hundred yards around this side of the mountain, and help our defense so your soldiers can pull back safely," Young Oak continued. "I don't want to leave this place and have the enemy control the bridge."

Although Young Oak knew McCaffrey's and Sink's first concern was the safe retreat of Americans, he intentionally mentioned the safety of the Korean soldiers first. After listening silently, the major nodded his head. The major then began to stop Korean soldiers. A few soldiers ignored him, but most of them followed his orders. When other Korean soldiers running in the rear saw the tanks, they slowed down too, and a few of them even volunteered to join. About 150 Korean soldiers had stopped. Young Oak and the major put them in a blocking position on the hill behind the tanks. From their conversations and gestures, Young Oak knew that many of the soldiers were not from the major's unit. When Young Oak confirmed that the Korean soldiers' formation would be good enough, he went back down the hill to where the tanks were lined up. Many more Korean soldiers were still passing by, but he didn't stop them anymore. He deduced that the major's group would be enough to defend the bridge. At that moment, he was very grateful for those Korean infantry. Even though he had put the tanks in that formation, it was a gamble. If the enemy attacked, he knew that the tank platoon, without the support of infantry, couldn't defend the bridge for more than several minutes. Tanks could never have maneuvered freely enough because they were wedged between the steep valley in front and the hill in the back. If just one enemy company came, they would spread themselves out and attack. There would be no way for the five tanks to successfully defeat them. With the American tanks and South Korean infantry ready, they stood waiting for the enemy. But for hours, no one showed, with the exception of retreating South Korean soldiers. Young Oak surmised that the enemy must have either given up on attacking them or chosen another route after spotting the joint defense. From the enemy's perspective, it would be easier to chase retreating South Korean soldiers on the eastern flank, since their defense had already collapsed there.

  While waiting for the enemy, Young Oak kept hearing the sounds of artillery fire from the west going north. The area to the west belonged to American troops, so he knew that they were firing toward the Chinese in the north. As the regimental intelligence officer, he knew that in these days Chinese were attacking Americans and North Koreans were attacking South Koreans. However, he didn't hear anything to the east. The adjacent area to the east belonged to the South Korean 5th Division and the area next to it belonged to the South Korean 3rd Division. He guessed that they had either run out of ammunition or their defense lines had collapsed already. A message from the regiment headquarters came a little later. The crisis was over and he was ordered to retreat with the Korean soldiers from the bridge.

Chapter 18
Wild Grass

In May 1951, the Eighth Army decided to exchange the positions of the U.S. 7th Division, X Corps and the U.S. 2nd Division, IX Corps. As the 7th Division was now relocated to the "Central Line," the 31st Regiment moved towards Jipyong-ri. With the tank company in the lead, followed by the medical company taking care of the wounded soldiers and the 3rd Battalion in the rear, the 31st arrived at the destination in the middle of the night. The 31st had been reassigned as a reserve unit and slowly made its way north as the troops rested. Patrols were sent out in various directions, but no enemy troops were detected. On May 14, when the patrols crossed the Bukhan River, the situation changed. Whenever a patrol crossed the river, they encountered strong resistance. This was a clear indication that the Chinese forces considered the Bukhan River to be their line of defense and were going to defend it decisively. Meanwhile, intelligence from the Eighth Army headquarters and from the South Korean 6th Division were serious.

According to the U.S. Eighth Army headquarters, 30,864 enemy vehicles were confirmed to be heading south. Of these, 2,322 had been destroyed either by air strikes or artillery fire, but 22,185 were observed to be moving south April 12-30. In addition, it was noted that enemy movements were most active April 29-May 3. Transportation of military supplies had also decreased by about 35 percent in comparison to the previous period. The Eighth Army headquarters concluded that the Chinese forces must have secured sufficient military supplies in preparation for a major attack.

The South Korean 6th Division also reported that one of their companies engaged in a fierce battle with two

Chinese companies. During the battle, they took two prisoners of war who said, "The second major attack has begun." Furthermore, the 6th Division arrested a suspicious 11-year-old boy in possession of poison. The boy told them, "My objectives were to poison the drinking water of the U.N. forces and to obtain their secret codes. There are many children like me in this area."

Similarly, the Benedae group attached to the U.S. 31st Regiment interrogated a 15-year-old boy, who also turned out to be a spy. He testified that there were three other boys like him in the area. The U.N. forces also used young boys as spies with the code name "Blue Boys." The Benedae group arrested another North Korean spy who carried a "pass" issued by the U.S. 7th Division's intelligence section. He claimed to have bought it from a South Korean policeman.

Although Chinese forces had apparently completed preparations for a massive attack, they appeared to suffer from low morale and insufficient supplies. Korean refugees reported approximately 20,000 Chinese forces gathered near Gapyong, some of them crying out of hunger. A captured Chinese soldier said, "We don't want to die in Korea. We are suffering from hunger due to U.N. airstrikes. We want to surrender, but can't in fear of officers."

Yet another intelligence report said that some Chinese soldiers were found wearing American or South Korean military uniforms. The Chinese movements were more active along the Bukhan River, sending patrols deep down south across the river.

McCaffrey and Young Oak agreed with the analysis that the Chinese were avoiding contact and pretending to withdraw in order to disguise an imminent massive attack. The Chinese troops liked to attack when the enemies were moving or when they lacked the time to take defensive formation. They also preferred to attack at night. Taking these things into consideration, McCaffrey and Young Oak also agreed that the Chinese would make the most of May 18-21, when the moon would be visible from sunset to sunrise. They figured the enemy would definitely include May 20, the night of the fullest moon, in their attack plan. Division headquarters made the same assessment that the attack would be before the 20th of the month and warned the regiment to be ready. Major General Ferenbaugh himself called the regimental headquarters and ordered, "The enemy could attack anytime soon. Evacuate all civilians north of the main line of defense." After this call from the division commander, division headquarters called to order another search of all the abandoned empty houses and to burn all the blankets and comforters. Chinese troops often used the blankets to climb over barbed-wire fences.

The basic principle for evacuation was that everyone except local residents had to leave. Thus, refugees who were not local had to flee again. Once they left their hometown, they became refugees forever. In case of an imminent battle, the rule was to evacuate all the civilians. But soldiers wouldn't stop there. In addition to evacuation, they also burned houses.

Private First Class (Pfc.) Bill Quinn from Philadelphia was a young man who had volunteered to join the U.S. Army. A veteran of the Incheon Landing, he single-handedly burned several farmhouses. Some residents left without any resistance, but many others refused. In those cases, soldiers forcibly removed them and burned their houses. The grass-thatched roofs of the houses ignited quickly, and voices crying "Mother" or "Father" could be heard as the homes burned. American soldiers burned the houses fearing that Communist guerillas and infiltrators were getting supplies from the villagers. The razing of local Korean houses didn't stop until after the U.S. and Chinese troops began to fight again.

Dealing with civilians in the battle zone was really difficult. The 31st Regiment let the civilian affairs section handle this issue with the help of the CIC and South Korean police. Life for Koreans during the Korean War was much more brutal than that of the French or Italians during World War II. The declared "winner" of the war changed twice over a very short period of time. At the beginning of the war, which started in June 1950, the North Korean forces swiftly overtook nearly all of South Korea within two months. After the Incheon Landing in September 1951, the U.N. forces rapidly took hold of almost all of North Korea also within two months. Then, after the Chinese began their first massive attack in November 1951, the frontline moved back south of the 38th parallel, again in two months. Since the war started, South Korea's capital city, Seoul, had been in enemy hands twice. As a result, Koreans suffered drastically, caught in the crossfire. The story was the same with the residents in the vicinity of the Bukhan River.

According to First Lieutenant Lincoln Steigermolt, in charge of the civilian affairs section of the 31st, the residents had basic food for one to two months. But many of them lost their cows during the war and gave up farming. They suffered from malnutrition and there were many typhoid patients. There wasn't much Lieutenant Steigermolt could do other than spread DDT and distribute some rice. The refugees were handed over to the Korean police or sent to temporary holding camps. He reported that two female refugees had been raped by American soldiers. Another intelligence report cited Korean residents as saying that a group of Chinese soldiers came to their town and took a young girl. She had yet to be seen again.

As the 31st advanced northward, soldiers could often see dead bodies of Koreans with hands tied behind their backs and bullet holes in their heads. Private First

Class Frank Wise saw a leaflet stuck to a dead body's forehead. The leaflet, dropped by American airplanes, urged Chinese troops to surrender. Wise thought a Chinese officer had probably done it to warn his soldiers not to carry such leaflets.

Around this time, Young Oak went on patrol and had the chance to talk to an elderly Korean man who hadn't left his home. Young Oak asked him in Korean, "Do the residents of this village support communism or democracy?"

"We are like wild grass. Yesterday, a cow stepped over us. Today, it's a horse. It doesn't matter who steps over wild grass."

Young Oak never again asked which side a particular resident was supporting.

The 31st Regiment began sending long-range patrols to contact Chinese forces. Because the weather and roads were too hazardous, patrols had to be conducted on foot. Food and ammunition had to be airdropped. One day, the 2nd Platoon of A Company, led by First Lieutenant John Covach, reached a mountaintop, but they were too exhausted from a long-range patrol to dig foxholes, so they slept on the ground. Chinese forces found them and opened fire. The American soldiers, believing that if they were destined to die they would, ignored the enemy fire and kept on sleeping. Up until that moment, Lieutenant Covach, a second-generation Hungarian American, had never imagined himself sleeping on the ground without a foxhole in the middle of enemy fire. It was an utter miracle that when the sun rose, there were no casualties. After returning to the regiment, Lieutenant Covach led a patrol again, this time along the Bukhan River. As they were moving little by little to the north, they turned a curve and a chill went through his entire body. He saw the charred bodies of several hundred Chinese soldiers. They looked like charcoal. The poor enemies must have been killed instantly by American napalm. The next scene was even more horrific. It was so terrible that Covach would never forget it for the rest of his life. One Chinese soldier's blackened body looked like he was praying for his life, when he was instantly killed by napalm. His upper body lay back a little while his two hands were still stretched forward. There was something white and short stuck between his burned fingers. An American soldier must have placed a cigarette, probably a Lucky Strike, there. He might have done it for a joke, but Covach couldn't laugh.

Friendly fire is another nightmare in combat and the Korean War was no exception. During the Korean War, friendly fire frequently occurred between Americans, between Americans and South Koreans, between South Koreans, etc. Around this time, Pfc. Frank Wise witnessed a South Korean unit on a mountain mistake another South Korean unit below the mountain for a Chinese unit and attacked. Dozens of casualties instantly occurred to the unit down below. The first machinegun fire Lieutenant Covach ever experienced on the way south, after the Incheon Landing, was from the Americans.

The case was the same between Americans and South Koreans. One day, war correspondent Charles Weisenberg was with a Korean artillery battery on a central front to cover cooperation between American and Korean troops. That day, Korean artillery officers saw a column of tanks moving below the mountain, where the Korean artillery battery was. The officers consulted a chart of the flags of the nations that made up the U.N. forces prepared to help different countries distinguish friendly troops from the enemy. However, the Korean officers couldn't match any of the flags on the chart with the flags on the tanks below. They were so embarrassed and didn't know what to do, because they knew the flags on the tanks were neither Chinese, nor North Korean, but at the same time it wasn't on the chart. They gravely weighed the decision whether or not to fire at the tanks.

The flags on the tanks were red, with blue and white diagonal lines that crossed to form an "X." The "X" was dotted with 13 white stars. Alerting their soldiers to prepare to fire, the officers couldn't decide whether to open fire or not. In truth, the flag was the "Stars and Bars," the Confederate flag used during the Civil War of the 1860s. A U.S. unit from the south flew this flag on the tank. Frighteningly enough, since the Korean officers were not familiar with this flag and since it was not on the U.N. charts, the Korean artillery battery almost destroyed the American tanks. Fortunately, an American military advisor recognized the Confederate flag. Although this particular incident ended with a laugh, friendly fire happened all too often during the Korean War.

As contact with the Chinese troops became more frequent, the regimental commander, McCaffrey, began to consistently seek out Young Oak's thoughts on Operations Officer Major Clark's plans. One evening, when Major Clark's briefing was over, McCaffrey turned to Young Oak and asked, "Well, how would you do it?"

Young Oak offered his ideas briefly. McCaffrey turned to Major Clark again and ordered some modification that was somewhere between what Major Clark originally wanted and what Young Oak offered. That night, McCaffrey invited Young Oak to his tent again for a game of cards. McCaffrey began talking about the operations plans briefed by Major Clark during the day.

"What do you think about Major Clark's operations plan?"

"It looked good," Young Oak replied.

"If you were in his place, what would you do from the beginning?"

Young Oak knew that the regimental commander's question meant something significant this time.

"Devising an operations plan is not my responsibility," he said. Young Oak was a captain, and his official title was intelligence officer and so operations planning were not part of his job.

"I am asking you what you would do, if you were in charge of operations," McCaffrey pressed.

When Young Oak described his plan in more detail, the regimental commander questioned his rationale. Young Oak explained the reasons for his suggestions. Then McCaffrey ordered Young Oak to make the plans from then on.

"Clark is not only a major, but also has been the operations officer for a long time. When it comes to operations, he can make the documents backwards and forwards," McCaffrey said. "Of course, he can handle documents with both eyes closed. He is better than me, in terms of documents. Nobody can ever find fault in the documents prepared by him, as his grammar and regulations are perfect. However, the real problem hidden in that perfection is that he has no idea about combat."

"How did you handle it before I got here?" Young Oak asked.

"As you've seen, I went out on the front every day. When I came back, Major Clark explained his plan and I made changes. In actuality, it was like I made a plan from scratch and he wrote the orders. That was too much for me. I can see you make better plans than I do. Tonight, I liked your plan, but I didn't want to embarrass him. So I modified it to something in between. For a while, do both S-2 and S-3. From now on, make the basic plan, give it to him and let him polish it."

"Sir, I'll do what you're telling me to do. But both of us know that this isn't the way it's supposed to be."

"Don't worry too much. Soon I'll give you an appropriate position."

Although the regimental commander didn't explicitly mention it, he had a plan of his own. Because a regimental operations officer was a major's slot, McCaffrey was going to promote Young Oak to a major and make him S-3. From that moment on, Young Oak assumed the dual responsibilities of both intelligence officer and operations officer. Whether in a regiment, division or corps, the two most important positions in wartime were the operations officer and the intelligence officer. At this time, racial minorities suffered intense racial discrimination in American society. It was literally unprecedented in the history of the U.S. military for a minority captain to assume the double duty of intelligence and operations officer for a white regiment. McCaffrey's trust in Young Oak was something absolutely beyond common sense.

As McCaffrey ordered, Young Oak began to help Major Clark draw up operations plans. Clark must have heard something from the regimental commander, as it was not something he and Young Oak discussed. When Young Oak said something, Clark documented it. At first, Clark presented Young Oak's idea to McCaffrey and with McCaffrey's approval, Clark would prepare the official documentation. However, Clark soon began to prepare the official documents before Young Oak's idea was submitted to McCaffrey. Young Oak asked him why. Clark answered with a smile, "There is no reason for me to wait for his approval. I noticed he very rarely changes your plan. So there's no reason for us to waste time."

On May 17, McCaffrey officially made Young Oak the acting operations officer of the regiment. He knew there would soon be a massive counterattack by the U.N.

forces and that his regiment would have to play an important role. In preparation, he began to take steps to utilize Young Oak as the regimental operations officer. On the 18th, the regiment took over the U.S. Marine Corps 5th Regiment's zone. On the 19th, the division headquarters issued an order to attack beginning at 5:00 a.m.

Chapter 19
Mason and McCaffrey

On May 20, at 5 a.m., the U.S. Army 7th Division commenced a major attack. As it was the first major battle for the 31st Infantry since nearly being wiped out at the Battle of Chosin Reservoir the previous year, Young Oak had to be extremely careful. After the long rest and reorganization, the regiment had crossed the Soyang River for a counterattack about a month earlier. But as U.N. forces were ordered to retreat due to the Chinese Spring Offensives, the regiment had to retreat and wait another month. At 10:30 p.m. the night before the attack, Young Oak called each battalion to reconfirm all operation orders in detail.

"First Battalion, make sure to mobilize tanks to support B Company's patrol. Second Battalion, secure your current position and support 3rd Battalion's attack. Third Battalion, advance through 2nd Battalion's zone with A Company in the lead to begin attacking at 5:00 a.m. sharp."

Because the operations officer Major Clark was off-duty, Young Oak directly issued orders of attack as Acting S-3. That day everything went smoothly, with the exception of two Koreans from the Benedae group who were wounded when they entered a minefield by mistake. The problem was the next day; the 1st Battalion, under Battalion Commander, Lieutenant Colonel Kermit Mason's command, was scheduled to lead an attack.

Meanwhile, Young Oak was left in charge of the attack because Regimental Commander McCaffrey was suddenly called to go over to division headquarters and the regiment's executive officer and operations officer had both left for Tokyo on short leave right before the offensive.

The problem arose in A Company, which led the battalion's attack. While 2nd Platoon leader First Lieutenant John Covach was waiting for the order from A Company commander, Captain Harold Willecke, he struggled to rid his mind of the gruesome scenes from the previous day. One scene in particular bothered him.

His company had been passing through the northern region of the Bukhan River where grass-roof houses were scattered across a valley. Unlike other areas, there were several farmhouses where civilians had not been evacuated. Procedure dictated that civilians always be evacuated when troops moved in, but either due to negligence or an accident, such was not the case. A Company's advance was led by their tanks, which fired heavily. When Covach's platoon crossed the valley, they were told to dig in and wait for the next order. Covach was busily digging foxholes with his men, when he saw a Korean man who seemed to be a local farmer. The distraught man was holding a young boy in his arms, around 10 years old. The boy appeared to be dead. It was unbearable to witness the agony on the man's face. Covach thought the boy had been killed by American tank fire, though it was just as likely that Chinese artillery killed him.

Abruptly bringing Covach back to the battle of the moment, Captain Willecke's voice crackled over the radio.

"Today's objective is Hill 337. Re-cross the valley that you crossed yesterday, turn around on the road and first capture the hill in front of Hill 337." The first hill Captain Willecke ordered him to take was approximately half a mile to the north. Captain Willecke was a good man and a brave officer, but he could not read a map worth his salt. Knowing his commander's weakness, Covach made sure to memorize the terrain before taking his platoon to the destination. The 2nd Platoon left early the next morning. The platoon occupied the hill without resistance. The two staff officers from battalion headquarters verified it was the hill Willecke had ordered them to capture. At around 11:00 a.m., Captain Willecke appeared with the rest of the company and barked out, "2nd Platoon, follow the company in the rear."

Leading the company, Willecke marched in an unknown direction. Summer was approaching and the central front was beginning to fill out with lush forest foliage. The company soon disappeared into the deep forest. For more than 30 minutes, Willecke led the company deeper into the forest. Then, abruptly, he stopped and assembled the platoon leaders together: Artillery Liaison Officer First Lieutenant Steve Folkenberry; 1st Platoon Leader, First Lieutenant Tom Walker; 3rd Platoon Leader, Second Lieutenant Ward, and 2nd Platoon Leader, First Lieutenant Covach. When they all gathered, Willecke declared, "The hill right in front of us is Hill 337. Register the artillery first and attack immediately."

Covach strongly objected, recognizing right away that the company commander was making a grave mistake. But Willecke wouldn't listen and ordered Lieutenant Folkenberry to open fire at the purported Hill 337. Folkenberry took out his map and read the coordinates to the artillery unit. Four rounds of 105mm howitzer landed on the mountain to the company's right. This proved even more clearly that the mountain Willecke was ordering to attack was not Hill 337. Willecke insisted that the artillery liaison officer had misread the coordinates and ordered him to move the artillery fire closer to the mountain he assumed to be Hill 337. It took another 30 minutes to move the artillery fire to the hill in front of them. Following concentrated artillery fire, A Company commenced the attack. Fortunately or unfortunately, there was no one on the mountain. Nonplussed, Willecke, despite capturing the wrong hill, reported to the battalion headquarters, "We've captured Hill 337."

It was this report that began a chain of disasters.

The Chinese forces were actually on Hill 337. While A Company was attacking the wrong hill, B Company, trusting that A Company was to attack Hill 337 together with them, commenced attacking Hill 337 only to fail and retreat. Upon receiving Willecke's report that A Company had "captured Hill 337," battalion headquarters ordered B Company to join A Company, since they had apparently been successful. Because B Company had been told that friendly forces had already captured the hill, the company proceeded to mount the hill with no precaution. Tragically, they were ambushed by awaiting Chinese troops and suffered severe casualties. Among the injured was the company commander. To make matters worse, while this particular debacle was unfolding, C Company was under attack by friendly fire.

Young Oak could not believe his eyes as the reports came streaming in to regimental headquarters: "Communications with A Company lost...B Company ambushed by Chinese...C Company under friendly fire..." He frantically radioed the 1st Battalion commander, but there was no response. Then Young Oak called for the 1st Battalion operations officer, Captain Joe Conmy.

Young Oak had gotten to know Conmy quite well over card games at the regimental headquarters. More importantly, they both fought the Nazis in Europe during World War II, so they had become quite close in a short period of time. He could trust Conmy. Conmy had gone down to the 1st Battalion as its operations officer just before the offensive had begun. Unfortunately, Young Oak was unable to communicate with Conmy either. Instinctively knowing something had gone terribly awry, Young Oak immediately left the regimental headquarters to get to the 1st Battalion headquarters. However, since no "road" actually existed between the two headquarters, it took him three hours. At 3:00 p.m., he arrived at the 1st Battalion headquarters. He searched for Battalion Commander Mason, but couldn't find him. After Young Oak repeatedly demanded to know the whereabouts of Lieutenant Colonel Mason, the battalion staff officers reluctantly admitted, "Colonel Mason went to take a shower when the battle began and hasn't come back yet."

Young Oak couldn't believe his ears."

"The Lieutenant Colonel went to take a shower? In combat?" Young Oak said. "The nearest shower room is 20 miles from here!"

The battalion command post could not even locate the exact positions of A, B and C Companies. This meant that the battalion command post had lost track of all three rifle companies under its directive. If all three companies weren't entirely wiped out, they were about to be. At that moment, Conmy came into view, driving a jeep from the direction of the front. He was bleeding from his head and arms. Neither wound was serious, but both of them were pretty bad.

"What happened?" Young Oak asked.

"I just got back from Hill 337. Captain Willecke reported that he'd captured the hill, but the Chinese were there instead. I've been hit."

"I ordered the tank company to get down here right before I left regimental headquarters," Young Oak said. "They should be here soon. We can do something with 16 tanks. But we must locate the three companies as soon as possible."

A jeep came roaring up behind Young Oak. Lieutenant Colonel Mason jumped out, shouting, "What the hell's going on? Captain Kim, what're you doing in my battalion?"

"Sir, your battalion is in serious trouble," Young Oak replied.

"What the hell are you talking about?"

"I might be wrong, but from the report I received, your entire battalion is in grave danger. Tell me, where are your rifle companies, A, B and C?"

"It's none of your damn business!"

"It is my business. Tell me! Tell me where they are!"

"I don't have to tell you anything," Mason said.

"Where the hell have you been? You know your battalion's jumpstart was at 9:00 a.m. It's after 3:00 p.m. now. Where have you been for the last six hours, when you're supposed to be here?"

"None of your goddamn business."

"I hear you went back to take a shower."

"I'm going to tell you where your rifle companies are, or where I think they are," Young Oak said. "We must find them all."

Young Oak, to the best of his knowledge, explained the situation clearly and briefly.

"You're wrong," Mason said. "They're all okay."

"What are you going to do?" Young Oak pressed.

"I don't care, I'm not going to do anything," Mason insisted. "Everything is okay."

"I want you to find A Company. I want you to bring it back to the objective."

"Are you – just a captain – giving me orders? No, I'm not going to do that. Has Colonel McCaffrey returned?"

"I don't know where he is right now," Young Oak said. "He was beyond radio contact when I left the regiment."

Then Young Oak turned to Conmy and said, "True, you're wounded, Joe, but you're not wounded that badly.

You know the area. You know the terrain better than anybody. I want you to find C Company. I'm going to go find B Company."

"Okay," Conmy said.

"I guess C Company is located somewhere between our Marine Corps over here and the Chinese forces over here," Young Oak said, pointing to a map.

Young Oak found C Company's location based on its last report of being under friendly fire. He surmised that the U.S. Marines, positioned to the right of the 1st Battalion, might have mistakenly fired upon them. He turned to Lieutenant Colonel Mason once again.

"Even if A Company is on a wrong hill, there's no real danger," Young Oak stated. "If you want to do it, you go find them and bring them to the objective. If you don't want to do it, don't do it."

"I'm not going to do it," Mason said.

Young Oak volunteered to find B Company because he knew it would be the most difficult and dangerous task, as they had been under Chinese assault. He had suggested that Captain Conmy find C Company, because it was a task more dangerous than finding A Company. The lieutenant colonel still insisted that he wouldn't cooperate. Left with no recourse, Young Oak exited the tent, hopped into a jeep and ordered the driver to go. The jeep moved about five yards, when the lieutenant colonel dashed after him, yelling. So Kim stopped.

"Where are you going?" Mason yelled.

"I'm going to do exactly what I just told you."

"Now you listen to me! I'm a lieutenant colonel, and this is my battalion. I am the commander here! You can't do this. I don't give you the authority to do it. What the hell do you think you're doing, ordering me to do this or do that. I'm ordering you to leave now! This is a direct order. If you don't leave right now, I'm going to court-martial you!"

"Sir, yes, you are a lieutenant colonel and the battalion commander and I am a captain. However, I am here as the acting S-3 of the regiment and I'm giving you these orders in the name of Colonel McCaffrey. I'm not leaving until you have your battalion under control. It's not under control now. You've probably already seen the tanks up the valley on your way back here. They're coming. I have already committed them."

The battalion commander turned to Captain Conmy and bellowed, "You're seeing what's happening here. I want you to be my witness!"

"You know, Colonel, it's all screwed up and I don't care what you say," Conmy responded flatly. "Everything is fucked up, and if we don't do something pretty soon, it's going to be dark, and our troops are going to panic, and we're going to be in trouble. I'm going to go and do what Captain Kim tells me to do. I reckon he represents Colonel McCaffrey."

As Conmy got in his jeep, Mason shouted, "Wait! I'll go find A Company."

When Young Oak finally found B Company near Hill 337, they were scattered and panicked. They knew their company commander First Lieutenant Alfred Anderson had been ambushed by the Chinese and was severely wounded, but they didn't know whether he was alive or not. They didn't know whether to stay, retreat or fight. Young Oak quickly found an officer.

"Don't panic," Young Oak ordered. "Very soon, you'll see more than 15 tanks coming up here. They're our tank company. We're going to put five tanks across here and the rest across the flat area below that mountain. Gather soldiers and stop right on that southern hill. Stay there and get others there. Soon, we'll find A Company and bring them here. Everything will be okay."

Communication equipment wasn't very advanced during the Korean War; as the regimental S-2, Young Oak could directly radio division headquarters, the battalion commander and battalion operations officer, but not the company commander or platoon leader. Subsequently, he wasn't able to issue direct orders to the B Company commander or his platoon leaders.

With a thunderous roar and dust swirling in the air above them, tanks rolled in at the base of the mountain in a single imposing column. Night was beginning to fall, but things were still visible to the naked eye. Young Oak knew it was a gamble to commit the regiment's entire tank company to one location. However, he also knew from his World War II experience that soldiers had to feel safe psychologically in order to restore their morale. He took the calculated risk. Chinese troops were hiding nearby, but they didn't dare attack enemies armed with 16 tanks. Young Oak gave specific orders to the tank company commander to position the tanks. After staying with B Company for a little over an hour to put them in control, he then radioed Captain Conmy.

"Have you found C Company?" Young Oak asked.

"Yes, I've found them," Comny said. "They were right where you guessed they would be."

"Okay, I'm coming over there. I'm going to walk through the tanks to get there, so come over with the company commander."

As he made his way through the tanks, Conmy arrived with C Company commander Captain McCoy from the opposite direction.

"Your company is marching in the wrong direction," Young Oak ordered Captain McCoy. "Bring the entire company over here by the tanks, dig in and wait for the next order."

Just as he finished giving out his orders, Lieutenant Colonel Mason radioed in.

"I've found A Company," Mason said. "I'm taking them to your location."

Worried about the time, Young Oak maintained radio communication with Captain Willecke so he could assess A Company's situation. In the meantime, C Company arrived safely and dug in. Moments later, Captain Willecke radioed in, "We've made contact with B Company."

Young Oak let out a sigh of relief, as he reconfirmed with B Company that they had made contact with A Company. It was 11:00 p.m. Soon Lieutenant Colonel Mason reconvened with Young Oak and Conmy. All three went back to the tent that the 1st Battalion was using as its command post. Upon entering, Mason said in an agitated tone, "Captain Kim, I am sorry. I didn't mean, you know, what I said earlier. If you don't say anything to Colonel McCaffrey about what happened this afternoon, I won't report that you took over my command against my orders."

"It's up to you. I'll leave it to be business between you and Colonel McCaffrey. As long as the battalion is safe, I don't care," Young Oak replied, as he watched Conmy receive first-aid treatment. Then he exited the tent and got into his jeep.

Just as he was backing away, another jeep screeched up and came to a sudden halt right behind Young Oak's. The jeep approached so close that the two vehicles almost collided. Even before the jeep came to a complete stop, a man was jumping out. Bright headlights momentarily blinded Young Oak, but soon, he realized it was McCaffrey. Popping out of the jeep like a loaded spring, McCaffrey ordered Young Oak to follow him.

As the two officers entered the tent, McCaffrey's voice boomed out.

"What happened? I got some terrible reports back at division headquarters. I want to know exactly what happened."

"Nothing happened," Mason answered coyly.

"What the hell are you talking about? Something had to have happened. Otherwise, why is Captain Kim here? And why all these reports at the division? What happened?" McCaffery demanded. "I know what the division is saying and I know what the regiment is saying, but I want to hear it from you."

As soon as Young Oak had received reports that something had gone awry with the 1st Battalion, he had immediately called division headquarters searching for the regimental commander. When he received the report from Young Oak, McCaffrey had excused himself from a meeting and returned to headquarters. When the people at the regiment could finally contact him, McCaffrey had already heard the news.

"Oh, it's all just a big mix-up that got blown out of proportion," Mason said nonchalantly. "In fact, everything's okay now."

"I'm not going to accept that as an answer," McCaffrey said. Turning to Conmy, he asked, "What happened?"

McCaffrey trusted Conmy, as they'd known each other since World War II when they had fought together in Europe. In fact, McCaffrey had specifically requested Conmy to be reassigned to his unit when he was seeking experienced combat officers. Conmy spent about five days at the regimental headquarters after he arrived from the

U.S., getting abreast of the situation, before he was made 1st Battalion S-3.

"I'm going to tell you the truth. I don't care anymore where the chips may fall. I'm as much to blame as anybody for this whole mess, since I was the one who was here, and it was my plan. I'm the three, and this all happened under my watch," Conmy said.

Conmy proceeded to relate the exact events that had taken place over the course of the long and harrowing day.

McCaffrey turned to Young Oak and asked, "Is what Joe is saying true?"

"Yes sir," Young Oak replied.

"What do you have to say about this?" McCaffrey asked Mason.

"It's all exaggerated," Mason said. "None of it is true."

Mason outright lied, because he knew how serious the consequences would be. He knew he could be court-martialed. McCaffrey was silent, recalling the first day he had ever met Mason.

McCaffrey, who had just been appointed regimental commander, had ordered the 1st Battalion to move north. He went to see how they were doing. It was about 4:30 p.m., just getting dark and McCaffrey stopped an officer driving south in a jeep.

"I'm the new regiment commander," McCaffrey said. "Who are you?"

"I'm the 1st Battalion commander, sir."

"What? You left your battalion on the frontline? Where in the world are you going?"

"I'm going back to take a bath and go to sleep."

"My God! You've left your battalion behind to take a bath? Don't do this again."

McCaffrey then recalled another incident that had happened a few days after that. He was again inspecting the 1st Battalion. Having waited for the fog to dissipate, McCaffrey went to the line of departure, but there was nobody there. Suddenly, machinegun bullets were flying from the north. When McCaffrey ducked back about 50 to a 100 yards, a jeep came up the same track that he'd used that morning. It was Mason again. McCaffrey had asked him incredulously, "Aren't your rifle companies supposed to be on the line of departure? Where are they? What the hell is going on?"

"Sir, I don't know where they are. I guess they moved out this morning, but nobody woke me up."

McCaffrey, in the tent, stopped asking Mason questions. He stormed out, but not before grabbing Young Oak's arm.

"Come out with me," he growled to Young Oak.

Outside the tent, McCaffrey said, "Young, this is between you and me. I want you to stay as the battalion three. On paper, it's a demotion, because you're going from regimental three—acting three—down to the battalion three. But in reality, it's a promotion, because you're the battalion commander as far as I'm concerned. Your command will start at 6:00 a.m. tomorrow morning. Not a moment earlier."

Young Oak listened as McCaffery continued.

"You're only a captain. Nobody in the United States Army is going to let you command a battalion as a captain. I'm going to go find a young new major to be the battalion commander in name, but you're the one who's going to command the unit. You give all the orders. He will have orders to be there, to be the battalion commander in name, but he will do nothing, except what you order. "

"Yes sir," Young Oak said.

"I've got my own reasons for doing it this way. If I make you acting battalion commander, without a battalion commander, then people will know that a battalion commander slot is vacant. Then some high-ranking general is going to find a major among his fair-haired boys and put him down here. But I want you to run it."

McCaffrey was calculating multiple factors. According to U.S. Army regulations at the time, promotion to lieutenant colonel was automatic for any major who had commanded a battalion in combat for one month. In addition, a subsequent promotion to the rank of colonel was near-guaranteed on the condition that that individual didn't commit any egregious mistakes. If a colonel commanded a regiment in combat, he most likely would get a star on his helmet. This was why, whenever a vacancy for a battalion commander or regimental commander position opened up, everybody tried to pull strings.

McCaffrey was an outstanding and open-minded person. He didn't state it directly, but he had already made up his mind to promote Young Oak not only to major, but also to lieutenant colonel as quickly as he could. He had stressed 6:00 a.m. the next morning, as he had already calculated the time needed to process everything. As soon as he returned to regiment headquarters, McCaffrey spoke with Division Commander Ferenbaugh and Assistant Division Commander Sink and promptly received their approval. In addition, he also asked them to find a young major to be there as "window-dressing."

Meanwhile, Young Oak remained at the battalion. Once McCaffrey left the command post, Mason told Young Oak, "I don't know what's going to happen to me, but thanks for not saying anything. Since Colonel McCaffrey said you're going to command the battalion, you will. I know I'm a lieutenant colonel and you're a captain, but I'll support whatever you say as long as I'm here."

The next day, the 31st Infantry took over a South Korean Marine Corps zone and sustained an attack. The 1st Battalion's objective was Guman Mountain, also known as Hill 332 on the central front. Only about 10 miles north was the city of Chunchon. The battalion was scheduled to start the attack at 8:00 a.m. Young Oak awoke at 5:00 a.m. that morning and intently studied the map and deeply pondered the day's operations as he waited for 6:00 a.m. At 6:00 a.m. sharp, he stood up and headed over to the company commander's tent to wake Captain Claude McChesney.

"Who the hell are you?" McChesney sputtered, madder than hell.

"I'm Captain Kim. I'm the one who's going to give orders from now on in this battalion."

"What the...Well...I'm going to report you to the battalion commander!"

McChesney got up and stormed out of his tent to find Mason. He came back 15 minutes later and said, "I don't know what the hell's going on, but I guess you're in charge. What the hell do you want me to do?"

"I want you to get your company up and fed as fast as you can. We're supposed to launch our offensive at 8:00 a.m."

"It's already past 6:00 a.m. We can't do that!"

"We're going to try."

"It'll be noon by the time we're ready."

"No, we're going to attack long before noon. I don't know when, and I don't know where everybody is. But I want you to do the cooking and get the other officers. We don't have to have a full breakfast, just something quick to eat and drink so we can get going."

Soldiers were roused and hurried. At 9:43 a.m., C Company was on the line of departure to lead the attack. It was already one hour and forty-three minutes later than the jump-off time ordered by regimental headquarters. Young Oak made C Company lead the attack because it was the only one that didn't have any action the day before. It got shelled, but didn't lose anybody. Young Oak reported to the regiment over the radio.

"After two minutes, we're going to go," he said.

That day, he was particularly careful. To make the soldiers comfortable, he gave more than the necessary amount of motor and artillery fire. He had been concerned about the unusually heavy fog that morning, but the area's visibility was improving over time

Through his binoculars, Young Oak watched intently as C Company attacked the hill. At about 10:00 a.m., Young Oak saw that the company was a quarter of the way up the hill. He suddenly realized somebody was sitting next to him. It was Lieutenant Colonel Mason.

"How's it going?" Mason asked.

"Well, it seems to be going very well. We're going very slowly, but we started about an hour and a half late."

"Where are we?"

"C Company is about ready to pass Phase 1 and Phase 2. In another hour and a half, they will be on top of the hill."

"Young, I'm sorry about yesterday. I hope you won't hold what happened against me."

"No, as far as I'm concerned, what's done is done. It's over."

"I was way out of line yesterday. I'm aware that Colonel McCaffrey wants me relieved of my assignment. I don't know when it's going to happen. It may be today, tomorrow or a week from now. And I know you're going to run the battalion. I just wanted you to know that any decision you make is okay by me, as long as I'm here as the battalion commander. To tell you the truth, I'm glad you're doing this, because I don't know what the hell I'm doing. Honestly, I don't think I can be a combat commander. Just between you and me, you know, I was an adjutant general in a division during World War II and never up in the front lines. I never saw any combat. Korea is really my first combat. All that combat experience I had in North Korea is a lot of bullshit I made up."

Never having taken his eyes off C Company with the binoculars, Young Oak remained silent, as Mason struggled through his confession. Mason ended with an awkward declaration.

"Well, you seem to do a good job. I know that you're supposed to run the battalion and take the hill. It's all yours. To show you how much I trust you, I'm going back to the command post, and I'll be there to meet you later."

Lieutenant Colonel Mason got up and left. That was the last time Young Oak saw him. A few moments later, McCaffrey telephoned Young Oak, informing him that Mason had been relieved of his duties as battalion commander.

"You'll be commanding the battalion on your own, Young. I've found a major without any combat experience, but he's a fine and dandy lad. He'll be up there as battalion commander in name, but he's aware that you're in charge. He's fully prepped to be the window dressing and that's all. He won't get there, though, until tomorrow."

The next morning Major Irving Warden arrived as the new battalion commander. Immediately upon his arrival, he told Young Oak, "Colonel McCaffrey told me everything. Run this battalion as if it's your own."

McCaffrey finished the official personnel move by making Young Oak the 1st Battalion S-3 and Captain Conmy as the regimental S-2. McCaffrey also filled the vacancy of the B Company commander who had been evacuated due to a severe wound. It was a very unusual and aggressive personnel move in the U.S. Army for a regiment to change its regimental intelligence officer, a battalion commander, a battalion operations officer and a company commander all at the same time during combat. Although the U.N. forces were launching a counteroffensive, it was a time of turmoil and painstaking internal reorganization for the forces as well. It was also around this time when the South Korean Army left one of the most dishonorable marks in military history. General Van Fleet, Commander of the U.S. Eighth Army, disbanded the South Korean Army III Corps, when it helplessly collapsed under enemy attack and retreated in total chaos.

The battle at Hill 332 unfolded as Young Oak had anticipated. Lasting about four hours, it ended with C Company successfully capturing the hill. It was the first victory for the 1st Battalion under his command. Although the battalion suffered eight wounded, no one was killed in action. That day, the 31st Infantry captured four North Korean soldiers, between the ages of 15 and 22, who had been assigned to a Chinese unit to gather intelligence. The POWs told Young Oak, "Eight males and five females of our age were assigned to the Chinese 4th Division. Only one bag of rice is given to each company every month and the last distribution was exactly one month ago. The morale of the Chinese soldiers is extremely low because of hunger."

Mason and McCaffrey were U.S. Army lieutenant colonels, but they were complete opposites. Although Lieutenant Colonel Mason's full name was Kermit Mason, he was better known as "Red Mason" because of his red hair. He was known to be a brave soldier, as he was awarded a Silver Star for his military valor at the Battle of Chosin Reservoir in North Korea. But he had fabricated his heroism.

It's not hard to find people like Mason, who are irresponsible and deceptive. He was a liar who ultimately proved that he was not concerned with the safety of his subordinates and only cared about his own glory. McCaffrey had wanted to court-martial Mason, but Division Commander Ferenbaugh settled the issue by simply sending Mason back to America. A primary reason for this might have been that the U.S. Army in the Korean War was ill-prepared. If the U.S. Army had court-martialed soldiers like Mason, it would have revealed just how disorganized it really was for promoting a fool like Mason to lieutenant colonel, assigning him as battalion commander in the first place, and then awarding him a Silver Star on top of everything else.

In stark contrast, Lieutenant Colonel McCaffrey was an extraordinary officer. Promoted to full colonel at the age of 27, only six years after graduating from West Point, McCaffrey's record was a clear testament to his military aptitude. More importantly, McCaffrey was a soldier who was not bound by traditional mores, but rather highly valued individual ability and talent. The fact that he was willing to swap two white majors for one colored captain in an era when racial discrimination was legally incorporated and socially prevalent showed how little he regarded racial backgrounds. McCaffrey unabashedly assigned that minority captain as both the S-2 and Acting S-3 of his regiment. He was also a warm man with a beautiful heart. Once, while driving his jeep on his way back to the regiment, he encountered three Korean female refugees, a grandmother, mother and daughter, and went out of his way to take them to a safe haven, far from the frontlines.

McCaffrey had become a colonel quickly because it was wartime. Also, he had the absolute trust of General Edward Almond, who, as X Corps commander, successfully executed the Incheon Landing in 1950 under General MacArthur's orders. During World War II, Almond was the 92nd Division commander in Italy in 1945 when he made McCaffrey his chief of staff. At that time, McCaffrey had served as Almond's deputy chief of staff, as lieutenant colonel. Because a division chief of staff was a slot for a colonel, McCaffrey was instantly promoted. However, after the war, the U.S. Army reduced in size and McCaffrey, like many others, was demoted to lieutenant colonel on the grounds that his rank was considered too high for his age.

General Almond was General MacArthur's fair-haired boy as Colonel McCaffrey was General Almond's fair-haired boy. After Young Oak got better acquainted with McCaffrey in the Korean War, he became McCaffrey's fair-haired boy. In the military, particularly during wartime, it is crucial to devise good operations plans for victory. It is equally important to pick the right person to successfully implement those good plans.

After General MacArthur made up his mind to execute the Incheon Landing during the Korean War, he hastily formed the X Corps in Japan. He appointed Major General Almond, his chief of staff, to be in charge of the corps with absolute authority to choose anybody in the U.S. Army. Almond nominated Lieutenant Colonel McCaffrey as his deputy chief of staff. This was how McCaffrey, who was in America at the time, urgently crossed the Pacific to join the corps in time for the landing. From that point on, McCaffrey became Almond's right-hand man. After the landing, McCaffrey advanced into North Korea with Almond and became commander of the 31st Regiment.

One of the reasons Almond made McCaffrey the regimental commander was so he could promote McCaffrey. Almond wanted to promote him to colonel and eventually, to general down the road. By this time, however, U.S. Army regulations had changed, so even a corps commander couldn't promote somebody to colonel on a whim. Just as Almond had intended, McCaffrey was promoted again to colonel on the day Young Oak led the victorious battle at Guman Mountain.

Whether it's in political, military, or business circles, there are always politics and this type of "fair-haired boy" relationship in society. But the particular fair-haired boy relationship between MacArthur and Almond had a decisive impact on the Korean War, which resulted in changing the course of modern Korean history. Precisely speaking, the relationship between these two American generals was the seed that sowed a complicated destiny filled with fortunes and misfortunes for Korea.

The problem began when MacArthur allowed Almond to maintain the title as his chief of staff, although he had already made Almond the X Corps Commander for the Incheon Landing. This left Almond wearing two hats. At the time, Lieutenant General Walton Walker, U.S. Eighth Army Commander, was the highest-ranking general in charge of U.N. forces in Korea, including the U.S. forces. From the perspective of the U.S. forces in Korea, Walker was, of course, Almond's superior. But from the perspective of the Far Eastern Command in Tokyo, Almond was Walker's superior. Lieutenant General Walker was faced with a major dilemma, as Major General Almond was unwilling to be under his command.

This dual line of command defied common sense; there should have been only one chain of command in the military. Inevitably, the situation caused disaster. Walker was not comfortable with the scenario, as he was unable to take full control of the X Corps. As the "fair-haired boy" of MacArthur, who was like an emperor in the U.S. Army, Almond didn't give in to Walker as well. It became nearly impossible for three of the most important axes of the U.N. forces—the U.S. Army I Corps, the IX Corps, and the X Corps—to effectively coordinate with one another. What arose was a tragedy that no one anticipated, as the U.N.

forces marched onward to North Korea after the successful Incheon Landing.

When the U.N. forces crossed the 38th parallel after the landing, the U.S. Army I Corps and IX Corps were assigned to the western front, with the X Corps to the eastern front and the South Korean forces positioned between them. One of the reasons was that the U.S. forces were far better equipped and mechanized than the South Korean forces. Another reason might have been that the Americans didn't want to fight in the mountainous regions of the central Korean peninsula. But, behind the curtain of all those theories was the conflict between Walker and Almond. In a sense, the South Korean forces served as a buffer between the two U.S. forces.

This was one of the most serious mistakes that MacArthur made in the course of the Korean War. The Chinese forces took advantage of this weakness, and first attacked the vulnerable South Korean forces, which were clearly ill-equipped and poorly trained. Wiping out both South Korean Army 7th and 8th divisions overnight, the Chinese effectively split the Korean front into two, and pushed the divided U.N. forces south of the 38th parallel. Seoul fell into the hands of the Communists again. The war continued for two-and-a-half more years, shedding an almost endless amount of blood. From a military perspective, it was MacArthur's irrevocable mistake.

The Battle of Chosin Reservoir also occurred during the cruel winter of 1950 right after the Chinese intervention. The U.S. Army 7th Division advanced all the way to the Yalu River, which divides Manchuria and the Korean Peninsula, but it suffered massive casualties and barely managed to escape via the port of Hungnam. When Young Oak joined the division in March 1951, it was still struggling to recover from that aftermath. The debacle of

Red Mason's 1st Battalion on the eve of the battle at Hill 337 also took place on this continuum.

Chapter 20
Walking on the Ridge

When Young Oak took over the 1st Battalion, soldiers were suffering from a kind of chronic defeatist mentality. The men were traumatized and intimidated by the Chinese forces in what could be called "Chosin Reservoir Syndrome." The battalion was composed of essentially two groups of soldiers. One group was the old timers who had participated in the Incheon Landing and marched all the way north to the Sino-Korean border in North Korea. The other group was the replacements. Although the old timers had combat experience, they were still afraid of the Chinese forces. The replacements, easily influenced by the old timers, were also scared of the Chinese. On the battlefield, fear of the enemy is highly contagious, creating low troop morale. Once the troops began to suffer from low morale, it became a vicious cycle. But Young Oak, as the regimental intelligence officer, knew that the Chinese troops were suffering from their own low morale, intimidated by the technologically superior U.S. forces, who were the victors of World War II. However, his talks alone could not convince his soldiers that the Chinese feared them as well.

Although it is true that the success of the Incheon Landing was due to General MacArthur's military genius, the American troops were a mess in the early days of the Korean War. They were ill-trained, poorly prepared and nowhere near combat readiness. The 1st Battalion of the U.S. 31st Infantry was a shining example. When the Korean War first broke out, the battalion solely existed on paper. A U.S. infantry regiment was supposed to have three infantry battalions, but the 31st Infantry had only two. The state of the 7th Division—of which the 31st Infantry was a part—was equally unstable. Originally, the division was established during World War II when it was sent to the French-German border. During World War II, the division also fought against Japan in the Pacific. After the war, the U.S. assigned the division to be part of the occupation forces in South Korea. After World War II, the U.S. and the U.S.S.R. had agreed to send tandem occupation forces to the south and north areas of the 38th parallel under the pretext of disarming the Japanese troops. During the American Military Government period (1945-1948), the division was stationed in Korea. With the founding of the Republic of Korea in 1948, the division was then relocated to Hokkaido, Japan. When the U.S. forces committed to the Korean War, troops that were stationed in Japan were sent to Korea first. The 7th Division then became the reserve division for the Far Eastern Command. Unfortunately, the division ended up providing so many replacements to the units fighting in Korea that it grew substantially weaker. Subsequently, when General MacArthur decided to include the division in the Incheon Landing, its manpower was less than 50 percent. The Far Eastern Command tried desperately to muster additional troops by reactivating paper units such as the 31st Infantry's 1st Battalion. When it became too difficult to supply American replacements, the Far Eastern Command decided to use South Korean troops. These 8,653 South Koreans were randomly conscripted civilians from the streets of Korea.

   They were known as KATUSA— Korean Augmentation to the United States Army. In other words, although the U.S. 7th Division was officially a U.S. unit, in reality it was composed of Americans and Koreans. This was how the 7th Division was sent back to Korea during the war. It was a division that shed so much blood during the war that President Syngman Rhee, presented the famous Korean folk song "Arirang" to the division. As a result, the American soldiers sang "Arirang" whenever they marched and so earned the nickname of the "Arirang Division."

When the 1st Battalion was reactivated, its soldiers did not have time to receive proper training. The minute the Korean and American soldiers arrived at the training facilities at Mount Fuji, they were simply assigned to units and boarded onto ships headed for Korea. In many cases, American soldiers were left wandering around for days before they found their appropriate units on ships sailing for Incheon.

So when Pfc. Frank Wise volunteered to enlist into the U.S. Army on his 17th birthday, the boy had no idea what was about to happen to him. Three months later, the Korean War broke out and he was sent to Japan. He ended up participating in the Incheon Landing, as a soldier of the 1st Battalion. Unfortunately, during his basic training, he never even saw a bayonet or a grenade. Perhaps the U.S. had become too arrogant with its World War II victory.

At the time, although the U.S. government began conscription at the age of 18, a 17-year-old could volunteer for the army with parental consent. Often, boys younger than 17 would present fake birth certificates in order to enlist. Boys younger than 16 years also ended up fighting in the Korean War.

With the success of the Incheon Landing and the relatively easy marches into North Korea, the U.S. soldiers thought the Korean War was going to be quick and easy. However, after suffering several devastating defeats to the Chinese forces, the American soldiers developed an intense fear of the Chinese. Most of all, they feared night attacks by the Chinese forces, which nullified the superior air force and artillery fire power the U.S. had. During their attacks, the Chinese often blasted colorful flares into the sky, blew whistles and beat clanging gongs. These terrifying sounds were every American soldier's nightmare as he shivered with cold and fatigue in the middle of the night, deep in the mountains of Korea. Soldiers felt profoundly grateful for the rising sun after suffering such hell, crouched in a foxhole all night long.

When he took actual command of the battalion, Young Oak's first priority was to eradicate the defeatist attitude of the soldiers and their fear of the enemy. The previous day, Young Oak had C Company lead the attack and it tasted its first victory in the battle of Guman Mountain. This time, he wanted A Company to lead the attack. The objective was the southernmost summit of three mountain peaks, about three miles northwest of Guman Mountain. Since the height of this particular peak was 364 meters above sea elevation, it was named Hill 364. Hill 364 was neither a high mountain, nor a strategically important point, but the battle would have significant meaning to the battalion and the regiment. The former had just undergone drastic changes in their command structures, while the latter was still struggling to recover from the aftermath of the Battle of Chosin Reservoir. Although the soldiers were impressed by the clout of the artillery support they had witnessed in the previous battle, many thought it was a one-time occurrence, as they had never seen such firepower under the command of Lieutenant Colonel Mason. A report came in from regimental headquarters that at 10:00 a.m., a unit at the left flank of Young Oak's unit, the 1st Battalion of the South Korean Army 11th Regiment, began to engage in a fierce battle with Chinese troops.

At 12:45 p.m., when A Company was approaching Hill 364, artillery rounds suddenly began to fall on the lead platoon. Even though Chinese forces had opened fire, it was friendly fire that was hitting the lead platoon. In combat, soldiers panic when hit by enemy fire. But the degree of psychological terror intensifies when they are hit by friendly fire. In combat, panic is contagious. When a handful of soldiers begin to retreat in panic, others don't think or ask. The formation is broken swiftly and the situation moves beyond control.

The traditional attack formation of a U.S. rifle company was that the lead platoon leader initiated an attack behind two or three scouts. Immediately behind the lead platoon, the company commander controlled the entire company.

A Company was in this formation with Captain Willecke right behind the lead platoon, when the artillery rounds started landing. Unfortunately, Willecke couldn't stop his soldiers from turning around and running the other way. Willecke himself was surrounded by mass confusion and chaos as artillery rounds flew over his head. He couldn't even think about what was happening behind him.

At that moment, Young Oak had positioned himself right behind A Company to direct the battle with his radioman and the intelligence officer. Seeing soldiers suddenly hit by friendly fire, Young Oak instinctively ran towards where the artillery rounds were exploding. He tried to stop the panicking soldiers from retreating, but they were too hysterical to hear anything. Immediately, he pulled out his pistol, aimed it at a soldier running in front and yelled, "Stop, or I'll shoot!"

He didn't pull back the hammer as a precaution since he didn't want to accidentally fire in the midst of the confusion. Soldiers halted before his pistol. Even though the soldiers didn't know who he was, being a non-white officer might have helped draw their full attention.

"Don't panic. This is friendly fire. It'll stop soon. Do not retreat," he said, calming them down.

Young Oak knew that the incoming rounds were friendly fire from the direction they were coming from. He had already ordered his artillery liaison officer to stop. But it was only after several soldiers were wounded that the artillery ceased fire. Young Oak had a hard time convincing the soldiers that the friendly fire was not going to hurt them anymore.

"As you can see, enemy artillery is not accurate," Young Oak said reassuringly. "They are too far away to do any harm. They're saving their ammunition. Calm down. I'll stay here with you. I already ordered our artillery to stop and I'll call for artillery again. I'll show you that we can control it."

Young Oak had to find out which guns were fired, whether it was his own regimental artillery or somebody else's. It was verified that the gun was one of the regiment's 105mm howitzers supporting the attack. The original orders were for each of the six guns to shoot five rounds first and wait for the next order. By the time the artillery battery received Young Oak's order to quit firing, they had already stopped. But that was after five rounds from one gun had hit the lead platoon.

Rapidly evacuating the wounded soldiers and putting the unit back in formation, he ordered the artillery battery to fire again toward the initial target. This was not only to attack the enemy, but also to demonstrate to his men that friendly artillery rounds were not going to hit them anymore. After the second support fire, Young Oak ordered them to attack again. Shortly after, Hill 364 fell into the hands of the triumphant A Company.

Although the battle at Hill 364 ended within 40 minutes, the battle at Topgol, which lasted until late afternoon, faced vigorous Chinese resistance. This time the U.S. 31st Regiment's counterpart was the Chinese 538th Regiment, which bought time for its main forces to safely withdraw north of the Bukhan River. The main Chinese forces were sent down during the Second Spring Offensive. In fact, only three hours after the battalion's victory at Hill 364, the Chinese assigned an entire battalion to target A Company. It was as if the Chinese sought to shatter the unexpectedly sharp spearhead that the 1st Battalion had become. But the eventual victor at the battle at Topgol was, again, Young Oak's battalion.

The next morning, McCaffrey received a report of the 1st Battalion's victory. He called his personnel officer.

"Captain Kim has just led both battles to victory, I want to decorate him," McCaffrey said. "I don't care how you write it up, but just make sure he gets a Silver Star."

Just as Colonel McCaffrey intended, Young Oak received a Silver Star. It was Young Oak's first decoration during the Korean War and was his second Silver Star; he had received one in Italy during World War II. In truth, McCaffrey felt that Young Oak had long deserved a decoration on a number of occasions: when Young Oak had successfully led the long-range patrol leading the Korean guerilla unit; when Young Oak had saved G Company as they were about to be wiped out; and when Young Oak had made successful contact with the South Korean III Corps after perilously traversing Bangtae Mountain. However, McCaffrey wisely restrained himself from pursuing a decoration, because the general atmosphere had not been favorable.

He knew that if he tried to decorate Young Oak for successfully leading a Korean guerilla unit, he would have encountered objection and resistance. Later, McCaffrey wanted to decorate Young Oak for safely securing the small bridge, making it possible for the U.S. and South Korean troops to safely retreat, but he missed the opportunity. When Young Oak was at regimental headquarters, McCaffrey often expressed how Young Oak deserved decoration.

At around 8:00 p.m. after the battle at Topgol, McCaffrey called for Young Oak.

"Attack Hill 652 tomorrow morning," he said.

Hill 652 was labeled Chungbyung Mountain on the American operational map, but local Koreans called it Geumbyung Mountain.

"Isn't that the 2nd Battalion's zone?" Young Oak asked.

"I know, but it is going to be difficult for the 2nd Battalion to secure it alone. Help them," Colonel McCaffrey said.

"Yes sir."

"Since the 2nd Battalion will attack from the south to the north, you should also attack from the same direction."

Young Oak didn't respond.

"Why are you silent?" McCaffrey asked. The moment McCaffrey's order had been uttered, Young Oak's eyes had moved toward the map.

"I think we should attack from west to east," Young Oak finally said.

"You think so? Okay, do as you see fit."

Since C Company had tasted victory at Guman Mountain and A Company at Topgol, Young Oak decided to have B Company lead the attack this time. If B Company captured Hill 652, it would assuredly boost the morale of the entire battalion, as every rifle company would have experienced victory. Even more crucially, each soldier would palpably feel that he had played a key role in bringing about the victory. In addition, among the three rifle company commanders, Young Oak knew B Company commander First Lieutenant Charles Lonsford the best, and could trust him entirely. Although Lonsford had just taken over B Company two days earlier, he could read maps accurately and easily understood Young Oak's intentions.

When the regimental commander had relieved Lieutenant Colonel Mason of his duties, he told Young Oak to take any two officers in the regiment. Young Oak didn't hesitate in choosing Lieutenant Lonsford, the regiment's Intelligence and Reconnaissance platoon leader. Since the IR platoon was attached to regimental headquarters, it was under direct control of the regimental intelligence officer. As S-2 at the time, Young Oak could observe Lonsford closely.

When Young Oak picked Lonsford, McCaffrey groaned, "You know how to hurt people." But he issued an order to send him over to the 1st Battalion anyhow. Lonsford was a man of strength and honor. When he became B Company commander and found out that soldiers had abandoned weapons and communication equipment to hastily retreat under enemy fire, he made them go back to the mountain to pick them up.

For this battle, Young Oak established a command post between Sampo-ri and Daepyong-ri. B Company was on Hill 219, a small hill located a little more than one mile from the command post. Young Oak decided to go to Hill 219 himself because he was aware that Lonsford didn't have a map. The Korean War was already almost a year old, but it was still common for frontline company commanders of the U.S. forces in Korea to be were still fighting without maps. Young Oak and his driver left the command post for B Company on foot so that Chinese soldiers nearby wouldn't be able to hear them. At that moment, the houseboy Choi saw Young Oak's driver taking his carbine and radio and leaving the battalion command post with Young Oak. Choi hurriedly ran to grab his carbine. The rifle had been given to him by an American soldier. Choi had also learned how to shoot from

American soldiers and KATUSAs. Nearly an hour had passed since Young Oak had devised a plan after orders to attack. It was past 9:00 p.m. and the darkness of night had fallen.

A long and narrow flatland divided the two mountains where Young Oak and Lonsford were located. Along this strip of land there was a road that connected Palmi-ri and Sudong-ri. Young Oak had decided not to deploy troops along this road because spreading out the battalion too thin would endanger the entire unit. Coming down from the mountainside, Young Oak, his driver and Choi turned to the left and walked for about half a mile. Just before they reached the road connecting Palmi-ri and Sudong-ri, Young Oak heard a manmade sound in the darkness. Pulling out his pistol, he quietly ordered, "Be quiet. Stay right here, and don't make a sound."

Leaving his driver and Choi, Young Oak silently and swiftly walked 30 yards towards the road and hid. This time, the hammer of the pistol in his right hand was pulled back and ready to fire. The sound was coming from the north and getting louder as it approached where Young Oak was hiding. Straining to hear, Young Oak realized that it was a Chinese song. Overcome with concern, both the driver and Choi had quietly joined Young Oak and flanked him on each side, pointing their carbines into the darkness.

"Don't shoot until I order," Young Oak whispered.

A moment later, they saw the form of a man approaching in the darkness. It was a Chinese soldier. As if to overcome his fear, he was softly singing a song to himself. Since he was coming down the road all alone, Young Oak thought it was a clear indication that Chinese forces were somewhere nearby to the south. The soldier had his rifle on his shoulder and was carrying something in his hand, but it was too dark to make out what it was. Unwittingly, he approached Young Oak's party. When he was three to four yards away from them, he was shocked to see them. He tried to grab his rifle when two shots rang through the darkness. Bang! Bang! Choi had fired his carbine.

Just as the Chinese soldier had grabbed for his rifle, Choi had pulled the trigger despite Young Oak's order not to shoot. Since Young Oak pushed Choi's rifle muzzle up the moment he sensed that Choi was going to fire, the bullets shot through the darkness without hitting the Chinese soldier. Confused, Choi looked at Young Oak. The Chinese soldier turned and ran back up the road as fast as he could. Young Oak's driver couldn't believe what he had just seen.

"How come you just let him go?" the driver asked.

"Just let him go," Young Oak said. Ignoring Choi's resentful stare, he added, "Hurry up. Let's go quickly."

Young Oak hoped the gunshots would not provoke the Chinese. As the 31st Infantry engaged in combat every day with the Chinese, a firefight could erupt at any moment. While the driver and Choi couldn't understand why Young Oak had let the Chinese soldier escape, Young Oak had quickly weighed his options. He had concluded that it was best to spare the soldier's life: *Killing one enemy soldier isn't going to change the war. To kill him, I'll have to fire a single shot accurately. If I don't, he'll be severely wounded. If he is fatally wounded but still alive, I'll have to shoot him again to save him from his agony. If he is not fatally wounded, we'll have to take a wounded P.O.W. Then we'll have to carry him all the way back to battalion headquarters. And I won't be able to discuss tomorrow's attack with Lonsford. We won't be able to carry him back to B Company and return because it will delay our plans. In the meantime, the enemy might attack if we expose ourselves while trying to return to B Company. And even if the enemy doesn't attack, we won't be able to give him sufficient first aid, if it's too delayed.*

This is not a choice between firing and not firing, but between killing and not killing the man and I don't want to kill him if possible. More than anything else, we shouldn't provoke the enemy with gunshots. There's the possibility that gunshots in the darkness might provoke my men as well. The battalion headquarters or B Company soldiers might shoot in response to the gunshots even though it's against rules to return fire at unidentified fire—particularly in the darkness of night. But these men are still suffering from the aftermath of the Battle at Chosin Reservoir and there are too many replacements. These men are entirely different from the soldiers of the 100th in Italy and France. Even if this Chinese soldier returns to his unit with a minor wound and reports that he saw Americans commanded by an Asian, his commander probably wouldn't believe him anyway. And even if his commander does believe him, he's not likely to move his troops without gathering more facts on whether his enemy is American or Korean, how large his enemy forces are, and where his enemy is located.

While hustling towards B Company, Young Oak radioed Lonsford, "It was our houseboy who fired. Don't shoot. We're approaching your area."

When he finally got there, Young Oak discussed the next day's plan of attack in detail and then quickly left B Company. When Young Oak returned to the battalion command post, a memo informed him that the regimental commander had called him. When Young Oak called back, Young Oak discovered that McCaffrey was enraged.

"What the hell are you doing out there by yourself in the middle of the night? Don't you realize that there could be Chinese out there?!"

"Yeah, I know. I ran into one."

Hearing this, McCaffrey became even more irate.

"I don't want you ever going out like that again! Tell me before you go anywhere!"

The story of Young Oak letting an enemy get away alive spread quickly. Choi talked to KATUSA's members and his driver gossiped to American soldiers.

"What the hell happened out there? We've heard rumors. Are they true?" the intelligence officer, headquarters company commander, communications officer, and even the heavy weapons company commander all asked Young Oak. When Young Oak explained what happened, their responses were all the same: stunned disbelief.

"You're crazy to walk out there in the night! We didn't' even know you were gone..."

Since McCaffrey had authorized Young Oak to change the attack plan the previous night, B Company launched the attack on Hill 652 the next day from west to east. McCaffrey thought Young Oak miscalculated. In order for B Company to launch the attack according to Young Oak's plans, the line of departure had to be moved about two miles further to the west than the original plans. After moving B Company to the new line of departure in the morning, Young watched the attack with the battalion staff officers. But because of the previous debacle caused by Captain Willecke's false report that A Company had secured Hill 337, B Company's morale had been badly shaken; the company had suffered severe casualties.

Like a camel's back, Hill 652 had two peaks. The enemy was on the southern peak when the attack began. While the Chinese were busy shooting towards the south in response to the 2nd Battalion's attack, Lonsford initiated B Company's attack from the west. After, the Chinese troops didn't know what to do as they saw B Company suddenly appear from the west. At the same time, artillery rounds began to rain down upon the southern peak.

After the Chinese troops retreated to the northern peak, B Company occupied the southern peak without firing a single shot. However, when B Company approached a two mile-long ridge running along the southern peak, the repositioned Chinese troops opened fire from the northern peak. Immediately, B Company soldiers abandoned the ridge and took cover on the slope below. With their heads down below the ridge, the soldiers, who could not even see the enemy, shot in the air. Bullets flew helter-skelter into the sky. Lonsford tried to get his men to lift their heads and shoot, but nobody so much as budged. Then all of a sudden, Lonsford climbed atop the ridge, totally disregarding the Chinese bullets, and simply folded his arms across his chest. Young Oak understood what Lonsford was doing and dashed toward the southern ridge as well. In the meantime, Lonsford began to slowly walk along the ridge with his arms still crossed. When Young Oak reached Lonsford, he did the same thing. As both men strolled along the ridge, Lonsford tried to pump up his men.

"How are you going to hit the enemy without looking at them? Get up here!" Lonsford said.

"No, no, it's too dangerous," the soldiers replied.

"If it's so dangerous, how come we're not dead? We're still alive!"

Young Oak maintained a smile on his face as he overheard the conversation between Lonsford and his men. The Chinese soldiers were just plain baffled with the two officers, who were slowly striding along the ridge with crossed arms, as if they hadn't a care in the world for the bullets flying around them. Chinese soldiers continued to shoot at Young Oak and Lonsford, but the barrage of bullets all somehow missed both of them. Young Oak was a small man of medium height and build, but Lonsford, of

Norwegian ancestry, was an easy target as he was six feet tall and broadly built. Yet, bullets missed them both. Young Oak's and Lonsford's military serial numbers were not written on Chinese bullets that day.

After some time, two or three American soldiers crept a little higher until their heads reached the ridge. Out of embarrassment or guilt, they took random shots at the Chinese. Then, Lonsford suddenly sat down on the ridge, pulled out a K-ration, combat food for frontline soldiers, and calmly began to eat it while Chinese bullets continued to whiz all around him. In response to this even crazier stunt, his soldiers finally raised their heads above the ridge and began to shoot in earnest. The Chinese stopped shooting and began to retreat.

The Chinese positioned on the north peak appeared to be about two platoons in size. In order for them to retreat safely, these two platoons had to pass through an area about 100 yards from the south peak where the Americans were located. Ironically, the American soldiers could not hit a single Chinese soldier either. It was a miracle that the several dozen Chinese soldiers shooting at Young Oak and Lonsford did not hit the two men as they strolled across the ridge with crossed arms, but it was a phenomenon that about 150 American soldiers equipped with machine guns and automatic rifles could not hit a single Chinese soldier who were retreating from only 100 yards away. B Company soldiers were nervous, excited and scared. It was also the first time most of these soldiers were ever in a position to shoot at moving enemies.

"What the hell kind of soldiers are you? Nobody's shooting at you. They're running away!" Lonsford screamed as he pulled his hair in frustration. "They've got an entire 100 yards between you and them and you're missing every goddamn one of them!" (In actuality, there was one Chinese casualty in that battle. He had returned to pick something up from his group and he was shot and killed instantly).

Meanwhile, Young Oak was bent over, loudly guffawing.

"What's so funny?" Lonsford yelled at Young Oak.

"It's kind of comical if you think about it," ," Young Oak replied laughing. "Every single one of these men are shooting as fast as they can and not hitting anyone or anything. How could I not laugh? But I will say, it's an invaluable experience for the men. They finally beat the Chinese; they've finally seen Chinese soldiers retreating. We've captured two hills without any casualties. Let them enjoy the taste of victory for the first time. Now they'll be free of their fear of Chinese soldiers."

After the battle, curious soldiers approached Young Oak and Lonsford and inspected their uniforms. There were three holes in Young Oak's uniform and a few more in Lonsford's. Word of their insane behavior spread like wildfire. They quickly became legends and were viewed as phoenixes among the soldiers.

That day's victory was a turning point for both the battalion and the regiment. It was their third victory in a row. Since Young Oak had taken command of the battalion, it suffered only two KIAs and 46 WIAs, which was very low. The soldiers had rid themselves of their fear of the Chinese and morale flew sky high.

Chapter 21
Night March

That night around 8:00 p.m., the regimental S-2, Major Clark, called Young Oak and gave the order, "Move near Gumdae-ri tonight and attack the Chinese on Suan Mountain at 8:30 a.m. tomorrow morning."

Still on the phone and looking at the map, Young Oak immediately sensed that something was wrong with the order. Considering the terrain and the location of the enemy troops, it was a rather strange order. It appeared nearly impossible to move the battalion from where it was to where Major Clark was telling him to relocate and launch an attack at 8:00 a.m. The unit would have to move along the Bukhan River, which ran west and then turned almost 90 degrees to run south. The entire area was in the hands of the Chinese.

"It's already 8:00 p.m.," Young Oak said. "How do you want me to move the battalion near Gumdae-ri and launch an attack by 8:30 a.m. tomorrow morning?"

"Why don't you move to the south, then turn west to get around the Chinese?" Clark said.

Clark wanted Young Oak to find a way to move the battalion from where it was, to south of the Hongchon River, and then to move west along that river until it met the Bukhan River. He suggested that Young Oak then move the battalion northward along the Bukhan River. Young Oak knew that Major Clark was a poor map-reader, so he asked to speak to the regiment commander. When he heard McCaffrey's voice on the other end of the line, Young Oak asked, "How firm is the order?"

"It's firm, you've got to attack at 8:30 a.m."

"Yes sir, but it doesn't make any sense to follow Major Clark's plan."

"What do you want to do?"

"I don't know yet. I have to think about this."

Ending the radio communication with the regimental commander, Young Oak began to assess the critical situation while intently studying the map.

Regimental headquarters wants us to move along this route because of the Chinese. It's almost certain that the Chinese are positioned north of the Bukhan River. It's highly possible that they're still on the mountains south of the river, too. The high peak, north of the river, was what they used as their launching pad in the area for their Second Spring Offensive all across the Korean front, just a few days ago. Every day, we heavily bombed the mountains south of the river. I'm not sure, but I bet they're still there. But if I move the battalion along the path Major Clark is ordering, it'll be absolutely impossible to launch the attack at 8:30 a.m. tomorrow. What he doesn't realize is that the Hongchon River meanders so much that the distance to our destination is almost 40 miles. It'll be impossible to march that distance overnight. We'd have to attack in the afternoon, and if enemy resistance is strong, the battle will drag into the night. Then, it's highly unlikely that we will win. If the marching distance is too long, our men will have little time to eat, not to mention any time to rest. The men will have to fight fatigued and underfed. And they've already been in fierce combat with no rest for five consecutive days. Looking at the big picture, we're on the offensive; the enemy's on the defense. The Chinese have already begun to avoid aggressive engagement with U.N. forces. We don't know where the Chinese are because we don't have enough manpower to send out patrols. I bet it's the same with the Chinese. They can't possibly send patrols to the bottom of the mountain. Besides, they're feeling safe up in the mountains since we haven't attacked them, with the exception of air strikes.

Young Oak recalled the night in Italy when he penetrated the German lines to take German POWs during World War II. He also remembered the day he led the Korean guerilla unit back to regiment headquarters along the Bangtae River, which ran through enemy positions. It was almost summer in Korea and the wind was strong at night in the mountains of the central front. The moon had been full several nights earlier and it had shone brightly. However, that night, thick clouds obscured the moon, darkening the sky. Young Oak gathered the battalion staff officers and company commanders.

"I just received orders from the regiment to move near Gumdae-ri tonight to launch an attack against the Chinese on Suan Mountain at 8:30 a.m. tomorrow," Young Oak explained as he pointed to the map. "We don't have good intelligence on whether the enemy is on the mountains south of the Bukhan River or not. But it's a strong possibility. Even if they're not there, as you can see, there are many mountains without roads. We can't pass overnight. But if we go south first to avoid the enemy, we won't be able to make the jump-off at 8:30 a.m. And if we begin the attack too late, the battle will get tough. To launch the attack on time, we will march through enemy territory. We'll leave immediately, follow this road to the Bukhan River, then follow the river to the west. Past Gangchon, Baikyang and north of Gulbong Mountain, the river flows south. We'll continue to follow the river to the south. Our objective is here, near Gumdae-ri."

Stunned by Young Oak's orders to march through enemy territory in total darkness, the battalion staff officers and company commanders could do nothing but silently stare at him.

"Obviously there will be enemies to the north of the Bukhan River," Young Oak continued. "They may also be in the mountains to the south, so there will have to be absolute silence during the march. All the vehicles and tanks with the exception of three jeeps should leave to the south right now. When the vehicles and tanks hit the Hongchon River, they'll follow the river to the west to bypass the Chinese to join us at the line of departure tomorrow morning. The rest have to stay close in single file and move as quietly and as fast as possible. After transferring all of the equipment into the vehicles going south, the remaining three jeeps will turn off their headlights and follow the column to the rear."

Immediately, Young Oak issued the marching order and the vehicles and tanks moved in a hurry. In single file, the battalion began its night march of about 19 miles to penetrate enemy territory in total silence and darkness. It was a dangerous gamble, betting that the Chinese would never anticipate an entire enemy battalion daring to penetrate their territory with no prior artillery fire. After a while, radio communication from the regiment came in around midnight. Major Clark had been waiting for the report that the battalion had passed through the location he had recommended. When he discovered that the battalion had decided to infiltrate Chinese territory directly, he must have reported it to the regimental commander. Young Oak could tell even over the radio that Colonel McCaffrey was madder than hell.

"Where are you?" McCaffrey asked.

"We're passing Nam-do," Young Oak replied.

"What? Already passing Nam-do? What the hell are you doing? Are you crazy? You know the enemy is all around you!"

"I know."

"You know?"

"You told me I had to jump-off at 8:30 a.m. This is the only route that allows for the launch at 8:30 a.m."

"What? That's the reason you took the entire battalion into enemy territory? You are out of your goddamned mind! You should have asked me to delay the attack."

"Yeah, but they're all up there on top of the hill. They're not going to bother me."

"Goddamn you. You always fool me. You're crazy."

"We'd better turn off the radio."

Knowing that it would endanger the entire battalion if he continued to rant over the radio, Colonel McCaffrey turned it off. He was a man with quick and keen judgment. After hearing the confidence in Young Oak's voice, he was also able to calm down. The island marked as "Nam-do" on the U.S. military map during the war is now known as Nam-i Island. The regimental commander was shocked at the report that the battalion was passing Nam-do, because that meant that the unit had already covered 80 percent of their marching distance and had less than four miles to their destination. A U.S. Army infantry unit was usually trained to march at about two and a half miles per hour with full gear on. However, Young Oak knew from his experience in World War II that ordinary soldiers with no special training could march over four miles per hour for the first several hours in an emergency situation. This was a vital reason why Young Oak had calculated that the march would take four to four-and-a-half hours when issuing the order.

The night was windy and the marching sounds were lost in the howl of the wind. Auspiciously, the battalion did not encounter enemy resistance that night. The lead unit soon crossed the Bukhan River and was fast approaching Gumdae-ri. If everything went as planned, the other units would arrive shortly. Soldiers would have some time to rest before the attack.

"Let the men take a rest and have the company commanders assemble at 5:00 a.m.," Young Oak commanded, when they finally arrived.

The soldiers dug foxholes and tried to get some sleep in the cold night. Soldiers at the rear didn't have much time because they arrived later. But everybody felt fortunate and relieved that the entire battalion had passed safely through enemy territory without a single shot being fired.

Once the company commanders assembled before dawn, Young Oak crossed the Bukhan River in the predawn darkness and scaled Hill 445. He led the company commanders to the location where he had decided to establish the command post. Hill 445 was a mountain about two-and-a-half miles southeast of Suan Mountain across the Bukhan River where the Chinese were. Young Oak and his men climbed Hill 445 in order to check enemy positions and confirm the attack plans with their own eyes.

When they approached the summit, the sun was just beginning to rise. Because Hill 445 is 44 meters higher than Suan Mountain, it was an ideal location to establish the command post, as it was perfect for monitoring enemy movements. Young Oak did not have enough time to evaluate each of his company commander's capabilities, so instead of briefing the attack plan on the map, he explained each target in detail while pointing with his finger. That morning, A Company was going to lead the attack. Assessing that Captain Willecke lacked a sense of direction, Young Oak tried to make sure Willecke knew exactly where to begin the attack and in which direction. Young Oak also ordered that he report A Company's advance every 25 yards.

At 8:30 a.m., the very jump-off time ordered by regimental headquarters, Young Oak issued the attack order without hesitation. He was firmly convinced that the battle had already been won when the battalion successfully penetrated enemy territory during the night. The battle unfolded as planned and the battalion secured Suan Mountain before noon. Although Young Oak knew that the night march was an extremely dicey operation, sometimes such a risk had to be taken in order to secure victory. And such a decision was always a commander's responsibility.

Young Oak's decision to turn down the regiment's original plan and execute the night march was only one critical factor for the victory. There was another factor. It was a unique method of attack that he had used in World War II. After winning the battle the previous day, Young Oak gathered all the company commanders.

"From now on, have all the soldiers cut an orange artillery panel into smaller pieces," he ordered. "Make sure lead scouts attach a piece to their back, when they're attacking."

An artillery panel was a rectangular-shaped board about three yards high and about two feet wide with special fluorescent chemicals painted on the surface so that it could be easily seen day or night from the sky. The panels were given to ground troops by the air force to serve as markers for fighter planes and artillery liaison planes so they could avoid attacking friendly troops. Ground troops typically lay the panels side by side on the ground to signal airplanes not to attack below the line of panels. The panels came in many colors, and Young Oak chose orange panels because they could be seen easily from far away. The idea was that when the soldiers carried the orange pieces on their back, their positions would be seen quite efficaciously from the command post far away.

However, when Young Oak issued the order, initially the soldiers almost rebelled. They felt that carrying such markers on their backs would be suicidal, making them easy targets to the enemy. Officers argued that American artillery, such as the 105mm or the 155mm howitzer, could not fire with precision and needed the markers. Young Oak had already won battles in France during World War II by utilizing this method with minimum friendly casualties.

The idea originated from a Japanese American soldier during the battle in Bruyères, France. Young Oak had been controlling artillery fire from the rear to support a unit leading an attack into a forest. Suddenly he saw something brightly colored flash through his binoculars. As a result, he was able to guide the artillery fire much more precisely. After the battle, Young Oak sought out the soldier. The soldier told Young Oak that he had carried a piece of orange artillery panel on his back in order to make himself more visible so that the battalion command post could locate his position better. Afterward, Young Oak always utilized this method in every battle that was fought in France. Subsequently, he was always able to guide artillery fire more accurately; the results were favorable every time. A good idea had nothing to do with rank. If a good idea reduced casualties, it should be readily adopted regardless of the rank of the soldier who conjured it.

"You think carrying an artillery panel piece will make it easier for the enemy to detect you, but that is just not the case in real combat," Young Oak said. "As long as our men are not retreating with their backs turned to the enemy during an attack, it does not matter. Furthermore, even if the enemy is on higher peaks and is able to spot our men when we attack, it still doesn't matter, because our artillery provides fire support before our soldiers are within firing range of the enemy. As for the 105 and 155's precision problem, I have a plan, so don't worry."

Young Oak's plan to solve the accuracy problem of the howitzers was to use anti-aircraft guns. Even though the Chinese had begun to use air power during the Korean

War, the U.N. anti-aircraft units had little to do since Chinese fighter planes did not fly into the vicinity of the 38th parallel. Young Oak was able to secure "Bofors" and "Quad 50s" from the anti-aircraft units of the Division and Corps. The Bofors are 40 mm anti-aircraft guns that were designed by the Swedish company Bofors. During World War II, the U.S. had produced them under licensed contract with the company; these guns were reputed to be one of the best light anti-aircraft guns in the world. More specifically, they were called "Twin Bofors" because each was equipped with two guns. The firepower of Twin Bofors was formidable and each shell weighed about two pounds, as it could fire 120 rounds per minute. It was not only significantly accurate, but could also shoot planes up to approximately 3,600 yards above. In addition, a Twin Bofors was able to provide accurate fire support for up to 10 yards in front of a leading soldier. As the central and east central frontlines of Korea were crowded with mountains, a Twin Bofors on a mountaintop would easily hit targets on the next mountaintop.

A Quad 50, another anti-aircraft weapon, had four guns with a half-inch caliber, usually mounted on a half-track. Its primary function was to shoot down low-flying airplanes. The Quad 50 could fire 2,300 rounds per minute and because there was one tracer for every four rounds, one could see precisely where the bullets were going. It could also hit targets up to approximately 3,300 yards away on the ground.

Battles on the central and east-central frontlines of Korea were primarily over who was going to overtake the mountaintops. Mountaintop battles, whether in Korea, Italy or France, followed a general pattern. The attacking sides typically launched artillery fire or an air raid first. Then, foot soldiers would charge toward their enemies on the mountaintop. Therefore, it was critical to precisely calculate the distance between attacking friendly soldiers and defending enemy soldiers in order to know when to start or stop the artillery fire or bombing. If artillery fire or bombing ended too early, enemy soldiers hidden in trenches or foxholes could return fire. If artillery fire or bombing ended too late, units might suffer too many casualties from friendly fire. Subsequently, soldiers defending a mountaintop would stay crouched down until enemy artillery fire or bombing ended. They would raise their heads and begin firing at the approaching enemy soldiers once the artillery assault or air raid stopped or when shells started to land behind them. Naturally, the most dangerous moment for the attacking soldiers was right after artillery support stopped, as this was when the potential for the most casualties sharply increased. Reducing friendly fire casualties by minimizing exposure time was critical. Maximizing support fire while minimizing friendly casualties was the key issue. Balancing these two often determined the victory or loss of a battle.

Reducing exposure time to enemy fire was one of Young Oak's primary reasons for using the Twin Bofors and Quad 50s. When the battalion attacked, Young Oak used the 105mm and 155mm howitzers first. The howitzers could safely fire rounds up to 30 yards in front of the leading soldiers. To accomplish this, the artillery units and the foot soldiers had to be well trained and disciplined. Young Oak's rule of thumb was that once the distance between the attacking soldiers and the enemy narrowed to 50 yards, he stopped the howitzers. Then the Twin Bofors and Quad 50s opened fire immediately. Thanks to the precision of these two anti-aircraft guns, the Chinese soldiers were not able to even lift their heads until Young Oak's soldiers had narrowed the distance down to almost 10 yards. Young Oak had adopted this tactic from the

Germans during World War II. He had learned from the Germans to lower the firing angle of the anti-aircraft guns for ground battle, although they were designed to fire into the sky. During the battle for the liberation of Rome, Young Oak could see how the Germans were utilizing this tactic of using their 20 mm anti-aircraft guns against the American soldiers on the ground.

In theory, learning from the enemy should be easy, but in reality, it doesn't happen unless one has an open and flexible mind. A typical infantry officer would not have imagined borrowing anti-aircraft guns. In fact, officers in the 1st Battalion thought Young Oak must have had been mistaken when he tried to borrow anti-aircraft guns. Division and Corps anti-aircraft units refused his request at first. "What's the use of anti-aircraft guns when there are no enemy planes?" they asked. Finally, after several persistent requests, the anti-aircraft guns were authorized for loan. Young Oak had used only two Twin Bofors and two Quad 50s for the entire battalion at the Suan Mountain battle, but in every battle afterward, he made sure to assign two Twin Bofors and two Quad 50s per each company.

On top of this, Young Oak took additional steps. During the Korean War, a U.S. infantry regiment typically received artillery support from an artillery battalion just like during World War II. One infantry regiment consisted of three infantry battalions, and one artillery battalion consisted of three artillery batteries. This meant that one infantry battalion would receive fire support from one artillery battery. The case was the same with the 57th Artillery Battalion, which supported the 31st Infantry Regiment. However, when Young Oak took over the 1st Battalion, he changed that.

"From now on, when you ask for artillery fire, you must do as I tell you even if you don't like what I have to say," Young Oak directed his artillery liaison officer. "I'm going to say it anyway. When asking for artillery fire support, make sure you also request from the Corps and the Eighth Army."

"But asking for fire support from the Corps or Army for a battalion-sized operation, doesn't make any sense," came the expected response.

"I don't have time to discuss this and educate you. You either do it or leave the battalion."

"But I'm the artillery liaison officer of this battalion; I can't leave."

"I'm telling you one more time, either do it or leave."

"What do I tell my artillery battalion commander if I leave?"

"That's your problem. I'm going to demand somebody else."

"That's a demotion for me and I won't be able to explain what happened."

"Then do what I tell you to do."

"Just like that?"

"Yes, follow my orders a few times. If you still don't like it, we'll discuss it again later. But you must follow my orders."

When the artillery liaison officer requested and received artillery support from the X Corps and the Eighth Army Headquarters, he was so surprised that he yelled out, "I can't believe this! The Corps is going to provide artillery support for us! The Army is doing the same! Both the Corps and the Army are going to provide us an artillery battalion each! Two artillery battalions will give us 108 additional guns; adding up the 18 guns from my battery, I've now got 126 guns!"

With the additional artillery firepower from the Corps and Army units, the situation altered fundamentally. Young Oak's 1st Battalion was now capable of mobilizing greater fire support than any other U.S. infantry battalion in Korea. Young Oak was able to make this possible due to his experiences in Italy. He had discovered that if a commander is diligent, he could seek support from the division if he could not find a solution within his own regiment. A commander could also seek solutions from the Corps if he couldn't find it in his Division. On battlefields, where soldiers' lives were at stake, there was nothing like a "proper level of compromise." Young Oak's firm conviction was to always find a solution whenever, whatever and wherever he could. Once, Young Oak actually mobilized six artillery battalions for his battalion during the Korean War.

  The way Young Oak utilized artillery units was also fundamentally unique. When U.S. Army infantry commanders requested artillery support, they usually pre-calculated the jump-off time and the advancing speed of the soldiers. Then, the commanding officer had to figure out how and when his 18 guns would be fired or not, in accordance with the movements of the attacking unit. Of course, in real combat, directing precise artillery fire was extremely difficult, since the advancing speed of the foot soldiers always varied depending on enemy resistance. However, Young Oak devised highly detailed attack plans once he secured enough artillery firepower. He first divided the target area into a chessboard and assigned each battery to a specific area with a predetermined order of fire. This way, a battery did not have to waste time adjusting its firing angle in the middle of combat. In these crucial moments of life and death, Young Oak's artillery support units were able to coordinate precise turns to provide continuous fire support.

  Young Oak handled the situation with the tank unit in a similar fashion. Rarely did an infantry battalion commander request tanks, although the U.S. 7th Division had one tank battalion. The main reason was that infantry battalion commanders typically did not know how to use tanks for combat very well. Subsequently, tanks were generally always available for support.

Young Oak decided to proceed with his perilous night march during the battle at Suan Mountain because regimental headquarters ordered him to launch an attack at 8:30 a.m. But that was not the only reason. Another vital reason was that Young Oak tried to avoid night battles because the Chinese preferred to fight at night. Knowing this, Young Oak initiated every battle at Guman Mountain, Topgol village and Chungbyung Mountain in the morning and was able to finish the battle in daylight. Attacking during daylight may appear insignificant, but it made a drastic difference when there were battles every day. This was why Colonel McCaffrey, who also knew this very well, characteristically issued orders to begin attack usually between 7:00 a.m. and 9:00 a.m. But the 2nd and 3rd Battalions rarely began their attacks on time.

Procedurally, U.S. Army battalions launched their attacks upon official orders from the regiment. The regiment had to issue an official document to the battalion. One major problem during the Korean War was that the battalion typically received the document of order around 8:00 p.m. Since the 2nd and 3rd Battalions did not finish their battles before 6:00 p.m., the regimental headquarters could not issue documents of order any earlier. Upon receiving orders from the regiment around 8:00 p.m., the battalion had to analyze them and then devise its own specific operation plan for the next day.

Furthermore, the plan had to be recorded and documented as well. Consequently, company commanders would receive their orders at around 3:00 a.m. or 4:00 a.m. Company commanders would then have to issue their own orders to their platoon leaders based on the documents they had just received. All this was done in the dead of night; hence, the terrain was never verified by sight. Naturally, company commanders and platoon leaders needed their sleep and sustenance; thus, the earliest possible time either battalion could ever launch an operation was 11:00 a.m. Then, the operation would last until 6:00 p.m. and often dragged on for hours. Worse yet, the battalion sometimes had to give up the operation due to an ineffective plan of attack.

In contrast, Young Oak's 1st Battalion would begin operations in the early morning as directed by the regiment and was able to finish its battles by noon. Wrapping up its missions in a relatively short period of time meant it suffered fewer casualties. With such a low casualty rate, not only was there a smaller need for replacements, but soldiers gained courage and invaluable combat experience. In addition, since the battalion always finished its operation early, soldiers could rest and be ready to take on the next day's operation.

When a battle ended, the next order was typically to occupy one of the two mountains in the front. Even if the unit was not sure which one of the two should be attacked, it could devise a complete operation plan for at least one of them and a semi-complete one for the other. Most of the time, the next order was what Young Oak had anticipated.

After a day's operation, Young Oak would always spend about two hours studying the next day's operation plan along with the intelligence officer, the company commanders and the artillery liaison officer. As this was almost always done by 2:00 p.m. or 3:00 p.m., everything was verified in person. The artillery liaison officer could finish test firing, and the heavy weapons company commander could complete practice runs, aiming his mortars and machine guns at possible targets. By 3:00 p.m.

or 4:00 p.m., even the platoon leaders thoroughly understood the next day's operation.

Around 8:00 p.m., after dinner and the evening briefing, the battalion would receive an official order from the regiment. Once Young Oak received an official order document, he would analyze it and prepare his own attack plan in connection with the verbal orders he had made during the day. Most often, he would go to bed after midnight. On the other hand, company commanders, platoon leaders and soldiers were able to rest since they had been told what to do the next day. But Young Oak rarely caught more than three to four hours of sleep each night, and emergency telephone calls at night disturbed his rest. A conscientious and responsible commander on the battlefield never had five minutes of personal time a day.

Under Young Oak's brilliant leadership, the 1st Battalion was beginning to emerge as an invincible unit. The battalion won all its battles at Guman Mountain, Topgol village, Chungbyung Mountain and Suan Mountain. With the 1st Battalion ahead, the U.S. 31st Infantry Regiment began to lead the U.N. forces' Third Counteroffensive during the Korean War on the central front, after they successfully deterred the Chinese Second Spring Offensive—the final barrage of Chinese attacks during the Korean War. The battalion was also the first of the U.N. forces' regular infantry units to cross the 38th parallel again on May 27, 1951.

During the Korean War, the U.N. forces crossed the 38th parallel three times. The first crossing was right after the famous Incheon Landing in September 1950. The second crossing was made when the U.N. forces recaptured Seoul in the spring of 1951, after it was lost following Chinese intervention the previous year. The third and last time was in May 1951. Unlike the first crossing, the U.N. forces had not placed great political significance on the second or the third crossing. But Young Oak felt something quite profound as he crossed the line with his battalion.

Memories came flooding back: putting back on his military uniform after hearing news of the war in his father country; his mother telling him to be sure to visit President Syngman Rhee; insisting on coming to Korea as an infantry officer; trying to persuade Colonel Singles in Japan to let him come to Korea; seeing those hungry children at the Pusan train station; stopping panicked Korean troops from retreating at Soyang River; walking with his arms crossed on Chungbyung Mountain, and leading the dangerous night march toward the battle at Suan Mountain. Now he was crossing the 38th parallel leading a U.S. Army battalion.

The U.S. Eighth Army, which was in charge of the Korean War, updated the situation map every day. This map showed the positions of armies, corps, divisions, brigades and regiments, but typically did not specify the positions of all the battalions. However, the map dated May 31, 1951 clearly marks Young Oak's battalion as the unit most advanced to the north on the central front.

The legend that was born in Italy and flourished in France during World War II was reborn in Korea. Young Oak played a vital role in pushing the central front to the north by approximately 37 miles. This move became the backbone of the armistice line that still separates the Korean peninsula today.

On May 31, 1951, when Young Oak led his battalion to the northernmost position on the central front among the U.N. forces, the composition of the U.S. Army 31st Infantry Regiment was 3,522 American soldiers, 472 Korean soldiers including six liaison officers, 500 Korean civilian laborers who carried ammunition and food to the front, and approximately 100 Korean guerillas. The ratio between Americans and Koreans was approximately three to one, indicating that the U.S. 31st Infantry Regiment was actually a unit of both Americans and Koreans.

After crossing the 38th parallel, the U.N. forces continued pressing the enemy. The U.N. forces were able to safely secure the southern end of the road that connected Hwachon and Kumwha, and the 31st had managed to take Hwachon. However, when the U.N. forces intensified their attack towards Kumwha, Chinese forces mounted an uncharacteristically intense counterattack in defense of their occupation of the "Iron Triangle." In the beginning of the Korean War, North Korea had sent troops to this imaginary triangle, which connected Pyunggang, Chorlwon and Kumwha. China had also sent massive troops along the same route during the First Spring Offensive in 1951 in order to protect this strategic position that was the key to defending Pyongyang, the capital of North Korea. If the U.N. forces wanted to capture Pyongyang, they would need to secure the Iron Triangle first. Naturally, the Chinese were unwilling to give up this strategic position.

Crossing the 38th parallel as the lead unit of the U.N. forces, Young Oak's battalion kept pressing the Chinese. As the battalion neared the Iron Triangle, the Chinese mounted increasingly intense resistance. In June, it was difficult for the battalion to advance half a mile per day. Bloody battles were waged daily. Mountains and fields on the central front became wet with blood, shed by so many young soldiers of both friendly and enemy forces.

Civilians also suffered great hardships as the front line fluctuated back and forth, causing endless waves of chaos and destruction. Houses were destroyed to the point that not a single one remained intact. Some civilians were able to secure a little food in the midst of the extreme chaos, and the civilian affairs sector of the regiment tried to distribute rice, corn, salt and fish to the civilians, but wartime was traumatic for all. Psychological warfare unit members of the regiment tried to persuade many of the residents to leave their caves or other places of hiding, but the traumatized refugees persistently refused.

To the American soldiers, it was difficult to understand why these Koreans were so obsessed with their "hometowns." One case involved an eight-month-old baby found by a regiment medic. The civilian affairs section tried desperately to locate the parents, but their efforts were in vain. The child was eventually sent to a refugee camp in Chunchon; thus, another war orphan was born. Days later, three civilians wounded by shrapnel were brought in and sent to the same refugee camp. Nobody knew whether they had been hit by enemy or friendly fire.

Sadly, U.N. intervention was not always fortuitous. During the wartime chaos, a heinous incident shook up the 31st Regiment. In Yongam-ri, a small village just south of the Hwachon Reservoir, three U.S. soldiers raped two Korean women. It did not stop there. The three American soldiers murdered all three Korean men who had tried to protect the women. That was just six weeks after McCaffrey had court-martialed a soldier and gathered all three battalions, warning, "If a crime like this ever happens again, I'll make sure that the criminal will be shot to death regardless of rank."

Tragically, it happened again. Local civilians reported the incident to the regiment. Outraged upon receiving the report, Colonel McCaffrey ordered that the criminals be identified at any cost. To secure impartiality, he included the Korean police as members of the investigation team. But it was impossible to identify criminals whose trails were already cold in the chaos of war. As the victims could not identify the criminals, the case was closed.

After crossing the 38th parallel into North Korea, the 1st Battalion was heavily engaged in battle in a region north of the Hwachon Reservoir. Again the Chinese mounted strong resistance. It was the first time that Young Oak witnessed such intense enemy artillery fire during the Korean War. As the advance slowed, the U.N. forces began "Operation Piledriver" on June 5, 1951 in an effort to accelerate the advance. Young Oak was ordered to relocate the battalion and fight on the mountains near the Iron Triangle.

To keep the U.N. forces from advancing northward and to buy time to regroup in the Iron Triangle, the Chinese forces mounted fierce defensive resistance. The battle became even more ferocious and brutal. The battalion began to run out of 81 mm mortars and grenades. Orders were issued to limit mortar fire down to 15 rounds per day. Running out of grenades indicated how closely both sides were engaging. In combat, it's not easy for a soldier to throw a grenade farther than about 10 yards, since he had to hide behind some kind of object. Because a grenade was the weapon of choice against enemies hiding in caves, trenches or foxholes, the paucity of grenades revealed that the soldiers were fighting at close range against enemies who had many places to hide.

In spite of Young Oak's efforts to minimize fatalities, the battalion suffered casualties every day. On June 7, three were killed and 10 were wounded. Company Commander Captain Willecke was killed after being hit in the chest with six submachine gun bullets, when he was searching a cave in Nodong-ri. First Lieutenant Covach, 2nd Platoon leader of A Company, who had mourned the Korean farmer carrying a dead boy in his arms near the Bukhan River just days earlier, was also wounded and evacuated. A bullet had hit the lieutenant bar on his helmet, passing through the upper part of his skull. Had the bullet entered half an inch lower, Covach's name would have been on the KIA list. And although not a member of Young Oak's battalion, First Lieutenant Smock, who had originally organized and trained the Benedae Group, had been wounded a day earlier and then died on June 7. On June 8, four soldiers were killed and 10 wounded. One on the KIA list was a KATUSA. Young Oak almost got on the KIA list when facing a concentrated Chinese machinegun and mortar attack the day before "Operation Piledriver" commenced. It was a similar situation he had faced in Monte Cassino, Italy, when standing on the wrong side of a German sniper's rifle. He had to leave everything to the mercy of the goddess of fortune once again and simply hoped to see another day.

Chapter 22
Friendly Fire

While leading his battalion northward on the road connecting Hwachon and Kumwha in the same afternoon that Captain Willecke had been killed and First Lieutenant Covach had been wounded, Young Oak witnessed yet another tragic situation. At his right flank, the 2nd Battalion was valiantly fighting against innumerable Chinese. The Chinese had sent an entire regiment to solely target the battalion as if to cripple the 31st Regiment from further emerging as the spearhead of the U.N. forces on the central front. During the Korean War, the Chinese often tried to overpower their enemy with incomparably overwhelming amounts of manpower. When Young Oak's battalion emerged as the lead unit of the U.N. forces, the Chinese had focused a massive number of soldiers solely on the 1st Battalion. But then, on June 7, it looked as if the 2nd Battalion was the target of the Chinese troops. The brutal battle lasted from before dawn to late morning.

All of a sudden, American fighter planes appeared in the sky. The 2nd Battalion had barely managed to defeat the Chinese in the morning, so it requested air support. Just before 6:00 p.m., a U.S. Air Force squadron of F-80s screamed in from the south. Informed in advance that there would be a friendly air raid, Young Oak watched the approaching planes as he led his men to the north. But when the first F-80 dove to release a napalm bomb, it was not released properly. A napalm bomb was attached to a plane by two locks: one in front and the other in back. When the pilot pushed a button in the cockpit, the two locks were supposed to simultaneously unlock, thereby releasing the bomb. A properly released bomb would then fall in the same direction that the plane was flying. But on that terrible afternoon, when the pilot of that first F-80 pushed that button, only the back lock released. Then, as the bomb hung beneath the plane for a moment, the front lock unlocked. Instead of being delivered to the enemy position as intended, the bomb dropped far south of its original target area. Tragically, the napalm bomb landed on G Company of the 2nd Battalion. To make matters worse, the pilot was completely unaware of the drastic mishap. In those days, the U.S. Air Force squadron's rule was that fighter numbers two, three and four must also hit the same target that fighter number one had hit unless different orders were given. So fighter numbers two, three and four intentionally bombed the same target, which was G Company. This time, their bombs released without any problems.

When the Air Force had attempted to obtain permission from infantry commanders earlier that day for fighter planes to offer air support while flying in from the east, Young Oak had refused. This was because the 1st Battalion had already advanced much farther into the north. In the eyes of pilots flying in from the east, Young Oak's 1st Battalion would have been in line with the Chinese troops. Pilots flying fast in the sky would be unable to distinguish friendly forces from enemy forces. And although the rule of thumb was not to bomb troops signaling with friendly smoke, it was never as easy nor as simple as that. If friendly troops and enemy troops were in the same line of the pilot's vision, the likelihood of fatal friendly fire was high. Young Oak had witnessed such situations many times in both wars, so he tended to avoid air support for close-range battles.

The U.S. Air Force was required to coordinate air raids with ground troops in advance. That day, the Air Force made no move to attack from west to east. Perhaps the unit at the left flank of Young Oak's battalion rejected the plan. Since fighter planes had to slow down when getting closer to the ground to accurately bomb a target, fighter pilots had to put themselves in the vulnerable position of being within range of enemy anti-aircraft guns. Therefore, pilots preferred to fly in from the direction of friendly positions, drop their bombs and then immediately steer their planes upward to fly higher into the sky. That day, the only option left for the Air Force squadron had been to fly from the south.

G Company was the unit that Young Oak had saved while on long-distance patrol with his Korean guerilla unit, just before the company was about to be ambushed by North Koreans. Despite all precautions to avoid friendly fire, G Company suffered heavy casualties from the disastrous friendly bombing.

On June 9, U.N. forces sustained pressure from the enemy on all fronts. Their formation north of Hwachon from west to east was: U.S. Army 32nd Regiment, U.S. Army 31st Regiment and South Korean Army 7th Regiment. Orders for Young Oak's battalion were to secure two mountaintops by 3 p.m., control about two-and-a-half miles of the road that ran between Nodong-ri and Sanyang-ri. By this time, Young Oak's battalion was used to its characteristic attack method of utilizing heavy artillery support. After securing ammunition, the 1st Battalion had finished their mission around 11 a.m., four hours earlier than had been ordered. By 1:00 p.m., they had finished cleaning up the battlefield and established defense formations in preparation against a possible Chinese counterattack. Just then, the regimental headquarters called Young Oak, "Can you occupy Hill 541?"

"It's not part of today's operations plan," Young replied.

"Yeah, I know. Still, can you do it?"

"Yes."

Hill 541 was a mountain northwest of the 1st Battalion's position; it was also about one-and-a-half miles closer to Kumwha. Though Young Oak had acquiesced, he delayed the attack. Not only was the battalion not prepared, but even if the attack was successful, they would be placed in a dangerous position as they would be far into enemy territory. Both flanks of the battalion would be completely exposed to enemy attack. Two miles of the right flank were already exposed to the enemy, as the 3rd Battalion's advance to the right was slow. Taking over Hill 541 would expose that flank even more. It would endanger the entire unit, because the battalion would be surrounded by Chinese forces without an available exit. So Young Oak deliberately delayed the attack to buy time and waited for the situation to improve. The regimental headquarters called again. Unlike the gentle voice that asked for cooperation only a while earlier, the order was now not an option but an imperative to attack. Nevertheless, Young Oak continued to drag out initiating the attack while telling the regiment that the battalion would be attacking soon. Swiftly, he ordered the artillery liaison officer.

"The situation is entirely different this time. Contact the division, corps and army and secure as much artillery fire as you can. Get two artillery battalions per unit; that makes six. Don't give up until you've secured six. The moment we occupy Hill 541, we're going to be surrounded by the Chinese from three sides. The enemy will counterattack immediately. We've got to set aside enough artillery for that counterattack. I'm positive the Chinese will attack us from somewhere between the west and the north. Give the units the exact coordinates now and have them ready to fire at any moment."

Immediately after giving those orders, Young Oak tried to contact the tank company commander. Since an infantry battalion could not directly communicate with the tank company, he had to call Captain William Miller via a third party.

"Bill, the regiment wants us to attack Hill 541. Looking at the terrain, I have to begin the attack from Sanyang-ri. I'm sorry to have to ask this, but can you send your tanks over there?"

Young Oak knew very well how dangerous it would be for tanks to come to Sanyang-ri in such a situation. The 3rd Battalion was still engaged in battle just south of Sanyang-ri in a region through which the tanks would have to pass. If the tanks went just a little further north of the region and were ambushed by Chinese bazookas without the protection of foot soldiers, it would mean disaster. However, Young Oak could not afford to send his infantrymen to protect the tanks.

"Don't worry, Young," Miller said. "I'll send them right away."

Captain Miller was already aware that the 1st Battalion would soon have to launch an independent operation. Despite the fact that it was a risky mission, he was ready to accept Young Oak's request. However, retreating Chinese forces destroyed all the bridges over the Mahyun stream and installed obstacles on the road between Hwachon and Kumwha; it would not be easy for the tanks to get to Sanyang-ri. In fact, Captain Miller decided to lead the tanks himself. When the tanks arrived at Sanyang-ri in single column formation, he had them turn their guns toward Hill 541 and wait for Young Oak's signal. As soon as Young Oak ensured that the tanks and artillery units were ready to provide the support, he gave the signal.

Captain Miller ordered the tanks to open fire. The attack began at the base of the mountain and slowly moved upward. Simultaneously, artillery fire also slowly made its way up the mountainside. After scrutinizing Hill 541 for a long while, Young Oak finally ordered A Company to begin attacking. A Company then commenced its attack in coordination with its formidable tank and artillery support. Once the lead platoon climbed past the middle of the mountain, the tanks stopped firing, as they could not hit anything higher than the limited angles they were confined to. Then, seeing that the lead platoon was 50 yards below the summit of the mountain, Young Oak ceased the howitzers as well. In the same moment, the Twin Bofors and Quad 50s opened fire; two Twin Bofors and two Quad 50s poured approximately 5,000 anti-aircraft rounds per minute into the side of the mountain. At this point, this was all familiar procedure for the soldiers of the 1st Battalion. Backing up A Company 50 yards from the rear, C Company soon joined the approach to the summit. Prior to the attack, Young Oak had stressed again and again to Captain McCoy, C Company commander, "The attacking distance of A Company is longer than half a mile. Maintain no more than 50 yards from A Company. When A Company reaches the summit, join them immediately."

The reason why Young Oak had ordered Captain McCoy to maintain a 50-yard distance between the two companies was that by the time A Company secured the mountain summit, it was highly likely that the company would be out of ammunition. In those days, a U.S. Army infantryman carried enough ammunition to fight for about an hour. But if a panicked soldier held down his trigger, the ammunition could be gone in 20 minutes. An experienced soldier could fight for an hour in fierce combat. Young Oak had calculated that it would take about an hour for A Company to get to the summit from the line of departure. Therefore, having C Company was vital in order to stave off a Chinese counterattack. Just as he had predicted, the Chinese launched a counterattack in massive numbers. Through his binoculars, Young Oak assessed the lead counterattacking soldiers to be more than 200. He could see that the soldiers of A and C companies were just taking their first breather as they reached the mountaintop, but they were clearly anxious. A Company did not have enough ammunition.

Just when the faces of the American soldiers blanched in fear as they watched the Chinese forces roar in, the earth began to tremble. The American howitzers, ready for that moment, opened fire. The artillery assault lasted for about five minutes and the rear side of Hill 541 was covered thickly with dust. As the dust settled, not a single Chinese soldier was to be seen; it was as if all of them had evaporated with the dust or the surviving enemies had taken their dead in their rapid retreat.

The Chinese were well-known for doing everything in their power not to abandon their dead comrades. In this respect, American soldiers thought highly of their enemy. That day, the U.S. 32nd Regiment, fighting to the left of Young Oak's 31st, reported to the division that, upon securing their objective, they had discovered 70 Chinese bodies buried just beneath the earth. The Chinese had retreated in a hurry, evidenced by several abandoned 82 mm mortars and plenty of ammunition, but they had not neglected to bury the dead bodies of their comrades-in-arms.

Shortly after, Young Oak climbed Hill 541 with his command group. The Chinese were not going to return after their prepared counterattack failed. The battle at Hill 541 was over, just like that. Looking at his watch, it was 2:55 p.m. Young Oak radioed the regiment headquarters.

"We've just secured Hill 541."

"Thank you, Young. Thank you. I will be grateful to you forever."

Although it was odd for McCaffrey to say "thank you," rather than the usual "good job!" or "well done,"

Young Oak turned off the radio without giving it a further thought.

As was his routine, Young Oak began to set up the attack plans for the next day. Along with his command group, he left the summit for a location where he could better observe the next day's target. A non-military individual might think that a battalion command group would consist of two to three individuals, but in real combat, such a group easily exceeded 20. In those days, a battalion command group included the battalion commander, the operations officer, the intelligence officer, three rifle company commanders, the heavy weapons company commander and the artillery liaison officer—each accompanied by two radiomen, with the exception of the rifle company commanders, who were allowed only one apiece. There were 13 radiomen total. All told, there were 21 in the command group so far. However, since an artillery liaison officer's radio was so heavy, he could sometimes have four or five radiomen. Occasionally, artillery liaison officers from higher units and a tank officer joined, of course with their radiomen. In addition to that, if there were soldiers in charge of installing telephone wires, the size of a command group could grow exponentially.

Hill 541 had two long ridges, like rabbit ears, one extending to the north and the other traveling northeast, both about half a mile each. The ridges were smooth and flat, but then abruptly dropped off all the way to the bottom of the mountain. The road leading to the Iron Triangle ran through the middle of Jihye-dong village at the foot of the mountain. As it appeared that the edges of the rabbit ears provided an excellent view of the road from Hill 541, Young Oak's command group hastily made their way to the area. Just then, Young Oak got a call from regimental headquarters.

"Captain Kim, do you know why Colonel McCaffrey thanked you when you reported that you had occupied Hill 541?" the person said.

"No, I don't."

"It was because he was almost relieved, but you saved him."

"What do you mean?"

"As a matter of fact, the Corps commander, along with the Division commander, was at the CP."

The Corps commander referred to Lieutenant General Hoge of the IX Corps. The Division commander at the time was Major General Ferenbaugh.

"As you know, just like yesterday, the 3rd Battalion was advancing too slowly," the person continued. "General Hoge asked General Ferenbaugh twice when Hill 502 was supposed to be taken by the 3rd Battalion. General Ferenbaugh answered it'd already been passed. General Hoge then ordered General Ferenbaugh to relieve the regimental commander if the 3rd Battalion couldn't capture Hill 502 in 20 minutes. When he said that, he didn't even look at Colonel McCaffrey, who was standing right next to him.

"We were all standing in the back, scared as all hell. The 3rd Battalion was still having a tough time, and there was no way that it could have captured Hill 502 in 20 minutes. It was just like General Hoge was announcing that he was going to relieve Colonel McCaffrey," the person on the line continued.

"Really?" Young Oak asked.

"As a matter of fact, when General Hoge arrived at the CP, he asked General Ferenbaugh the same question about Hill 502. When General Ferenbaugh gave him the answer, General Hoge told him to relieve Colonel McCaffrey if the 3rd Battalion couldn't take the hill as scheduled. But looking at the situation, we knew the 3rd

Battalion would never be able to do it. That's why we asked you to capture Hill 541 even though it wasn't part of today's operation plans."

"I see," Young Oak said.

"Yeah, see, both your battalion and the 1st Battalion of the 32nd had finished their missions before noon. The 2nd Battalion of the R.O.K. 7th Regiment to the east of our 3rd Battalion also finished their mission by noon. So the front line was moving north with the exception of the 3rd Battalion, which made the overall advance slow. That's why General Hoge was madder than hell. Honestly, we felt sorry asking you to capture Hill 541 like that, but we had no other option. But Captain Kim, you did much better than we could have hoped for! It was 2:55 p.m. when you reported the capture—only five minutes before the scheduled deadline!"

"Is everything okay now?"

"Everything's more than okay now. When Colonel McCaffrey relayed your report, General Hoge whooped and even shook hands with Colonel McCaffrey and General Ferenbaugh to congratulate them. It appeared he'd completely forgotten about the 3rd Battalion and Hill 502 and just left immediately. Same with General Ferenbaugh, who was able to save face thanks to you."

If a regimental commander was to be relieved during combat due to slow advancement of a unit under his command, he wouldn't be stripped of his uniform, but promotion to a general would be pretty much impossible. To Colonel McCaffrey, the proud and promising graduate of West Point, nothing would have been more dishonorable. Considering his personality, he would have put himself out of service, had that been the case.

At that moment, the South Korean Army 6th Division was fighting to the right of the U.S. Army 7th Division. The 6th Division was the first South Korean unit that reached the Sino-Korean border the previous year. Around then, the U.S. 7th Division became the first American division to reach the border. So the only two divisions among the U.N. forces, which had advanced all the way to the Sino-Korean border in the previous year, were fighting side-by-side at that time.

After communicating with regimental headquarters, Young Oak moved with the command group to the observation location he had chosen, which offered an optimal view of the terrain. There, he discussed the next day's operation plans. Unless unforeseen circumstances were to arise, it was obvious that the next day's targets would be one of two possibilities. If the attack were to go northeast, the target would be Hill 667 where one could clearly see Jihye-dong. If the direction of attack were to go northwest, the target would be Hill 637 where one could see Shinwol-dong. Considering the current direction of the attack that the regiment had been taking, Young Oak surmised that the more probable target would be Hill 667. After thoroughly preparing for the attack of Hill 667 and roughly discussing for the attack of the other hill, the command group began to return to the battalion CP.

Everybody had not had a moment to rest since dawn. After fighting two battles in one day and finishing preparations for the next battle, everybody suddenly felt exhausted. When someone suggested a short rest, everyone agreed. Young Oak also willingly accepted the suggestion. Everyone was already either lying or sitting on the ground to enjoy the short break. Finding a space next to the battalion commander Major I. D. Warden, Young Oak lied down on the ground and almost fell asleep. But then he noticed two American airplanes flying in a circular pattern directly above. One was flying approximately 200 to 250 yards above and the other was flying approximately 2,000 to 2,500 yards above the ground. He felt okay with the lower airplane, which was an artillery observation aircraft of his own regiment. But somehow he was uncomfortable with the higher airplane, which was also an artillery observation aircraft.

Twisting his body to the direction of his artillery liaison officer, Young Oak asked him, "Those two airplanes are American, aren't they? What the hell are they doing up there?"

"The one flying low is ours."

"I know, but the other one's also an artillery plane. Don't they know they don't have the right to fly high over there? Is it going to fire at us?"

"No, I don't think so, sir. We've placed an artillery panel."

"Then, why do they keep circling around us? It's very annoying."

"Maybe they have their own business up there. Plus, that plane should be able to see our plane down below. See? I'm already in contact with them."

While trying to reassure Young Oak, the artillery liaison officer had his radioman call the regiment's artillery plane and began talking with the pilot. Hearing the conversation reassured Young Oak and he dozed off and even began to snore.

But the rest didn't last for long. Soon, artillery rounds started landing on the group. The 155mm howitzer rounds were coming from the south. It was American friendly fire that was being concentrated on the summit of Hill 541 and the central area between the two edges of the rabbit-ear ridge formation. The barrage lasted for about two minutes, only stopping when the artillery liaison officer's frantic request was finally relayed. But it was too late, as the friendly fire had already wounded many of the command group, including Young Oak and Major Warden. Bloodied bodies were scattered everywhere. The news of severe casualties suffered by the battalion command group due to friendly fire reached the regimental headquarters rapidly. Colonel McCaffrey was stunned with the unbelievable report: "1st Battalion command group devastated by friendly fire...Major Warden and Captain Kim seriously wounded..."

Colonel McCaffrey hastily reported to the division commander and requested a helicopter. Major General Ferenbaugh, who was also well aware of how valuable Young Oak was to the division, was equally dismayed. Feeling the urgency of life and death, General Ferenbaugh ordered his aide to call the Eighth Army Medical Corps.

Captain Kim? Wasn't he the one who helped me save face just an hour ago when General Hoge was driving me crazy by telling me to relieve McCaffrey? General Ferenbaugh thought.

His aide handed over the phone to him.

"This is the 7th Division commander, General Ferenbaugh. Send me a chopper immediately."

The general briefly explained the situation and gave the coordinates where he wanted the chopper to go. But the soldier on the other end of the line was reluctant.

"We can't do that, General. Our pilots don't want to fly there."

"What the hell are you talking about?"

"That location's too deep into enemy territory. Our choppers are unarmed and slow; it's too dangerous for them to go in there. Also, Hill 541 means its 541 meters above sea level. The air's so thin up there that a medic chopper might be able to land, but there's no guarantee that it could take off again."

"Shut up you son of a bitch! What the hell is it with your excuses? When I say send a chopper, just send one. Go get the wounded, but make sure you bring back a bloodied major and captain first! Understand? You've got to bring back these two, no matter what! While you send the chopper, I'll tell my men to bring the wounded down the hill. Send a chopper now!"

When the wounded made it halfway down the mountain on stretchers, a chopper arrived. Young Oak had been hit in both legs by shrapnel, just above the right knee, piercing through the leg and shredding his left knee and left ankle. Moreover, he was bleeding heavily. So was Major Warden, whose right cheekbone was torn where shrapnel had passed through his face underneath the left side of his chin.

After receiving the report that Young Oak and Major Warden were still alive, Colonel McCaffrey insisted to General Ferenbaugh that the person responsible for the friendly fire had to be court-martialed. The division commander, equally outraged, agreed. The Eighth Army's investigation revealed that the unit responsible for the friendly fire was the U.S. Army 555th Artillery Battalion of the IX Corps. The higher plane that Young Oak had been nervous about just before dozing off was the Corps artillery. Young Oak's artillery liaison officer did communicate with the regimental artillery plane, but he couldn't communicate with the Corps artillery plane due to radio frequency differences.

Furthermore, even though the Corps artillery plane's pilot had seen the no-fire line north of the battalion command group, he didn't believe that the group was really friendly forces. Because Young Oak's battalion had burrowed so deeply into enemy territory, the pilot assumed that the enemy was pretending to be friendly forces by using American artillery panels. After receiving the coordinates from their plane, the 555th Artillery Battalion decided to try Variable Time fuze artillery to maximize impact. VT artillery rounds were vastly different from ordinary rounds in that an ordinary round exploded on contact with its target or anything solid, whereas a VT fuze exploded in the air above its target to maximize shrapnel fragments. A VT round was a nightmare for foot soldiers. With regular rounds, soldiers could at least attempt to hit the ground to avoid shrapnel. With VT rounds, there was little a soldier could do except hope for minimal damage. Around 25 rounds had landed within two minutes. In this, the Corps artillery unit violated the rules of engagement.

In those days, according to U.S. Army regulations, a division, corps or army artillery unit was obligated to consult with the infantry regiment responsible for the area before opening fire. This particular Corps artillery battalion, nicknamed "Triple Nickel" for its official name of 555th Artillery Battalion, was notorious for "short" rounds—landing short of the target. In a perverse twist of fate, the battalion's fire that day was accurate. The 555th Artillery Battalion testified to the Eighth Army investigation team that Young Oak's command group was protruding by six kilometers—approximately 3.7 miles—north of the IX Corps frontline. However, either the artillery observation pilot had miscalculated or exaggerated the distance, as the command group had actually been located a mere one-and-a-half miles north of their neighboring friendly units.

When the investigation ended, Colonel McCaffrey and General Ferenbaugh insisted on a court-martial for the artillery battalion commander. But the corps commander didn't move. It was rumored that this was because the artillery battalion belonged to his IX Corps, and if the artillery battalion commander was to receive a court-martial, the general himself would have to admit at least partial responsibility as well.

The next day's target for Young Oak's battalion was Hill 667, just as anticipated. The battalion began its attack, without Young Oak, early in the morning. However, it eventually withdrew after suffering 18 casualties. The battalion, which had never lost a single battle under Young Oak's command, lost a battle that day. The very next day, the 31st Infantry handed over the frontline to the 17th Infantry and became the division reserve.

Chapter 23
Osaka Hospital

As soon as his bleeding was stanched, Young Oak was rushed to a hospital in Pusan. When a U.S. Army doctor cut open the bandages, Young Oak's wounds began to bleed profusely and he passed out. The situation was grim. Doctors didn't know what to do. Out of desperation, they bandaged him up, put him on an airplane, and sent him to a general hospital in the outskirts of Osaka, Japan.

When Young Oak finally came to, he was facing the Army physician who initially examined him upon his arrival in Osaka. The doctor was quiet for a long time. Young Oak had received so much morphine that he was too dazed to know whether it was day or night. He couldn't even answer the doctor's questions, because he couldn't remember anything.

"It looks very, very bad," the doctor said. "There's not only extensive muscle and nerve damage, but you bled too much. There's still a large piece of shrapnel in your knee and smaller fragments of shrapnel are scattered all over the place and badly infected. I may not be able to save your right leg."

"Is there any chance?" Young Oak asked.

"Yes, there is, but since the infection is so severe, a conventional treatment is not going to work. In order not to amputate, we have been working on a new experimental procedure. We haven't come to definite conclusions yet, but we think it's promising. But even if we do succeed, you've got to follow my instructions to save your leg. It's going to take a lot of self-discipline on your part."

The doctor picked up a small clear bag and showed it to Young Oak.

"What we're going to do is fill this bag with saline solution to disinfect your wound," the doctor continued.

"Once we feel it's somewhat sterilized, we'll open the wound and try to clean it again. I can't go directly inside the wound to clean it now. There's no guarantee that this will work. If it doesn't work, I'll have to amputate your right leg."

The doctor explained the procedure he was going to administer and began treating him accordingly. After a while, the doctor performed the surgical operation and inserted a saline solution bag inside the wound.

"The object of this surgical procedure is to cleanse, so we won't know for another week whether we'll have to amputate your leg or not," the doctor said. "Let's keep our fingers crossed."

After the surgery, a nurse changed the saline solution every 30 minutes for two days. Then she changed it every hour and a half. After several days, she said, "From now on, I'll be changing the bag every two and a half hours." Guessing that his wound was getting better, Young Oak dared to become optimistic. The doctor visited him every day. Finally, hope became a reality. Young Oak was able to keep his leg. One day, the doctor, who had been giving him the utmost intensive care, said, "Your leg is saved, but you probably won't be able to walk again. I am sorry. We tried our best, but…"

"I have to walk," Young Oak interjected. "I will walk again."

He was very fortunate to meet the doctors and nurses there. They were from Johns Hopkins University Hospital, one of the best medical facilities in the world. As the Korean War dragged on, the United States military began to activate reserve medical people. Many of the medical staff at the Osaka hospital were from Johns Hopkins. In other words, Young Oak had been taken care of by one of the world's best medical teams. If he had been in any other average military hospital, he might have had to amputate his leg.

However, although the expert medical team had given their all to save Young Oak's right leg, they had paid very little attention to the left leg. Since the wound on his left leg had not been as serious, a different surgeon operated. The left leg surgery didn't go well and another surgery needed to be performed. Still, the doctors couldn't completely cure the wound in his left leg. Despite the fact that the left leg wound was relatively less serious, shrapnel had penetrated the ankle and had cut nerves. The resulting pain from this wound was nearly unbearable.

Nurses' aides at the hospital were young Japanese girls. Although the United States government activated reserve U.S. Army nurses, the acute shortage of medical staffing posed major problems as the Korean War intensified and the number of wounded increased. As the situation got worse, Japanese doctors and nurses were also mobilized, but still it was not enough, and the hospitals became increasingly dependent on these Japanese nurse aides.

Because the U.S. Army didn't have sufficient time to provide them with proper nursing education, the hospitals adopted a system of labor division that relegated each aide with only one task. One girl would brush teeth for the patients, another would wash their faces and hands, while another one washed their bodies, and another massaged them. Another took blood pressure and another gave injections.

So even though a doctor would come once a day accompanied by a nurse to check each patient's condition, everything else was taken care of by these Japanese girls. One team consisted of about 20 aides. None of them could speak English. They were surprised that Young Oak was of Korean ancestry. They treated him especially well, even though it was a mystery to them how a Korean could be an American officer. Young Oak felt deeply grateful to these Japanese aides who took care of his every need when the doctors had put casts on both of his legs, rendering him unable to move at all. Two weeks after his surgery, Young Oak's condition had improved enough for him to go outside on a wheelchair for some fresh air. When the aides pushed his wheelchair outside, they would laugh heartily and teach him simple greetings and basic Japanese words, such as "ichi, ni, san, si," meaning "one, two, three, four."

The patients at the hospital were wounded soldiers from the Korean War. One day, a young first lieutenant approached Young Oak and saluted him.

"Sir, I'm Lieutenant John Covach of the 1st Battalion, 31st Infantry. Do you recognize me?"

"I'm sorry, but I don't."

The 22-year-old lieutenant had belonged to A Company and had been wounded three days before Young Oak during the battle at Nodong-ri, where Captain Willecke had been killed. He too had been evacuated to the hospital due to a serious wound. Like Young Oak, he was also a son of immigrant parents. The second son among three sons and three daughters of Hungarian immigrants, he was born in Saint Clair, Pennsylvania. The Korean War broke out only 10 days after he had been commissioned as a second lieutenant upon graduating from Pennsylvania Military School. After participating in the Incheon Landing, he went into North Korea as part of the X Corps, where he almost lost his life. Several months later, he got wounded again and was hospitalized in Japan.

"Sir, what are you going to do after you're released from the hospital?" he asked Young Oak.

"I want to go back to Korea."

"Me too sir, I'm sure you're going to be the battalion commander after your return. Could you give me a company?"

Lieutenant Covach was asking Young Oak to make him a company commander. Through their conversation, Young Oak could see that Covach, who had already been awarded a Bronze Star in North Korea, was an excellent combat leader. Young Oak liked the young man's frank manner.

"If I become a battalion commander, I will," Young Oak answered.

Two weeks later, Young Oak was able to get up from his wheelchair and begin hobbling about on crutches. During his recovery, the hospital frequently sent him on convalescent leaves to Tokyo, Kyoto and other places, in order for him to get up and move around. Each time he returned from his leaves, the doctors would check his improvement. Finally, the day arrived when his doctor checked him for the last time and said, "You're okay. I'm sending you to the States."

"No. I want to go back to Korea."

The doctor was surprised to hear his response. The war was still going on. When Young Oak was evacuated from the frontline, the U.N. forces were winning the war. There was no way Young Oak was going to leave Korea like that. Besides, he wanted to build a good track record as an officer. During his hospitalization, Colonel McCaffrey had sent him letters, urging him to come back to Korea with the promise that he would make him a major and battalion commander upon return. Severely wounded, Major Warden didn't return to Korea, and instead, was hospitalized for several more years after he was evacuated to America.

If Young Oak had not been wounded at Hill 541, he would have stayed for one more week in Korea and been promoted to major. When Colonel McCaffrey had given him actual command of the battalion, the regimental commander had taken the necessary steps to promote him. McCaffrey was going to make him a battalion commander at the same time as his promotion. In the U.S. Army, in those days, it was almost impossible for a brand new major to become a battalion commander on a battlefield. It was more than simply a matter of experience. U.S. Army regulations dictated that a major who commanded a battalion in combat for at least one month was guaranteed promotion to lieutenant colonel. And even though Army regulation didn't guarantee a major or lieutenant colonel, who had commanded a battalion in combat the promotion to colonel, it was nearly guaranteed, as long as no egregious mistakes were made. On the other hand, if a major or lieutenant colonel never served as a battalion commander during wartime, he was rarely promoted to the rank of general. Thus, strings were pulled whenever a battalion commander position became vacant.

In theory, naming a battalion commander was within a regimental commander's jurisdiction. In reality, however, generals wanted to make their "fair-haired boys" battalion commanders. A U.S. Army infantry division had only nine infantry battalion commanders, but there were several tens of majors and lieutenant colonels in a division. Naturally, competition became stiff, whenever such a spot opened up. Even if somebody was a general officer, he had to be a lieutenant general to make his "fair-haired boy" a battalion commander in a division that was not under his command.

Well aware of the situation, in order to make Young Oak a battalion commander simultaneously with a promotion to major, Colonel McCaffrey had already secured prior consent from Assistant Division Commander Sink, Division Commander Ferenbaugh, Corps

Commander Hoge and even Eighth Army Commander Van Fleet. All of them had agreed with McCaffrey, as they were well aware of the invaluable contribution made by the 1st Battalion under Young Oak's command during the successful counterattack of the U.N. forces after the Chinese Second Spring Offensive. Although it had not been necessary to secure General Van Fleet's consent in regard to selecting a battalion commander, McCaffrey had decided to get his permission out of courtesy. As evident from the extraordinary measures that McCaffrey had taken, it was exceptionally rare for a brand new major to become a battalion commander.

However, by U.S. Army regulations, if a candidate for promotion was wounded and evacuated to the rear, the promotion process stopped immediately. When the candidate returned, the entire process had to start over from scratch. In Young Oak's case, his official title on document was the "battalion operations officer" despite the de facto role he had carried out as battalion commander. If he had not been wounded on Hill 541, he would have been promoted to a major sometime in mid-June and made battalion commander. This meant he would have been promoted to a lieutenant colonel by mid-July.

But Captain Conmy, who had given his position as battalion operations officer to Young Oak and become the regimental intelligence officer, had been promoted to a major. He went on to become a lieutenant colonel after commanding a battalion for a month. Yet Young Oak still remained a captain due to his serious wounds. Furthermore, by the time Young Oak was discharged from Osaka Hospital, the U.S. Army had discarded the rule that guaranteed promotion of a major who commanded a battalion for a month in combat to lieutenant colonel. To Young Oak, the serious wound at Hill 541 was not only a tragedy in and of itself, but also a great misfortune for his military career.

Chapter 24
Back to Korea

After being discharged from the hospital in Osaka, Japan, Young Oak returned to Korea on August 27, 1951. While he had been hospitalized, truce talks had begun in Korea. The war had entered a stalemate and little had changed on the frontline in the two-and-a-half months since Young Oak was evacuated. The regimental headquarters was located in Jihye-dong, the same village at the bottom of the mountain where Young Oak had been wounded. There were many new faces. Almost a year had passed since the regiment had joined the Korean War.

During the war, the U.S. Army had a "point system" to rotate troops. A frontline soldier received four points a month, while a soldier in the rear was awarded three points. Soldiers who accumulated 36 points were eligible to leave Korea — at least, in theory. The general idea was to send back a frontline soldier after nine months of tour and the others after a year. Perhaps due to the truce talks, the soldiers were becoming increasingly lax as the atmosphere of the war changed drastically. Bob Gibson was a war correspondent for the UPI. He was with the U.S. Army 17th Infantry when Young Oak was hospitalized. He described the changing attitudes of the American soldiers once the truce talks began:

"Out of nowhere, Regimental Commander Bill Quinn began to sport a handlebar moustache. One day, he gathered the entire regiment and ordered every soldier to grow handlebar moustaches just like his. Since most of the soldiers were 18 to 20 years old, some only 16 and 17, it was not easy for them to grow and maintain handlebar moustaches. Since boredom is a soldier's worst enemy in a combat situation, it was one of the many comedic stunts

Colonel Quinn would stage to prevent his soldiers from getting bored."

As if a family member had come back from the dead, Colonel McCaffrey excitedly welcomed Young Oak's return. McCaffrey called in the personnel officer on the spot.

"Make Captain Kim 'Two' immediately, and begin the promotion process right away. You don't have to start from scratch. Start from where it stopped and get it done as fast as you can. Don't worry about the division; I'll talk to them."

'Two' meant the regimental intelligence officer.

The reason why McCaffrey took care of Young Oak's promotion so hastily was because he knew he was going to return to America on the first day of the next month. He only had five days before he was to leave the regiment and he was not sure if his successor would take good care of Young Oak. Therefore, McCaffrey wanted to maximize his jurisdiction as the regimental commander. He turned to Young Oak and said, "I could give you the 1st Battalion today, that's not a problem. But your health is not so good. So stay here and pay attention to your health. Even if your official title is S-2, you don't need to think about it."

Under the sporadic sounds of artillery fire, Young Oak practiced walking and running to get reacquainted with the battlefield. The next day, McCaffrey changed Young Oak's official title to the 1st Battalion XO, executive officer. McCaffrey, who was very bright and considerate, gave Young Oak the time to recover without having the direct responsibility of command. As Colonel McCaffrey hastily tried to promote Young Oak to major and officially made him the battalion executive officer, rumor spread quickly that he would soon be the battalion commander.

Several veteran lieutenants asked him to consider them first if he needed a company commander.

Although Young Oak was not born tall, he was born strong. With daily exercise, in addition to a little time in the hospital, he recovered quickly day by day. Young Oak chose Jeokkun Mountain to exercise and test his legs. The mountain, at 3,250 feet, was the tallest in the regiment's area. On his first attempt, the mountain was so steep that he had to sit down and rest several times. However, by the third attempt, he was able to come down the mountain without rest. He felt as if he had gained almost all of his strength back.

While Young Oak was trying to restore his health, the official order for his promotion to major was issued September 1, only six days after the regimental commander had first given orders to the personnel officer. Although race relations had improved since World War II, overt racial discrimination was still a deep-seeded problem for the United States of America. It was still nearly impossible for an Asian immigrant's son to become a major in the U.S. military, one of the most conservative societies in America. So his promotion to major had historical significance.

There had been a few Asian American majors before him, and Young Oak, a son of an immigrant from Korea, truly understood the meaning of this promotion. When he saluted McCaffrey, McCaffrey congratulated him as if he himself had been promoted. McCaffrey was supposed to leave Korea that day, but due to his successor's unexpected reassignment to the IX Corps G-2 the previous day, his stay was extended.

When Young Oak arrived at the battalion command post after reporting to the regimental commander, Battalion commander Major Jacobson welcomed him warmly. Major Jacobson was a good man and a wonderful administrator, but he knew he wasn't a combat leader. He desired reassignment more than anyone else, and greeted Young Oak with two hands, grateful that Young Oak was to replace him as the battalion commander.

That afternoon an operations meeting was held at the battalion command post. As a newcomer to the battalion, Young Oak silently observed. Perhaps because there had not been a real battle since the truce talks, the meeting was relaxed and without tension. Operations Officer Captain Rice gave a brief and Major Jacobson approved his plan with no further questions. Just before the meeting was about to adjourn, Young Oak asked, "Captain Rice, aren't the mortars of the heavy weapons company a little too far from the frontline company? Don't you think it might be tough to defend the position if the Chinese were to attack?"

"Major, I was told you've been in the hospital for more than two months. You've just arrived today; you may not know the situation here. I've been here for two months. If it's all right with you, how about letting me plan this the way I see fit?"

As if deeply annoyed by the sudden appearance of a superior officer of color with an oak leaf on his shoulders, Captain Rice didn't even try to disguise his disgust and contempt. Young Oak simply assented without saying anything more and the meeting ended without further discussion.

But as irony would have it, the Chinese who had been inactive for some time, chose to attack in the darkness of that very night. It was around 2:30 a.m. when the Chinese concentrated their attack on B Company, which had been thinly deployed around Hudong-ri. Initiating battle with only two platoons at first, enemy forces rapidly reinforced and increased to a battalion-sized attack within minutes. B Company reported 10 rounds of enemy 76 mm mortars hitting the company command post and repeatedly requested for a withdrawal order. Soon, B Company deserted their position and retreated. First Lieutenant Lonsford, who had encouraged his men by walking on the ridge of Chungbyung Mountain with his arms crossed in battle, was no longer in charge of B Company.

As soon as Lieutenant Lonsford had accumulated more than 36 points, Colonel McCaffrey had brought him back to regimental headquarters in order for him to avoid a pointless death, as he highly valued Lonsford's leadership and personal character. In fact, after the truce talks began, McCaffrey brought back to regimental headquarters other young officers who he thought would be pillars in the future of the U.S. Army, if they agreed to go back to America after accumulating their 36 points. He also ordered them not to go near the frontlines.

Upon receiving the report that B Company had deserted their position and was retreating, Young Oak left the battalion headquarters with Captain Rod Lindow to search for them. Moments later, a group of about 100 U.S. soldiers appeared in the darkness; it was soldiers of B Company who were retreating in the direction of battalion headquarters.

Of course, it went without saying that if the heavy weapons company had positioned mortars closer to B Company, the situation would have been better, but it was too late. If the B Company commander had been competent, the situation would have been better. Young Oak ordered Captain Lindow to give them ammunition and to take over B Company. Despite having met him for the first time that very afternoon, Young Oak immediately recognized the World War II veteran to be a highly competent officer. As Young Oak was going to be the battalion commander soon, he knew that the B Company commander was going to be relieved. Young Oak thought of having Lindow as the new commander.

Young Oak instructed Lindow where to position B Company, while repositioning the heavy weapons company as well. Fortunately, the 1st Platoon of B Company was at least holding its position. After quickly stabilizing the situation to an extent, Young Oak turned back to go to battalion headquarters. At that moment, a helicopter appeared and landed near him. Just like at the small cement bridge near Soyang River, it was again Brigadier General Sink, the Deputy Division Commander.

"It's you, Young! It's been a while," Sink said. "Congratulations on your promotion! How is your health?"

"I'm alright, sir. How are you?"

"Fine! When did you get back to the battalion?"

"Yesterday, general."

"How's the situation?"

"I don't know for sure yet. I just sent B Company back to the hill. Would you like to go to the battalion CP?"

"No," Sink said calmly. "Let's go find a cup of coffee."

Entering the battalion mess hall, General Sink casually inquired about the hospital in Osaka, but not the battle situation. After a while, General Sink made to leave.

"Now would you like to go to the battalion CP?" Young Oak asked.

"No. Since you're in charge, I'm not going to worry about the battalion anymore. Take care of everything like before."

He then got back in the helicopter and disappeared into the darkness with the sound of loudly beating propellers. The next morning, the battalion sent A Company to the hill that B Company had lost and recaptured it.

Learning a bitter lesson that day by allowing Captain Rice to neglect Young Oak's advice concerning the mortar position, Battalion Commander Jacobson readily accepted his recommendation to replace the B Company commander with Captain Lindow. The Chinese continued intermittent attacks for two more days, and the battalion suffered 16 KIAs and 26 WIAs that day.

But the frontlines remained unaltered. The Korean War had been changed from a mobile war where both parties waged all-out battles for complete military victory, to a trench war where both parties endlessly shed blood over the dream that truce talks would end the conflict at any given moment. Once they heard the news that truce talks had begun, soldiers expected to go home within a month. Yet, truce talks dragged on into a fourth month while fighting continued. Soldiers started to think they would have to once again spend Christmas in Korea.

The position of the U.S. Army 7th Division changed from the central front to the east-central front when it became part of the X Corps again on October 22, 1951. The 31st Regiment, which had stayed in the rear as the division reserve for the past 15 days, was also ordered to relocate. The destination was Moondeung Valley.

As the regiment was assigned to the frontlines once again, Colonel McCaffrey immediately appointed Young Oak as commander of the 1st Battalion. It was a pre-planned personnel move. Young Oak becoming the battalion commander had much more meaning than his promotion to a major. He became the first minority officer to command a battalion on the battlefield in U.S. military history. On a personal level, he now belonged to an elite group of U.S. military officers. It also assured him promotion to the rank of colonel as well, if he didn't make serious mistakes. However the appointment was much more significant than such promotions.

Military culture is a unique and distinct facet of American tradition. Inheriting the European value that military officers were aristocrats, America has been a nation that has considered and treated its military very preciously. "Warrior culture" is one of the many important faces of American culture. In the U.S. military, tradition dictated that only Caucasians could be commanders. This was why the U.S. Army promoted Japanese Americans to captain, but was very reluctant to make them company commanders at the beginning of World War II. However, people like Young Oak and Sakae Takahashi proved that Asian Americans could also be competent officers and commanders.

In the course of World War II, Asian Americans were made company commanders or battalion operations officer, but never beyond that. Now in the course of the Korean War, a battalion commander of Asian ancestry was born. In other words, during World War II America accepted an Asian American company commander and put him in charge of about 200 Asian American lives. Now, during the Korean War, America accepted an Asian American battalion commander in charge of about 800 Caucasian lives. In this respect, Young Oak becoming a battalion commander had significance, not only in terms of military history but also in the progress of racial equality in America.

When the 31st Regiment was ordered to move, Lieutenant Colonel Jacobson said to Young Oak, "I learned a lot from you that night the Chinese forces attacked us. If I'm ever asked to command a unit again in the future, I'll refuse it. It doesn't fit me. I don't like to make decisions that determine life and death."

Early afternoon, the next day, Young Oak left for Moondeung Valley with his battalion. Young Oak was impressed by the beauty of Korea, and he felt that fall was the most beautiful season of the year.

The village where the regiment had been staying was especially beautiful. But even more beautiful was the color of the autumn leaves covering the mountains and valleys that stretched from Hwachon Reservoir to Moondeung Valley. Perhaps the scenic beauty of Korea during the fall felt different from Italy's because of Young Oak's age and Korean heritage. There was a sense of sadness to the beauty of Korea that permeated the dust of the artillery fire.

The persimmon trees that lined the roads distinguished fall in Korea for Young Oak. The trees had so many ripe persimmons that it looked like somebody had set fires everywhere. The persimmon trees reminded him of his mother.

Mother, who particularly liked persimmons, would always buy four to five of them when they began to appear at the market, even if they were not ripe enough. She then put them on sunny windowsills and waited for them to ripen. As a child, I would be scolded for trying to eat them when they were still unripe. The time that the family spent laughing and chatting over several ripe persimmons was some of the happiest times. At this moment, it's night in America, so Mother is probably sleeping. But tomorrow morning, she will get up early to pray to God and open the store as she always does.

Darkness fell and Young Oak's jeep passed a village near his destination. About half a mile from there, was the place that he chose to set up the battalion command post. Young Oak quickly realized upon his return from the hospital in Japan, the battalion had changed a lot since the truce talks had begun. Not knowing whether the war was going to continue or not, officers gave up their determination for victory, and soldiers were aimless. Consequently, morale became very low. Yet skirmishes still happened frequently. As battalion commander, Young Oak's top priority was to reform battalion leadership and to boost morale. The first step he took was to change the operations officer. Rice, who had recently been promoted to a major, also wanted a transfer when he saw Young Oak become the battalion commander. In consultation with Colonel McCaffrey, Young Oak replaced him as well as the company commander, and then assembled the soldiers. With the regimental commander present, Young Oak spoke to them:

"I'll make one thing very clear. Under no circumstances will you ever harm civilians. In particular, I will not tolerate rape. Such will be punished by the highest possible martial law. This is not only my policy, but also that of our commander who is here. We are at war and you have weapons with live ammunition. Therefore, there will be absolutely no excuse."

Then he added a joke.

"You people are in your twenties? You've had most of the good times in your life and from now on you're more likely to have bad times. So, there's nothing to weep about if you were to die now. Dismissed!"

At that moment, suddenly machinegun fire rang through the air. The regimental commander and others threw themselves to the side of the mountain. But Young Oak kept turning his hat around on a fingertip and was rhythmically hopping as if he was dancing to the music of the machinegun fire. Miraculously, he was not hit.

To boost morale, it's important to remove the soldier's fear of the enemy. But it's also important for soldiers to know and understand each other and develop a sense of unity. What was equally important were fair rewards and punishments. Undeserved rewards were a direct cause of low morale. In turn, soldiers who were killed or wounded in action were not fairly appreciated. In combat, it was impossible to know who did what. After it was over, it was just as impossible to gather exactly what had happened. Soldiers often received medals based on how well letters of recommendations were written rather than how bravely they fought. Sometimes rank determined the level of decoration. For a similar action, a high-ranking officer would receive a Silver Star, when a low-ranking soldier would get a Bronze Star. It was a sort of medal inflation based on rank, rather than facts. In an effort to minimize such frustrations, Young Oak called for Personnel Officer Captain Eugene McCoy, who had been C Company commander until Young Oak was sent to the hospital in Osaka.

"Find me a good writer," Young Oak directed.

Captain McCoy brought several personnel cards to Young Oak. One of them belonged to Corporal Tom Shihan, who had majored in communications in college. Young Oak called him to his office.

"You are our battalion reporter now," Young Oak said to Shihan. "You have two responsibilities. First, find interesting stories and publish them in the Bear Facts. Second, if you come across a soldier who has fought bravely or displayed an exemplary act of courage, you must write it in official documentation accordingly so that he can get a medal. You must also secure the signatures of eyewitnesses. This goes for everybody. But, in this regard, never fail to take care of enlisted men."

The Bear Facts was a newsletter published by the 31st Regiment. Shihan, who became a poet after returning to America, was a diligent and competent writer. He wrote many stories about the men of the 1st Battalion. Sometimes stories of the 1st Battalion dominated the newsletter. Stories of the 1st Battalion also began to frequently appear in the Hour Glass, the 7th Division newsletter, and in the Stars and Stripes, the U.S. military newspaper. Consequently, there was an increase in 1st Battalion soldiers receiving medals. Although there was no official position of a battalion reporter in the U.S. Army, other battalions began to follow in the footsteps of the 1st Battalion.

Another measure taken by Young Oak was the bold sharing of information among his men. One day, Young Oak called up his communications officer and supplies officer and said, "Here's a list of equipment; high-quality microphone, speaker, amplifier, generator...find them as quickly as possible."

Young Oak used the equipment to broadcast communication between the battalion and regimental headquarters. Soldiers could listen to the communication between their battalion commander and regimental commander. When Young Oak gave orders, they understood exactly why he gave them.

According to U.S. Army regulations in those days, an infantry battalion was not allowed to possess a generator of its own or broadcast communications the way Young Oak did, but on battlefields victory triumphed over regulations. The rationale was that Chinese forces couldn't understand English communications anyway and speakers were placed in locations where the the enemy couldn't hear. Furthermore, the speakers could always be turned off, if secrecy was critical. Young Oak firmly believed that the more everyone knew what their commander was thinking and what was going on, the more the battalion could function as one body and ultimately enhance its fighting power.

While Young Oak was busy reorganizing the battalion, Colonel McCaffrey called him.

"Young, will you do me a favor?" McCaffrey asked.
"Yes sir."
"A few days ago, a captain came to the regiment. His name is Frederick Haight. I made him S-2 and he seems intelligent and good. He wants to be a rifle company commander, despite his good family background. His only

drawback is he doesn't have combat experience. How about it? Will you give him a company if you think he is okay?"

Young Oak agreed.

When Captain Haight came, Young Oak asked him, "So, you want to be a rifle company commander? We're at the frontline, and I was told you didn't have combat experience. Aren't you afraid?"

"No sir."

"Really?"

But Young Oak had seen many officers who talked big but performed poorly when real bullets flew. Young Oak decided to watch him for a while and made him the battalion intelligence officer.

McCaffrey had known that Young Oak was looking for a new A Company commander. The incumbent company commander Jerry Lauer was very good. He had been the company commander since Captain Willecke was killed, but he was being transferred to the IX Corps as the aide-de-camp of the Corps commander. Indeed, Young Oak had been looking for the right person to lead Company A for some time.

Young Oak had thought about First Lieutenant Covach. When Young Oak was laid up at the hospital in Japan, Covach was there too and had requested an appointment as company commander from him. At that time, Covach was the A Company executive officer. So making him the company commander might have been an option. However, Covach had only been a first lieutenant for less than a year. Captain Haight was faithful in his duty as intelligence officer, and frequently visited the frontlines to mingle with the soldiers there. When Young Oak noticed soldiers readily following Captain Haight, he decided to give him A Company.

At that time, the U.S. Army 31st Regiment was positioned south of Moondeung Valley. Young Oak's battalion was in charge of the left side, while the 2nd Battalion was in charge of the right side. The valley to the north split the Chinese forces to the west and the North Korean forces to the east. Subsequently, Young Oak's battalion was positioned against the Chinese, with the 2nd Battalion against the North Koreans. So it was a kind of strange situation in that one American regiment was confronting two different enemies. The distance between the American troops and the North Korean troops was so little that there was a fight every week.

There was a small stream called Naedong Stream flowing east to west. South of the stream, Young Oak's battalion was positioned on the mountain whose Korean name meant "General's Hill." North of the stream, the Chinese troops were on Hill 642. The hill had two mountaintops. The higher top was further to the north and 642 meters high—approximately 2,100 feet. Half a mile from there, the lower top stood 500 meters high—approximately 1,640 feet high. The Chinese had only been on the higher top, and on its back side. But just before Young Oak's battalion arrived, they had made a new trench with many curves connecting the two tops.

Young Oak climbed to the top of "General's Hill." As soon as he put the binoculars to his eyes, he instinctively realized that the new Chinese trench was posing fundamental problems. With the trench, the distance between the troops shrank to 1,100 yards. The small Naedong Stream was so shallow that foot soldiers could cross it anytime. This meant a battle could break out very easily at any moment. It would not be a relatively big battle, where a battalion or regiment would engage, and where the outcome could be predicted to a certain extent. Rather, it would be a platoon or company-sized skirmish that would inevitably incur unnecessary casualties to both sides.

On the one hand, Young Oak could not retreat. But on the other hand, he didn't want to engage in such wasteful skirmishes that would unavoidably cost lives with no specific military objective. He concluded that the only solution to avoid such repetitive skirmishes would be to demolish the new trench and increase the distance between the two sides.

So he ordered Captain Haight to demolish the trench and added, "Remember. Begin the attack in the morning when the fog starts to disappear. It's already November and the morning fog is very thick. But if you start the attack too early, the fog will cover the battlefield, so you won't be able to see or call for artillery."

Not every commander was as cautious as Young Oak, but he considered every detail when devising an attack plan. A competent commander had to be a "bean counter," when it came to battle.

On November 4, A Company was east of the Moondeung Valley. Early that morning, it crossed the stream down in the valley, and moved to the line of departure under the cover of the morning fog. As the fog began to disappear, the temperature rose. A Company commenced the attack. On the top of "General's Hill," where Young Oak was following the attack with his binoculars, mortars and machine guns opened fire. Those were the support fire of the heavy weapons company commanded by First Lieutenant Andrew Drenken. The Chinese forces fought back by firing their own machine guns, mortars and artillery, not to mention small arms. Both sides already started suffering severe casualties. Before the attack, regulations had changed, and A Company couldn't have full artillery because Young Oak couldn't mobilize any.

Around that time, the Eighth Army headquarters strictly limited how much artillery could be fired. No matter which side opened fire first, only a certain number of shells could be fired. If a unit's frontline was penetrated and the situation became really serious, then the division commander or corps commander allowed more shells. And that was only for defense, not for offense.

Even before A Company secured the southern mountaintop, soldiers fell like leaves as the enemy ruthlessly fired at them. At a moment like that, life and death was beyond human will. In the midst of heavy enemy fire, A Company occupied the southern mountaintop, and the lead platoon advanced around halfway up the Chinese trench connected to the northern mountaintop. At that moment, Young Oak's face suddenly twitched, as he saw Captain Haight fall. However, he appeared to still be alive, as Young Oak could see Haight's radio operator handing the radio to him. Captain Haight appeared to be talking to someone. Since Young Oak's radio was silent, he thought Haight was giving orders to the company executive officer or platoon leaders. In those days, a U.S. Army company commander carried two different radios: one to communicate with the battalion commander and the other to communicate with the company executive officer and platoon leaders.

As Captain Haight was saying something into the radio, an officer from the rear shot up the ridge like an arrow. Since a U.S. Army officer wore a helmet with a short white horizontal line in the back, it was possible to identify an officer. It was Company Executive Officer First Lieutenant Covach. In the U.S. Army, a company commander typically led an attack just behind the lead platoon, and the company executive officer backed him up in the rear of the company. So Lieutenant Covach had been in the rear. When a commander was killed or severely wounded in combat, morale plummeted. A company-sized battle was no exception. If the company commander was popular among his men, as Captain Haight was, the impact was more detrimental. The company could have collapsed unless effective emergency measures were taken. Lieutenant Covach arrived quickly, and kneeled to see Captain Haight's wound. Painfully breathing, Haight managed to talk to Covach, "You…take…over."

Once he took over the company, Lieutenant Covach exhibited brilliant leadership during the battle, leaving a lasting impression on Young Oak. First, Covach ordered a soldier to carry the severely wounded Haight down the mountain. Then, he took swift actions to lead the attack. Despite bullets flying everywhere, Covach tapped a soldier's back while pointing at a target to shoot with the other hand. He evacuated all the severely wounded. To that extent, Young Oak couldn't believe Covach had been commissioned only a year and a half earlier. Covach calmly led the attack toward the top of Hill 642 like a veteran. Then Covach picked up his radio and this time Young Oak's radio rang.

"Sir, this is it, give me the order to withdraw," Covach said.

"Okay, that's enough," Young Oak said. "Withdraw."

As the company stopped attacking and began to retreat, the Chinese concentrated more fire as if to finish off their ammunition. As a result, many more soldiers were either killed or wounded during the retreat than during the attack. Nonetheless, Lieutenant Covach evacuated all the killed and wounded. He was the last to come down from the mountain.

Company A had taken a severe blow from the battle. Four soldiers were killed, including the company commander, and fifty were wounded. Since Captain

Haight had not explained the objective of the original mission, Lieutenant Covach thought he had failed to accomplish the mission and felt guilty. However, A Company successfully accomplished its mission.

The purpose of the attack was to destroy the new enemy trench and force them to retreat to their original position on the top of and behind Hill 642. The main idea was to get rid of the source of repetitive battles to come. For that reason, Young Oak was ready to send in the other two companies as well, if necessary.

Lieutenant Covach received a Bronze Star for his heroic actions in this battle. It was his second Bronze Star during the Korean War. Later, as a retired colonel, he recalled this battle:

"Major Kim was inspecting our company the day before we were to launch the attack. All of a sudden, artillery shells came pouring over our heads. Everyone hit the ground except one man. Major Kim was still standing and looking into his binoculars to find where the artillery was coming from. He wanted to know exactly where the Chinese artillery was positioned. Artillery shells kept exploding. He was trying to boost our morale."

After the battle, a road was built all the way to the battalion CP on the top of "General's Hill." The road was used for many VIPs from the western world because the CP commanded a good view of the Chinese and North Koreans. When the road was built, Young Oak brought two M4 Sherman tanks to the top. This meant that regardless of the restriction on artillery fire, the battalion was now ready to fire 130 rounds of 76 mm tank shell at any moment. They could penetrate four-inch thick armor with formidable accuracy, if a target was within half a mile—the distance between the destroyed Chinese trench and Young Oak's battalion. The Chinese tried to rebuild the trench several times, but each time, the Sherman tanks opened fire. The

Chinese were not able to rebuild the trench until Young Oak's unit left the valley. As a result, Young Oak's unit didn't have to engage in another battle and avoided further casualties.

The stalemate continued until the Korean War was over a year and eight months later. The area where the American forces were is now part of South Korea and the area where the Chinese forces were is now part of North Korea. "General's Hill" is now in the middle of the DMZ—Demilitarized Zone—still dividing the Korean peninsula today.

Captain Haight was a relative of Sir Winston Churchill, the famous British Prime Minister. His grandmother was related to Churchill's mother by blood. Haight's family made a great fortune in the textile business. The wealth was passed on from generation to generation. The family was influential in America as well as in Europe. After Captain Haight suffered a head wound during the battle at Moondeung Valley, he was evacuated to a Swedish hospital ship off Pusan. After surgery, the U.S. Secretary of Defense Robert Lovett personally called the hospital commander to ask how he was doing. During World War II, Haight had been a liaison officer between American troops and French troops. His persistence took him to Korea during the Korean War.

Haight had always considered his service as a liaison officer in the rear during World War II dishonorable. He secretly went to the Pentagon to go to Korea without letting his family know it. When his father became aware of this and tried to stop him, he told his father that he would inform the media of his interference. When he arrived at the 31st Regiment in Korea, Colonel McCaffrey suggested that he stay at the headquarters, but Haight insisted on going to the frontline. So he came to Young Oak's battalion and got wounded.

In addition to Captain Haight, other people from families of world leaders fought in the Korean War, and some of them were killed or wounded. A son of the Chinese leader Mao Zedong was killed. A son of General Van Fleet, the U.S. Eighth Army Commander, lost his life in Korea too. When General Eisenhower was elected as the President of the United States, his son Lieutenant Colonel John Eisenhower was fighting in Korea. All this showed, from a different angle, another face of the Korean War; it was a battleground of superpowers at the beginning of the Cold War Era.

Chapter 25
Orphanage

When the Korean War entered its second winter and as the truce talks dragged on, Colonel McCaffrey was getting ready to leave Korea. Just like Singles had done for Young Oak during World War II, McCaffrey took special care of Young Oak during the Korean War. Aware of his imminent departure from Korea, McCaffrey invited Young Oak to the regimental headquarters. After a long conversation, McCaffrey finally got around to what was really on his mind.

"Young, I knew that you played an important role in the regiment, however, I hadn't realized just how vital it was until you got wounded," McCaffrey said. "After you were wounded, the company commanders were the same, and other staff officers were the same. But after you left, the battalion was totally different the very next day. Frankly, up until that moment, I'd never thought a single man, whoever he might be, could have so much impact over an entire unit. But after careful consideration, I realized the regiment was successful thanks to you. I don't know whether other people know it or not, but I know it. So, I want to give you a Distinguished Service Cross. Take it."

The Distinguished Service Cross was the second highest military decoration in the U.S., right after the Medal of Honor. It was the highest military decoration that the commanding officer of the U.S. forces in Korea was able to bestow within his jurisdiction. If the commanding officer of the U.S. forces in Korea had recommended the Medal of Honor to a soldier under his command, it could have been given, but it would have required a long process. But a Distinguished Service Cross was not something that a regimental commander could easily hand out either. But both the division commander and the corps commander were well aware of Young Oak's contributions, a DSC to him would be uncontested. It was a decoration that Young Oak had received once in Europe.

"Thank you sir, but I don't want it," Young Oak said.

"What did you say?"

"I said I don't want it."

"What? You... People are dying to get it and you're saying you don't want it? During my entire military career, I've never seen anybody who doesn't want a DSC. Why in the hell don't you want it?"

"You see, I got enough decorations. I got a DSC in Italy. And you already gave me a Silver Star several months ago. One more decoration doesn't make me a braver soldier, so you don't need to take pains to do such a thing. But I really appreciate your offer, sir."

"Young, you're a truly outstanding soldier, but you don't know the Army well. You're from the Officer Candidate School. Since I know you well, I don't care where you're from, but that doesn't mean the entire U.S. Army wouldn't care about it. One more DSC would be helpful in your future career."

"I don't care about it," Young Oak insisted. "If you want to give it, please give it to one of my men, sir."

In the U.S. Army back in those days, to be an officer, you had to graduate from the Military Academy, from ROTC or from OCS. You could also become an officer by battlefield commission, but it was rare. It was not easy for an OCS graduate to become a high-ranking officer and it was almost impossible for him to be a general officer. (Note: A "general officer" is a military term in the U.S. Army to call the rank of all generals collectively). McCaffrey was trying to take care of Young Oak's future career, as he believed Young Oak was a good candidate for a general, but simultaneously knew his being a colored officer from OCS would be an obstacle. McCaffrey respected Young Oak's opinion and finally left Korea before Christmas without giving him the DSC.

On Christmas Day that same winter, Battalion Chaplain Sam Neal came to see Young Oak at battalion headquarters. Captain Neal was staring at Young Oak for a while with a mischievous smile on his face and said, "Major Kim, you're a Korean, aren't you?"

"Yes, I am. But why do you ask?"

Curious to know why the chaplain would bring up his ethnic background, Young Oak waited for him to continue. Although Neal was a captain, he was the battalion chaplain and five years senior to Young Oak, who treated him like an elder brother. Reactivated from the reserve during the Korean War, Neal came to the battalion while Young Oak was at Osaka hospital. Following in the footsteps of his reverend father, Neal was a professor of theology back home in the U.S. during World War II. Despite the fact that he was exempt from active duty, he voluntarily joined the Army. He was captured by Germans during the Battle of the Bulge in 1944, and met the end of the war in a German POW camp. In the camp, he encouraged other prisoners of war with songs he himself composed and was a pillar of optimism and hope. Likewise in Korea, he always stayed with soldiers on the front, even though his hearing was severely damaged by the noise of artillery fire.

"Today our soldiers found a boy; he is only 11 years old and lost his parents in the war," Neal said. "Consequently, they brought the orphan back with them."

Even if Young Oak didn't say anything right away, he understood why Captain Neal was trying to tug at his ethnic heartstrings. The chaplain wanted to take care of the orphan and he needed Young Oak's approval. The word "orphan" brought Young Oak back to the snow-covered

Pusan train station full of children reaching out their small cold hands for help. Young Oak and other officers had given their C-rations to the children, throwing the cans out far from the danger of the moving train.

"They named him Jimmy," Neal continued.

The words coming out of Neal's mouth awakened Young Oak. The decision had already been made. The two officers then began to discuss in detail how to take care of Jimmy. Although it was a good thing to care for a war orphan, he couldn't be kept in a frontline unit. The best solution was to find an orphanage for Jimmy and then provide financial and material support.

"Make sure you ask all the soldiers. Do everything as they want under the condition that they make their own choice. It's not something that is going to be done by orders. Officers should not be involved in the decision-making," Young Oak said to Neal, who was stepping out of the headquarters.

During his sermon the very next Sunday, Chaplain Neal told Jimmy's story and how he was found on a snow-covered road on Christmas Day. His speech was short, but impressive enough to move the soldiers. After the speech, the soldiers held a meeting without any officers involved, as directed by Young Oak. When Chaplain Neal conveyed to Young Oak what the soldiers wanted to do, Young Oak approved it.

The soldiers decided to find a trustworthy orphanage, send Jimmy there and provide the necessary financial support. Each and every soldier agreed to pitch in fifty cents. A delegation was formed to find a proper orphanage. The delegation excluded officers, except for Captain Neal, who was to lead it. After the delegation consulted with higher commands and several Methodist church organizations, it came up with a list. The delegation inspected every orphanage on the list and came to the final selection: the Kyung Chun Ae In Sa. The Korean name meant "Respect heaven and love mankind."

Located in Seoul, the orphanage was established by a Methodist pastor, Chang Shi-wha. In those days, it was known as "Orphanage No. 18" among the U.S. soldiers in Korea. Another Methodist pastor, Leonard Anderson, was in charge of the orphanage. The fact that the orphanage was under the supervision of the Methodist church was one of the reasons why the delegation selected it. When visiting other orphanages, the delegation had discovered that some were clearly more invested in turning a profit than caring for war orphans. Although the Kyung Chun Ae In Sa was the best choice, its financial situation was bleak at best. When the delegation first visited the orphanage, it was already housing 192 children. The orphanage was struggling just to provide warm winter clothes and three meals a day.

Chaplain Neal and Sergeant Thomas Croker entrusted Jimmy to the orphanage with $145 donated by the soldiers. When they returned to the unit, they shared their account of the poor conditions of the orphanage with the others. Soldiers began writing letters to their families back home in America. Soon, their families began to send toys and children's clothes to Korea. Chaplain Neal also sought aid from church organizations in America.

As Young Oak witnessed his men voluntarily helping the orphanage, he pondered a way to provide longer-term financial support. The U.S. Army had just begun issuing cans of beer for its troops in Korea, but Young Oak assessed that his unit was receiving a bit too much alcohol for a frontline unit. He called for the supply officer.

"We have too much beer," Young Oak said to the officer. "Get rid of half the supply. Take care of it and you don't need to report to me."

So, 50 percent of the beer supply was put on the aid list for the orphanage. Many soldiers didn't smoke, including Young Oak himself, who had quit right after World War II. The surplus cigarette supply was put on the list as well. Beer and cigarettes were regular supplies to U.S. soldiers and they were very popular on the Korean black market. Consequently, financial support to the orphanage significantly increased.

While Young Oak's battalion provided cash, beer and cigarettes to the orphanage via the Methodist church, soldiers visited the orphanage from time to time and brought candy and chocolates, which were regular combat rations. When Young Oak saw them carrying too many candies, he ordered the soldiers to take only a limited amount and to give the rest to the church to sell. He was concerned about the children rotting their teeth from too much sugar.

Helping the orphanage was like killing two birds with one stone. Again, officers were not included in the delegation to take goods to the children. For soldiers, visiting the orphanage was like R&R from the frontline. Soldiers who were selected as the "Exemplary Soldier of the Month" were given the privilege to visit the orphanage over several days leave of absence; everybody was waiting for his turn. Leaving the battlefield, soldiers took cash and other goods to the church. They filled their jeeps with chocolates, candies, toys, baseball bats, balls, musical instruments, etc., and went to the orphanage, where they played baseball or sang with the children. It was both good for the children and the soldiers. Without the boring moral lessons, the soldiers learned unconsciously what they were fighting for. They felt immensely proud that they were helping the war orphans. A unit's morale soared when it had a clear goal.

Moon Kwan-ook of Hanam City (in Korea) and Cho Young-ja of Seoul were orphans at the Kyung Chun Ae In Sa during the Korean War and have since become successful citizens. About half a century after the Korean War, they were reunited with Young Oak in Seoul, when he visited Korea after receiving a civilian decoration from the Korean government in Los Angeles in 2003 for over 30 years of community service in America.

"One bitter winter day during the Korean War, my mother was carrying me on her back in a refugee column," Mrs. Cho recalled while sobbing. "It was snowing heavily and it was very cold. Then all of a sudden, airplanes appeared and bombs exploded everywhere. Everybody was killed, including my entire family. When I was crying from hunger and fear in the middle of the snow, I saw soldiers coming from far away. They were Americans. They took me to an orphanage, which was the Kyung Chun Ae In Sa. There, I learned to play the harmonica from American soldiers. I am who I am today because of them, and I sincerely thank those men."

"My family lived in Seoul, when the Korean War broke out," Moon recalled while shedding tears. "Before the Incheon Landing in September 1950, an air raid killed my parents and my youngest sibling. The remaining five brothers and sisters were separated. The Korean police found me and sent me to the Kyung Chun Ae In Sa. I remember U.S. soldiers teaching me songs in English there."

Perhaps, since Cho majored in music in college and Moon dreamed of becoming a vocalist, they might have been musically inspired by the songs and harmonicas in the orphanage. Cho later became a reverend's wife, and Moon majored in mathematics in college and eventually became a successful businessman. However, the tragic irony was that both of them lost their parents to American air raids.

The 1st Battalion was the only unit of the U.S. Army on the frontline in Korea to adopt an orphanage. With its consistent support, the orphanage became one of the most financially stable orphanages in Korea at the time. It grew exponentially, taking in around 500 children during the war who all grew up to become artists, musicians, scientists, pastors and successful businessmen in Korea or in the U.S.

Young Oak only visited the orphanage once. He wanted to make sure that his battalion would support the orphanage not only because its commander happened to be of Korean ancestry. The battalion's support continued for several years after his departure from Korea. American soldiers, who later met with him in the U.S. after serving in the battalion in Korea, gave him news about the orphanage. But the news discontinued after the mid-1950s, when the orphanage closed down due to an unfortunate litigation regarding property ownership. The children were dispersed to other orphanages in Korea. Today, the site is occupied by a Catholic church.

Chapter 26
The Iron Triangle

In the summer of 1952, the Korean War entered its third year, the truce talks dragged on, and nobody knew when it would end. The talks endlessly debated where the military demarcation line would be drawn. When both sides almost agreed upon the outline, they disagreed over POW exchanges. The U.N. forces wanted to not send back anti-communist POWs, and the Communists wanted a package deal, insisting there could not be any anti-communists among POWs in the custody of the U.N. forces.

While waiting for the truce talks to end, both sides made their respective frontlines invincible fortresses across the Korean peninsula. Both sides had to make huge sacrifices to occupy one mountain. In this situation, where neither side could finish the war with a total military victory, the conflict shifted from a military war into a political war. Depending on the progress of the truce talks, the battles became fierce or dormant. The truce talks were meant to end the war, but whenever progress in the talks stalled, fierce battles took place. The regimental or division newspapers carried news about the truce talks every day, but over time, the soldiers stopped paying attention to them.

Around this time, the Iron Triangle, the most important strategic area in the central front, was divided in two. The upper part of the triangle was occupied by the Chinese forces and the lower part was occupied by Young Oak's U.S. Army 7th Division. Since the end of April 1952, the 31st Regiment moved to Kumwha, at the bottom right point of the triangle. Ninety days after the relocation, Regimental Commander Noel Cox was wounded by a Chinese mortar. Colonel Cox was personally directing tanks attacking the Chinese. His executive officer, who was with him, was also wounded. When Colonel Cox was evacuated, the regiment was notified that "Jade 3" was going to replace him. "Jade 3" was a code name for the X Corps operations officer. So the regiment had a new commander, Colonel Lloyd Moses. Since the exchange of a regimental commander took place in every war, people didn't pay much attention to this one. But when Colonel Moses took over the 31st regiment, he made an enormous impact on the war. As the stalemate continued and as the war devolved into a war without decisive victory or defeat, high-ranking, ambitious U.S. officers began to use the war as a launch pad for their own promotions.

Around that time, Young Oak met Colonel William Westmoreland for the first time.

After Colonel Moses became the regimental commander of the 31st, the U.S. Army 187th Regiment was suddenly attached to Young Oak's division and came to the Iron Triangle. This parachute regiment had fought all over Korea and suffered severe casualties, so it had moved to a rear area in the south to rest when the frontline stabilized. But as soon as Colonel Westmoreland became the regimental commander, the regiment moved again to the frontline. Then, a rumor circulated among American soldiers, saying that the regiment was relocated to the frontline because the U.S. Army wanted to take care of Colonel Westmoreland's military career, on record. Even though Westmoreland had many supporters in the U.S. Army, he had never commanded a regiment in combat; this was an obstacle to his promotion to a general officer. Westmoreland was three years senior to McCaffrey at West Point. Thanks to World War II, both were promoted to colonel within several years after commission, but later demoted to lieutenant colonels after the war.

When the 187th Regiment came to the triangle, it was placed between the 31st and the 32nd. Whenever there was a new formation, the commanders of two neighboring units had to agree exactly where their units physically met. This was to make sure there was no empty space between the two friendly forces. At that time, the 2nd Battalion of the 187th Regiment and the 1st Battalion of the 31st Regiment had to remain side-by-side. So the two battalion commanders had to agree upon an actual contact position between their battalions. As the 2nd Battalion of the 187th Regiment arrived earlier than the rest of the regiment, Young Oak and the 2nd Battalion commander inspected the frontline together, and agreed upon their contact point.

The 2nd Battalion commander was a lieutenant colonel, who got a battlefield commission during World War II. He was a very competent officer. They walked the terrain for more than two hours to find a proper place. It was located south of the northernmost position of Young Oak's battalion and north of where the parachute regiment was originally scheduled to be. So the two battalion commanders picked a point somewhere midway between the two battalions. With such an easy compromise, they shook hands and departed. That night, Colonel Moses called Young Oak.

"Westmoreland didn't like that agreement. Would you be willing to meet him up there next morning?"

"I think the agreement was made, sir," Young Oak replied.

"I don't think you understand. All four of us will meet there again tomorrow."

The next day, Moses, Westmoreland, the 2nd Battalion commander of the 187th Regiment and Young Oak met at the contact point. The four officers repeated what the two battalion commanders had done the previous day. They discussed all the pros and cons, and all the different scenarios. During the discussion, Young Oak was very surprised. He was also familiar with Westmoreland's wonderful reputation of being a very bright officer and a rising star in the U.S. Army. But that day, when Westmoreland was enumerating his reasons why the contact point had to be moved to a place of his preference, there was absolutely nothing reasonable about it from a military viewpoint. In Young Oak's eyes, Westmoreland was an officer who actually knew nothing about the infantry, which was different from his reputation, or he was simply an officer who cared about his own record and not the safety of the soldiers. When the discussion was over, Westmoreland turned to his battalion commander and asked, "Don't you agree we're better off back here?"

The new point suggested by Westmoreland would have made his regiment impregnable, but would have easily exposed Young Oak's battalion to the Chinese. Young Oak guessed Westmoreland might have talked to Moses and to his battalion commander as well. But Westmoreland hadn't judged his battalion commander right. The World War II veteran, who had come up through the ranks from NCO, answered straightforwardly.

"No, sir, I still stick to what I had agreed upon."

Then Moses asked Young Oak, "Wouldn't you be willing to change?"

"No sir," Young Oak answered.

So they left there. During the middle of the night, Moses called Young Oak again.

"You know, I talked to Westmoreland, and I agreed to the change," Moses said.

"Sir, I would like you to put that in writing because if anything should happen, and we get overrun, I want it clear that this was an agreement between you and Colonel Westmoreland."

Young Oak's battalion would be in an untenable position, making its flank very vulnerable. Fortunately, the enemy didn't attack. After this experience, Young Oak assumed Westmoreland would become a general someday. Young Oak also thought Westmoreland was someone who would sacrifice his men at any moment for his own glory. From a broader perspective, men of the 31st Regiment were also his subordinates. But in this instance, Westmoreland at least took care of his own soldiers. But what was worse was Moses' decision. If American troops had suffered casualties because of this, it would have been on Moses.

Moses had made the compromise to make Westmoreland happy. Both were colonels, but their respective influence within the U.S. Army was different. Long before the incident, many people in the U.S. Army knew Westmoreland was a rising star. The 187th Regiment was actually sent back to Japan only a couple of months after this incident and Westmoreland, with his record of having commanded a frontline regiment during the Korean War, became a brigadier general. It was later known that Westmoreland's name had already been on the so-called "rocket list."

The list was created by General Dwight Eisenhower. People said General Eisenhower had ordered his personnel officer to come up with a list of 10 of the most young and promising high-ranking officers who had made outstanding accomplishments during World War II. Some said he originally ordered 12 and others said 15. Westmoreland eventually became a four-star general and commanded the U.S. troops in Vietnam during the Vietnam War.

Moses' ambition, which risked his soldiers to make Westmoreland happy, actually brought about a disaster. It was already germinating when he visited Young Oak that summer. As he looked at Triangle Hill, stretched from the "Papa San," Moses asked Young Oak, "Major Kim, what do you think about attacking the Twin Hills?"

"Papa San" was a nickname that American soldiers called the Osung Mountain. "San" means mountain in

Korean. They might have called it "Papa San," because the mountain was the highest in the region, meaning "Father Mountain" of all the mountains in the region. Triangle Hill was a group of hills with a shape of an upside-down triangle, composed of three hills. American soldiers called Hill 598, Pike's Peak and Jane Russell Hill. They stretched from "Osung Mountain."

Immediately understanding what Moses had in mind, Young Oak was very surprised. The Twin Hills referred to Hill 598 and Pike's Peak. American soldiers called the two hills "Twin Hills" because the third hill was not easily visible from the American position. Although Moses took the formality of asking Young Oak's opinion, in actuality, he was asking for Young Oak's consent. Among the three battalion commanders under Moses' command, Young Oak was the only one who had combat experience, particularly in attacking enemies. Even though Moses' question was short, Young Oak could read his mind.

Colonel Moses was a very brave World War II veteran. After he came to the Iron Triangle as the regimental commander, he was wounded in the stomach while inspecting a new position. Even though he was the regimental commander, he also took part several times in patrols behind the enemy line. But he was not from West Point. He was from the University of South Dakota ROTC. Back in those days, it wasn't easy for an ROTC graduate to become a general officer in the U.S. Army, even if he had a record of commanding a regiment in combat. Although Moses was a full colonel, he had been relatively, recently promoted. On top of that, at 48 years old, there was almost no possibility of his becoming a general.

But he was very ambitious and wanted a star on his helmet. There was nothing wrong with a soldier's wish to be a general. But in his case, it was already almost impossible, unless he somehow caught the special attention of high-ranking generals. This was why he said he wouldn't need the airplane, when he was flying an L-17 to come to the 31st Regiment from the X Corps Headquarters. He had desperately wanted a position where he could prove his ability. The commanding officer of the 31st Regiment, which had confrontations with the Chinese, was such a position.

Since Young Oak's battalion had moved to the region several months prior, he knew the terrain very well. As the American troops' position was lower than Twin Hills and the Chinese position was higher than Twin Hills, it would be a difficult and dangerous attack. Even if Americans succeeded in taking Twin Hills, they would be closer and more exposed to the enemy because they would have nothing to hide behind. Even with a victory, there was nothing to gain. To be able to stay on Twin Hills, Americans had to secure the third hill, Jane Russell Hill. But then, even after occupying all three hills, the highest possible mountain that Americans would be able to have was 598 meters high. On the other hand, the Chinese would be still on Papa San, which was 1,062 meters high.

A bigger problem was that beyond Papa San, the road went straight to Pyongyang, capital of North Korea. From the viewpoint of the U.N. forces, occupying Papa San would allow them to attack Pyongyang. From the viewpoint of the Communists, giving up Papa San to the U.N. forces would mean that the next real battle would be the defense of Pyongyang. Because of this, Young Oak already had the answer to Colonel Moses' question, long before he came in as the new regimental commander. Washington did not want to escalate the war, and it would not approve of such a major operation.

As the Chinese had finished strengthening their positions utilizing the truce talks, driving them out of there would not be easy. If the destination were Pyongyang, then the U.N. forces would execute an all-out attack all across the frontline. In that case, the story might have been different. Otherwise, taking one or two hills was not worth sacrificing lives. It would be obvious that Washington would not reinforce soldiers and equipment, because it would not allow such an attack.

"No, that's not a good idea, sir," Young Oak replied to Moses. "We must not do that. No. 1, even though Triangle Hill is only tens of meters higher than us, to attack the hill, we will have to come down the hill where we are now, then go up the hill toward Triangle Hill. Besides, its ridge is too narrow for soldiers to attack abreast. This means we will have lots of casualties. No. 2, one battalion will not be enough to take it. Two battalions won't do it and most likely, a full regiment couldn't do it. No. 3, even if we successfully take the hill, we can't stay there. Papa San is so strategically important that the entire 7th Division wouldn't do it. Unless the Eight Army wants Pyongyang and more, a frontal attack of the mountain, which the enemy made a fortress of, would be suicide. Even if Pyongyang is the destination, we would have to avoid a frontal attack of the mountain. If we want to attack Papa San, we should turn around and attack from the rear. We should mobilize at least two divisions and the Air Force as well. If we don't want to go to Pyongyang, we shouldn't touch Papa San."

Moses listened quietly as Young Oak continued.

"If we are to succeed in taking Triangle Hill, we would have no choice but to retreat. Then, why would we take it from the start? But if we go to Triangle Hill, we would be more than 460 meters lower than the enemy, we will lose the distance and there will be nowhere to hide. We will be exposed to the enemy. If you really want to advance, you should do it with Washington's approval. Frontal attack of a prepared enemy is absolutely not an option. Two divisions won't do it. If our government and the U.S. Army decided to occupy Pyongyang, it'd be different. But any other objective falling short of it wouldn't justify attacking Triangle Hill."

Colonel Moses was silent. But it didn't mean he consented. Instead, he broke the silence by alluding to the Civil War.

"General Grant forced enemy casualties by continuous engagements," said Colonel Moses. "He needed a complete victory, because the Lincoln Administration wanted it."

The conversation continued, but neither side gave in. After that day, Moses came back to Young Oak two or three times more to argue his point, but they reached an impasse. Several days later, Moses came back again to restart the talks.

"Sir, I've already told you my position many times," Young Oak said decisively. "Attacking Triangle Hill would waste lives and time."

Colonel Moses never raised the issue again with Young Oak. Ten days later, Young Oak became aware that the regimental staff officers were designing a plan to attack Triangle Hill. Even though he was not involved in the attack plan, Young Oak knew that once such a plan was established, it would be implemented and his battalion would be a part of it.

Around this time, Young Oak accumulated more than enough points for rotation. As he came to Korea in March of the previous year, he scored 36 points around Christmas. During the Korean War, the U.S. Army made it a rule to send a soldier with 36 points back to America, if he wanted. Young Oak chose to stay in Korea, because he wanted to fight for Korea. Promotion was another motivation. Colonel Cox, who came as the regimental commander after Colonel McCaffrey, had said to him, "If you stay with me, I'll make you a lieutenant colonel."

But the situation was changing fundamentally. If he stayed longer, he would have to issue attack orders to his soldiers for a battle without a proper cause and many of them would never come back alive. At any rate, the Korean War was already a war that neither side could finish with a thorough military victory. Young Oak decided to leave Korea. When he went to Colonel Moses, the regimental commander mentioned the promotion again.

"If you stay, I'll make you a lieutenant colonel," Moses said.

"Thank you sir, but I heard the same promise before and it was not kept," Young Oak said. "I don't think Colonel Cox didn't keep his promise because he didn't want to. I could have gone home more than six months ago. Among all the U.S. battalion commanders in Korea today, I am probably the only one who fought all over the peninsula. All those who fought with me have left already. Now, I want to go home too."

By U.S. Army regulations, Moses had no choice but to let him go. On September 1, Young Oak left the Iron Triangle to take a flight to Japan. Korea, his father's country, which was getting smaller and smaller down below the airplane, was still a heartbreaking war-torn land.

Young Oak's document said his next destination was the U.S. Army Infantry School at Fort Benning, Georgia. War heroes were selected as instructors at the infantry school and it was a position promising a promotion. One day in Fort Benning, Georgia, a sergeant came up to Young Oak and introduced himself.

"You don't remember me, but I was the C Company First Sergeant of the 31st Infantry in Korea in the summer of 1951. You were my battalion commander."

"No, I was three. Major Warden was the battalion commander."

"No, he was the battalion commander on paper. Don't give me that bullshit. You can bullshit other people, but you can't bullshit soldiers. I know who gave the orders and I know who made the plans and all that. I just want you to know you were the best battalion commander I ever had during my 30-year service in the Army. Everybody in Fort Benning knows that you were my battalion commander and you were the best battalion commander in the United States Army."

While at Fort Benning, Young Oak heard about "Operation Showdown." It was a joint operation of the U.S. Army 7th Division and the Korean Army 2nd Division. Originally the operation's objective was that one U.S. battalion would take Triangle Hill and one Korean battalion would take another hill to the east in five days. The operation unfolded exactly as Young Oak had predicted while objecting to Colonel Moses' attack plan. Looking at the original plan, it was unlikely to begin the operation with two battalions and finish within five days. Instead, two divisions were mobilized and the operation lasted for 42 days with tremendous casualties to both sides. The U.N. forces suffered 8,000 casualties, which was 40 times more than the initial expectation. Chinese casualties were 12,000.

The 1st Battalion, which was under a new commander after Young Oak left, was also involved, and suffered many casualties. The American troops once took more than two-thirds of Triangle Hill, but they couldn't defend it. So the U.S. Army came up with a "smart" exit plan. The IX Corps ordered the U.S. Army 7th Division to hand the battle over to the Korean Army 2nd Division, this way, the American's direct involvement in the battle was over. But the problem was the Korean division was already involved in another fierce battle in "Operation Showdown."

Considering the overall situation, leaving both battles to the Korean division was absolutely unreasonable from a military point of view. The Chinese retook the two hills within one week. Several days later, the IX Corps ordered the Korean division to give up the battle at Triangle Hill. So the battle at Triangle Hill was won by the Chinese. Two weeks later, "Operation Showdown" finished. The frontline around Triangle Hill was exactly the same as before the operation, and it remained like that until the war came to a halt in an armistice agreement.

But Colonel Moses boasted of his "victory," saying that Triangle Hill was in the hands of Americans when it was handed over to the Koreans. His own assessment was different from that of General Mark Clark, U.N. forces Commander in Tokyo, who didn't consider it a success. Later, the Russian Army analyzed this battle in detail and concluded that the winner was the Chinese. With this battle, the U.S. 31st Regiment suffered devastating damage, but Colonel Moses got the star that he so desperately wanted. He was eventually promoted to a major general.

"Operation Showdown" was the last offensive operation of the U.N. forces that year. It inflicted 20,000 casualties in total to both sides. The truce talks were postponed until the next spring.

Chapter 27
Blue House

Exactly 10 years after the Korean War ended in an armistice agreement, Young Oak went back to Korea in the summer of 1963. This time, he was a military advisor to the Korean Army. He had been promoted to lieutenant colonel when he was in the 7th Army in Europe after being an instructor at Fort Benning. It was a promotion from "below the zone." In the U.S. Army in those days there was a certain zone of seniority that a lieutenant colonel was picked from, but 10 percent of the promotion came from below the zone.

When Young Oak got to his office in Korea, everybody was standing around the table as he was being introduced. Then the phone rang; it was for him.

"Goddamn it, you dumb son of bitch," someone was shouting through the phone. "What the hell are you doing over there?"

At first, Young Oak didn't know who it was. But soon, he recognized the voice. It was Mel Hughston, the man who kicked Young Oak out of the G-3 tent, when he first arrived at the 7th Division Headquarters in Korea. Later, when Young Oak was commanding the 1st Battalion, Hughston thought Young Oak was the greatest battalion commander he'd ever met. Since then, Young Oak became one of his fair-haired boys. Through Hughston's military career, he always took special care of Young Oak. At the time, when he called Young Oak, he was Brigadier General, G-3 of the Eighth Army.

"Shit, if you're going to go anywhere, you should be across the street working for me," Hughston yelled.

The Eighth Army Headquarters was across the street from KMAG, the Korean Military Advisory Group.

"You're dumber than I ever thought you were," Hughston continued. "Shit, if you're over here, you can have any job you want in the G-3 section. I'm one of your best supporters. I'm so goddamned mad, I can't talk. Get your ass over here across the street in five minutes."

"Thank you, Mel..."

"Don't give me any of that shit. You get your ass over here, right now."

General Hughston's voice was so loud that the other people in the office could hear it. When Young Oak hung up the phone, they asked him, "Who the hell is that? He sounds mad as hell."

"Oh, that's General Mel Hughston."

"General Hughston? You mean the Eighth Army G-3?"

"Yes, I'd better go. I've got to go over and see him."

It took Young Oak about 10 minutes to find Hughston's office. He knew it was right across the street, but didn't know what office he was in. When he finally found it, he went in and said, "I am very delighted to see you, Mel, it's been a long time."

"Good thing 10 minutes has passed. I was so goddamned mad, I couldn't talk, I still can't. You dumb little snot," he yelled. "Goddamn you, why the hell aren't you over here? You could be the Eighth Army plans officer, which is one of the most important jobs in Korea. Instead you're over there, being an advisor to some goddamned...I don't give a goddamn what the hell his rank is. Sit down and explain to me why you're over there."

Young Oak's original assignment was to be the operations officer of the Eighth Army Headquarters, but a family matter changed it. When Young Oak got through explaining everything to him, Hughston said, "This is a big mistake on your part. Militarily, your future depends upon what kind of jobs you have. I'm not saying you can't do a great job over there, you will. But no matter how good it is, it's not the same as working over here. If you work here, I am going to make all the difference in the world to you. If you work for me, you will get the absolute highest rating possible. I would recommend you to be a general, and over there, you're working for second-rate officers. Sure, a lot of them are full colonels and West Pointers, but none of them are going to make general. They all know it. They're bitter. Bitter people don't give good efficiency reports. So, be prepared for a bad report, no matter how great a job you do. I'm just sick that you're over there, wasting your talent, instead of being over here. Regardless of what happens, I want you to stay in close touch with me while I'm here."

One day General Hamilton Howze, Commander-in-Chief of the U.N. Command, called Major General Yancey, Commander of the KMAG.

"Come see me now with Lieutenant Colonel Kim. Don't tell anybody about this."

Yancey got Young Oak and reported to General Howze.

"Major General Yancey, I have a special assignment for Lieutenant Colonel Kim. I can't tell you what it is. Just keep in mind that he is my special envoy from now on. He is to report directly to me. So don't try to understand it," Howze said. "If Kim thinks it necessary, he can leave his office at any time for this matter. Once again, you have to keep this confidential. You can leave now."

When Yancey left, General Howze said to Young Oak, "You did a wonderful job on the emergency mobilization plan last time."

"Thank you, sir."

General Howze appreciated Young Oak's service at KMAG when he had overhauled the Korean military's emergency mobilization plan in preparation for another war in Korea. He also launched the first two missile units of the Korean Army in 1964; the 111th Antiaircraft Battalion and the 222nd Antiaircraft Battalion.

"I hadn't been aware of it, but you were also famous in Italy during WWII," Howze said.

General Howze, who also fought in Italy during World War II, mentioned several things about Italy during the war, and then got to the point.

"You know General Myung-shin Chae well, don't you?" he asked.

It seemed that General Howze had done a thorough background check on Young Oak. He knew Young Oak and Major General Chae of the Korean Army were comrades-in-arms during the Korean War; Young Oak commanded a U.S. Army battalion when Chae commanded a Korean regiment right next to his battalion. The two war heroes met each other again, when Chae went to Fort Benning after the war. General Howze began to explain everything.

At that time, the U.S. was in charge of all the supplies to the Korean military. Suddenly the U.S. found out that the Korean Army was getting double supplies for two infantry battalions. The Eighth Army began investigating and soon the truth was revealed. When President Chung-hee Park initiated a military coup in 1961, two Army battalions from the frontline were also mobilized. After the coup was successful, they weren't sent back, but were kept to guard him and the Blue House of Korea. In the meantime, the divisions that the two battalions had belonged to, fell short two battalions. So they formed two new battalions with the same name as the old battalions and didn't inform the U.S. Eighth Army.

Samuel Burger, the American Ambassador to Korea, and General Howze insisted that the two battalions had to be dissolved. General Howze's position was that frontline units couldn't take any losses. To President Park, it would remove the most reliable protection he had. So he strongly objected and the U.S. threatened to cut off all military assistance. All three—Ambassador Burger, General Howze and President Park—were very stubborn. This initially minor issue was mixed with their egos and pride and became a complicated diplomatic issue between the U.S. and Korea. General Howze was trying to find a solution to the problem by relying on Young Oak and General Chae's friendship.

Even though the process was rough and took several months, it worked. The compromise made between the two friends and approved by their respective bosses was very simple: the two old battalions would change names and stay to protect President Park and the Blue House and the two new battalions would carry the old names. The two old battalions were later merged into one unit, which became the most important military force protecting the Blue House.

Chapter 28
Candlelight

Young Oak retired as a colonel in 1972. Some people who knew him and the U.S. Army very well said that one of the biggest reasons he was not promoted to a general officer was his health; he suffered from too many war wounds, particularly the one inflicted during the Korean War. It was a possibility because he retired officially with 85 percent disability. Young Oak himself also believed this. Yet others like Colonel John Covach (Ret., U.S. Army) believed Young Oak's racial background was another major obstacle. The Civil Rights Act was legislated in 1964, the same year Young Oak got the order for promotion to a colonel, but the legislation didn't mean actual equality in every corner of American society.

What was waiting for Young Oak after his discharge from the military was a daily struggle with the aftereffects of his war injuries. After he was wounded in Korea, he underwent approximately 40 major surgical procedures. Nerves were cut in eleven parts of his body, including two in the spine. He developed a significant limp.

His primary and immediate concern was to deal with the unbearable pain. Doctors injected morphine to reduce the discomfort temporarily. Young Oak knew these periodic injections, without any other treatment, meant doctors had given up searching for a medical solution. This went on for more than a year and he became increasingly exhausted and demoralized from the pain he had to fight daily. Naturally, Young Oak couldn't think about his future. He was simply tired from the wounds that wouldn't go away. Wounds he had suffered during the Korean War and had hindered his promotion to even the rank of lieutenant colonel for eight years and likely played a large part in denying his promotion to the rank of general officer.

His wounds were so severe they ultimately compelled him to retire from the military, and continually haunted him with unbearable agony.

When Young Oak had reached a time of deep despair, the UCLA School of Medicine offered him a glimmer of hope. The school was experimenting with traditional Chinese medicine. However, since the UCLA School of Medicine was concerned with its reputation as a world-renowned western medical facility, the Chinese medical research was done in an obscure basement of the university. Nonetheless, having heard of the new program, Young Oak visited the UCLA Medical Center. They recommended acupuncture treatment. At first, treatment seemed dubious at best. When the doctors put the needles into his body, the pain went away, but returned as soon as they pulled the needles back out. The doctors then recommended self-hypnosis treatment in conjunction with the acupuncture treatment. Of course, self-hypnosis treatment was not as simple as it sounded; Young Oak had to completely alter his lifestyle, dietary needs and exercise regimen. But if it was possible to find reprieve from his unbearable physical suffering, Young Oak was willing to make drastic changes in his life. After a few months, inexplicably, the compound treatment worked. Young Oak was remarkably free from pain and began to live a new life, like a normal person, almost.

When it was apparent that Young Oak was finally able to resume a normal life, both political and business communities tried to lure the war hero to champion their causes. Refusing all their generous offers, Young Oak instead, dedicated his entire life and resources to helping others and serving communities in need.

He kept the promise he had made to himself when he witnessed the heroic deaths of Takeba, Eaton and others in the Battle of Monte Cassino in Italy during World War II:

"If I survive this war, I will devote my life to the betterment of the community I belong to."

He had also decided long ago that he would never look back at the glory of the past. He became a lifelong defender of the civil rights of children, youth, elders, victims of domestic violence, the disabled and racial minorities. During wartime, he was a shield protecting freedom and democracy with the power of guns and artillery. After his retirement, Young Oak became a candle that shined in the world through the power of his love and service. For more than 30 of his retired years, Young Oak dedicated his life to serving and helping minorities and underprivileged individuals.

This chapter briefly discusses Young Oak's public service records in three different sections: for the Korean American community, the Japanese American community, and the communities of minorities, women and children.

Young Oak was the founding father of the Korean Health Education and Information Research Center (KHEIR). At first, KHEIR was a non-profit health organization that provided health-related information and services to first-generation Korean immigrants with limited English-language abilities. Today, KHEIR also provides rehabilitation services for handicapped and convalescent patients, regardless of their race and ethnicity. KHEIR has become a highly reputable non-profit organization that serves underprivileged populations mainly in the Los Angeles area, including but not limited to Korean Americans.

Young Oak had managed to persuade Los Angeles County Supervisor Kenneth Hahn, who was one of his closest friends and the father of former Los Angeles City Mayor James Hahn, to provide financial support for the

Korean American community. Because of the recession at the time, Los Angeles County and city governments were trying to cut back on existing programs, making it nearly impossible to receive funding for a new program. Yet, Young Oak went in person to see Kenneth Hahn and somehow successfully requested and received $60,000 to conduct a research survey on assessing the needs of the Korean American community.

It turned out the most desperately needed agency in the Korean American community was a health clinic. Accordingly, funds were allocated to establish KHEIR in 1986. Despite the widespread skepticism concerning his plan, Young Oak pursued his vision steadfastly and ultimately succeeded in launching KHEIR.

"We had a very good plan," Young Oak recalled. "Although a clinic was something our government should have been providing in the first place, it wasn't just going to happen, because the government lacked the budget. I knew we could do it at half the cost of a governmental organization. If we could just prove that we had a solidly effective program, the government would have to provide us with the necessary support."

He not only successfully secured funding but efficiently educated others on how to build an infrastructure and networks with mainstream American society to ensure longevity for the center. Consequently, KHEIR emerged as one of the most prominent and visible non-profit organizations of the Korean American community in the U.S with an average annual budget of approximately $4.5 million.

A quintessential adage Young Oak left was: "Do all the groundwork, but let others take the credit for it. It's important to allow a person to take pride in what he or she has done for an organization. Nobody can do it alone and everybody has to work as a team. It doesn't matter who came up with the idea. I've never claimed ownership of anything myself."

Thus, only a handful of Korean Americans in Los Angeles are even aware of Young Oak's role in building the many non-profit organizations that exist or prosper because of him today. Young Oak wanted others to take the credit; he knew he could stay behind the scenes and still inspire others to keep going. It's shameful that the Korean American community simply did not give him the credit he deserved, nor did it ever quite properly show its appreciation for someone so dedicated to its causes.

Young Oak also played a major role in securing funding for the Koreatown Youth and Community Center (KYCC) in Los Angeles. As a board member of the Los Angeles chapter of the United Way, Young Oak helped obtain initial funding to get KYCC on its feet. As a result, KYCC has emerged as a well-known non-profit youth organization with an average annual budget of approximately $4 million that serves not only the Korean American community but more importantly, promotes the participation of multiracial and multiethnic youth communities in Los Angeles. Young Oak also played a key role in founding the Korean American Museum (KAM), a place dedicated to housing, recording and displaying Korean American immigration history. At 84, Young Oak was once again asked to serve as chairman of the Board of Directors of KAM in 2003.

Young Oak also played an instrumental role in developing the Korean American Coalition (KAC) which has become one of the most important national voices for the Korean American community in the United States. The KAC has established a wide national network and emerged as one of the most vital Korean American political organizations in America today. The Korean American community learned invaluable lessons on the importance of maintaining their ethnic identity and heritage in the aftermath of the Los Angeles civil unrest of 1992. These four non-profit organizations founded or raised under Young Oak's leadership, along with the Korean American Family Service Center (KAFSC), serve as the most central and influential Korean American organizations in the United States. Young Oak most fruitfully dedicated his life to serving the Korean American community.

Young Oak also served as chairman of the "Go For Broke Foundation," which was the World War II Japanese American Veterans Association. This organization was developed into the "Go For Broke National Education Center" today. As chairman, he fought for and successfully led the civil rights campaign of Japanese Americans, which naturally resulted in benefiting other minorities. This organization has been the heart and pride of Japanese Americans. Although the Japanese American population constitutes only about 0.5% of the entire population of the United States, the Japanese American community has generated many high-ranking political leaders among all the racial minority groups in the United States.

Today, one U.S. cabinet member, one U.S. Senator and three U.S. Representatives of the House are Japanese Americans. The first Asian American Chief of Staff of the U.S. Army was a Japanese American as well. Utilizing their political clout, Japanese Americans have been able to exert tremendous influence over the formulation and implementation of policies positively affecting the Japanese American community. In addition, the Japanese American community has been able to influence both America's foreign policies over northeast Asia and domestic policies concerning minority issues in America. The Japanese American community has become increasingly influential after World War II due to the sacrifices and contributions made by the Japanese American soldiers who fought in the war and also due to the rise of Japan as a major international force. Although Young Oak is a Korean American, he was able to transcend his ethnic background and serve as one of the most important leaders of Japanese Americans.

Young Oak made significant contributions not only to the Japanese American community, but ultimately to the progress of civil rights of all racial minority communities in the United States.

One of the most invaluable contributions made by him was the successful establishment of the "Go For Broke Monument," erected in downtown Los Angeles in 1999, to commemorate the sacrifices and contributions of all the Japanese American soldiers who served during World War II. Unlike the Korean War Veterans Memorial dedicated in 1995 in Washington D.C., which commemorates the sacrifices and contributions of all American soldiers in the Korean War, the "Go For Broke Monument" is a symbol of the progress of civil rights for minorities.

After the attack on Pearl Harbor on December 7, 1941, more than 120,000 Japanese Americans were forcibly sent to internment camps without due process of the law. Their loyalties to America in question, Japanese Americans were labeled as "enemy aliens." To prove their loyalties to America, approximately 20,000 Japanese Americans fought in Europe or in the Pacific during World War II. "Go for broke" was the motto of one of the Japanese American units—the 442nd Regimental Combat Team.

Ultimately, the Japanese American community's demand for an official apology and reparation finally paid off when President Ronald Reagan signed a redress and reparation act in 1988. The next year, the Japanese American veterans of World War II established the foundation, now better known as the "Go For Broke

National Education Center." The monument became a symbol for seeking retribution and ultimate protection of the civil rights of all Japanese Americans, Asian Americans and racial minorities in America.

"In American history books or even in school textbooks, you can't find a page that describes Asian American's contribution to America's progress and prosperity," Young Oak said about the monument. "I wanted to build and leave it as evidence that proves Asian Americans contribution to America."

To commemorate Young Oak's contributions, the Japanese American community engraved his name on a small copper plate mounted on a separate small structure nearby the monument: "Colonel Young O. Kim Chairman." This copper plate is a reminder of another copper plate on a church wall in Biffontaine, France. Accepting him as their friend and leader, the Japanese Americans honored him, even though he was the only Korean American among the 20,000 Japanese American soldiers who served during World War II.

Another example of his service for the Japanese American community was his contribution to the Japanese American National Museum. According to the museum, Young Oak became one of the founding fathers when he signed the museum's incorporation papers in 1985, together with Mr. Y. B. "Buddy" Mamiya, Mr. George Aratani and Mr. Toy Kanegai, among others. The institution was actually born before the incorporation when two community groups merged their individual efforts to create a museum in the early 1980s. Young Oak led a group of World War II veterans who were intent on preserving the stories of Japanese American military service. His group joined forces with several Japanese American businessmen, led by Mr. Bruce Kaji to create an organization whose mission is to permanently preserve and share the story of Japanese Americans as an integral part of U.S. history.

Former U.S. Ambassador to Korea, Donald Gregg, said the relationship between Young Oak and the Japanese Americans, which was one of mutual trust, would be an exemplary model for Japanese and Koreans in the future.

Young Oak's service as a board member for the Special Service for Groups during the 1970s showed that his humanitarian work went beyond the Korean American and Japanese American communities. This organization began during World War II, as a result of the infamous "Zoot Suit Riots" in Los Angeles. American sailors had attacked a Mexican American youth on the streets of Los Angeles causing a national outrage. To alleviate the issue, the United Way formed a "special services unit" to attend to youth recreational and social issues. Eight years later, the Special Service for Groups was incorporated. SSG has been a non-profit organization dedicated to providing quality human services to a diverse and multicultural community. It also offers community-based solutions for the social and economic issues facing those in greatest need.

During the war, Young Oak had always taken extra care of women and children, including female POWs and war orphans. Young Oak left a long-lasting legacy of helping women and children even after his military service. "Every Woman's Shelter" in the Metropolitan Los Angeles area is another example of Young Oak's compassion for women and children. This shelter has been a home for Asian and Pacific Islander women victimized by domestic violence. The women and their children can stay at the shelter for a certain period of time while preparing for a new future. Starting in the mid-1980s, Young Oak served as the shelter's chairman for about ten years.

"That period was the most difficult among various community services of mine," Young Oak later recalled. "Domestic violence was a major social problem for every community. However, in those days communities never wanted to publicly admit that domestic violence existed in their own backyards. Therefore, it was extremely difficult to obtain support. Even if you successfully persuade people to donate, they wanted to do it anonymously."

Other existing domestic violence centers in Southern California were not of much service to Asian American victims, because many women would not stay long enough to receive adequate help, due to language barriers and cultural differences. Social service agencies in Los Angeles recognized that there was a desperate need to provide adequate support for Asian American victims of domestic violence. Such a shelter would take a large burden off existing mainstream organizations. Under his leadership, together with the collaboration of mainly the Filipino American community, Every Woman's Shelter emerged as the largest shelter of its kind in California. During the 1990s, the U.S. federal government and California state government recognized the imperative need of such shelters and subsequently increased funding for them. Many counties also increased marriage certificate fees to provide more funding for such victims.

As a humanitarian, Young Oak was a compassionate man with a huge heart. He was also resolutely unwilling to yield to the injustice of war crimes, such as sexual slavery by the Japanese military during World War II and the massacre of civilians by the Korean military and police during the Korean War. Young Oak also played a key role in the process that led the California State Assembly to pass the 1999 resolution demanding the official apology and reparation by the Japanese government to the victims of sexual slavery committed by the Japanese military during World War II. The resolution was initiated by then-California State Assemblyman Michael Honda, who is a third-generation Japanese American and now a U.S. Representative of the House. The resolution was adopted unanimously and paved the way for the U.S. House of Representatives to adopt another resolution of similar nature in 2007.

In 1999, the Associated Press ran a series of shocking articles about a civilian massacre of South Koreans by American soldiers during the early stages of the Korean War. President Bill Clinton ordered an investigation into the incident. At the request of the U.S. Department of Defense, Young Oak served as a member of the outside experts committee in order to secure credibility for the fact-finding mission. He went to Korea again for this mission, accompanying U.S. Secretary of the Army Louis Caldera.

Many individuals who had ever spent time with Young Oak during war or peacetime have expressed a deep appreciation for who he was. One such individual, was a soldier named Douglas, who was a private first class Japanese American soldier during World War II and also a sincere and honest man. Many years after the war ended, he told Young Oak, "I was able to safely return home because of you. I got married and have three sons. They're all grown now. They could be born into this world because of you and each one of them knows it very well."

A few years ago, when Young Oak moved from Las Vegas to Los Angeles, a group of Korean Americans handed him a small white envelop, which contained a small amount of money for a fruit tree. It was because they remembered Young Oak saying, "Whenever I see a persimmon tree, it reminds me of my mother and Korea. I should like to plant a persimmon tree someday."

Persimmons brought fond memories of his mother back to him. Young Oak's Japanese American friends from Central or Northern California sent him boxes of ripe persimmons every year.

Young Oak's contribution to World War II was recognized again, years later, by France. The French consulate in Los Angeles held a ceremony in February 2005 to honor Young Oak. The ceremony was held in front of the "Go For Broke Monument" by the Consulate General of France in Los Angeles to show appreciation to Young Oak with France's highest military decoration—Legion d'Honneur.

"France never forgot you and will never forget you," the Consul General of France in Los Angeles said when he awarded Young Oak with the decoration. After the war, France had awarded him with a "le Croix de Guerre"—the Cross of War—which is its second-highest military decoration. More than 57 years after the war ended, France reevaluated his contributions and decided to award him its highest decoration. Long before the ceremony, France requested his choice of where the ceremony would be held. Young Oak intentionally picked the monument in downtown Los Angeles to share the glory with his comrades-in-arms. At the ceremony, Young Oak said, "I honorably receive this medal on behalf of all the soldiers who fought together in France."

At the ceremony Dr. Sammy Lee, two-time Olympic gold medalist and Young Oak's lifelong friend, gave a speech representing the Korean American community.

"Without Young Oak, I could not have won any medal in the Olympic Games," Dr. Lee said. What he meant was that he had wanted to become an Olympic diver, but could not freely enter a public pool because of racial discrimination at the time. He was only allowed to use the pool on Wednesdays. During the London Olympics of 1948 and the Helsinki Olympics of 1952, Sammy won two gold medals in a row in platform diving.

France was not the only country to honor Young Oak. Italy had awarded Young Oak with its highest honor in 1946, one year after World War II ended. Korea also honored him. In September 2005, the President of Korea signed a document which awarded him with its highest military decoration of Korea—"Taeguk Order of Military Merit." It was more than 52 years after the Korean War ended. In addition, Korea had awarded him in 2003 with its second-highest civilian decoration for his community services.

Young Oak is perhaps the only person to have fought two different wars in three different countries and received the highest military decorations from all of them. Yet his own country—the U.S.—has not given him its highest military honor.

On October 21, 2005, the news of his being awarded Korea's Taeguk Order of Military Merit was wired all over the world by the AP, together with the tale of his having cared for hundreds of war orphans during the Korean War. It was 62 years after UPI had wired the news of him capturing two German POWs in the battle for the liberation of Rome in 1944.

When President Roh Moo-hyun of Korea signed the award document, Young Oak was still unconscious from his third operation for cancer treatment. When Young Oak heard of the signing a few days later, he thought he might never be able to have an opportunity to thank the president, and decided to write a letter. He who often emphasized that he was 100 percent American and simultaneously 100 percent Korean, wrote a thank you letter to everyone.

INDEX

A

Aachen...............................110
Acheson, Dean......... 171, 172
Adriatic Sea 1, 106
Ahn Chang Ho IX, XII, XIII, 17, 147
Ahn, Philip............................XIII
Akahoshi 4, 5, 6, 7, 8, 9, 10, 11, 44, 73, 85, 89
Alien Land Law.....................22
Almond, Edward 204, 205, 207, 208, 247, 248, 249, 250
Anderson, Alfred 236
Anzio............... 1, 3, 81, 97, 142
Army Security Agency 174
Arno XXVIII, 100, 101, 103, 105, 106, 107

B

Battle of Chosin Reservoir 188, 203, 229, 246, 250, 255
Battle of the Bulge .. 141, 142, 143, 335
Battle of the Lost Battalion 150
Belmont High School 20
Belvedere 85, 86, 87, 94, 95
Bendix..................................169
Biffontaine . XX, 125, 126, 127, 128, 129, 134, 135, 142, 172, 365
Boodry, James...80, 102, 111, 112, 130
Bright, William.............. 67, 238
Browning Automatic Rifle 5
Bruyères ...XIX, XX, XXVIII, 110, 111, 114, 120, 121, 124, 125, 126, 135, 142, 275

Burger, Samuel..................356

C

Camp Bill.................... 156, 157
Camp Drake ... 175, 176, 178, 179
Camp Robert 158, 159
Camp Shelby .. 25, 28, 34, 44, 49, 68, 142
Candy, First Lieutenant....See Tanaka
Central Middle School........ 19
Chae, Myung-shin 356
Chang, In-hwan................... IX
Cho, Young-ja 339
Churchill, Winston 38, 44, 140, 331
Civitavecchia...................... 82
Clark, Mark 1, 65, 75, 184, 188, 352
Clark, William 203
Clinton, Bill...........................368
Clough, Casper 67, 68, 69, 70, 71, 72, 73, 77, 78, 202
Conmy, Joe 203, 232, 233, 234, 235, 236, 237, 238, 239, 240, 245, 311
Connor, Gary 76, 77
Corbin, Paul......................... 69
Counterintelligence Corps 209
Covach, John . XXII, 223, 224, 230, 231, 287, 288, 289, 308, 309, 325, 328, 329, 330, 358
Cox, Noel 341
Croker, Thomas 337
Cross of Military Valor......... 12

D

Dahlquist, John 116, 121, 123, 124, 126, 128, 150
De Maiolo, Frank 80, 102, 116, 150, 151, 159
Dongjihoe 15, 147
Donovan, Joseph 158, 159
Donovin, Joseph 95
Drenken, Andrew 327

E

Eaton, Kenneth 68, 69, 73, 74, 359
Eisenhower, Dwight .. 67, 109, 116, 332, 345
Eisenhower, John 332
Emmanuel III, Victor 39
Ensminger, Ralph 86
Ethridge, Harold 90
Every Woman's Shelter 366
Ewha Woman's University.. 13
Executive Order 9066 26

F

Feibelman, Charles 89, 90, 92, 93, 94, 102, 105, 113, 114, 127
Ferenbaugh, Claude 208, 221, 242, 247, 297, 298, 301, 302, 303, 310
Fifth Army Headquarters.. 2, 3
First Spring Offensive 210, 285
Fleming, Alexander 140
Florey 140
Folkenberry, Steve 231
Fort Benning ... 24, 25, 91, 171, 176, 350, 351, 353, 356
Frayburg, Bernard 75
French Riviera .. 142, 149, 151, 154, 156
Froning, Paul 40

Fukuda, Mits 78

G

Gillespie, James 51, 52, 55, 56, 59, 61, 64
Go For Broke Foundation 363
Go For Broke Monument XXX, 364, 369
Gothic Line 85, 100, 201
Gurka Unit 79
Gustav Line 1, 45, 73, 81

H

Hagiwara, George 134
Hahn, James 360, 361
Hahn, Kenneth 360
Haight, Frederick 324, 325, 327, 328, 329, 330, 331, 332
Honda, Michael 368
Houston, Mel 192
Howze, Hamilton 355
Hyun, David XII

I

Incheon Landing ..... XXII, 203, 221, 222, 224, 247, 248, 249, 250, 252, 254, 283, 308, 339
Iron Triangle 285, 287, 296, 341, 342, 346, 350

J

Jaisohn, Philip V
Japanese American National Museum 365
Johnson, Clarence 30
Johnson, Jack . 43, 63, 64, 73, 191, 192

K

Kaneko, Kenneth 49, 61
Kim, Chong Rim .... XI, XII
Kim, Ida 142, 143, 144, 146, 147, 148, 166
Kim, Soon Kwon VIII
  Soon Kwon 13, 187
Kim, Willa 18, 19
King, Oscar 39, 86
Kitaoka, Takashi 31, 32
Koh, Nora
  Nora .... VIII, 13
Kometani, Katsumi 28, 29, 42, 136, 137, 138, 144
Korean American Coalition 362
Korean American Day VI
Korean American Family Service Center 363
Korean American Museum 362
Korean Aviation School X, XI, XII
Korean Health Education and Information Research Center 360
Korean Health Education Information and Research Center XXIII
Korean Provisional Government X
Korean War Veterans Memorial 364
Koreatown Youth and Community Center 362
Kubokawa, James 4, 5, 44, 73
Kyung Chun Ae In Sa 337, 339
Kyungshin High School 13

L

Lauer, Jerry 325

Lee, Sammy .... XII, 15, 369
Lee, Soon Ki 15
Legion d'Honneur ... XXX, 369
Lindow, Rod 317
Lonsford, Charles 259, 260, 261, 262, 263, 264, 265, 266, 267, 317
Los Angeles Civil Unrest .. XVII, XXIV
Lovell, James 42
Lovett, Robert 331
Lucas, John 1

M

Mansei Movement IX
Marzano, Rocco 52, 64, 67
Mason, Kermit . 229, 233, 234, 235, 236, 238, 239, 240, 241, 242, 243, 244, 245, 246, 247, 251, 255, 260
McCaffrey, William .. 194, 199, 200, 201, 202, 203, 204, 205, 206, 207, 208, 210, 211, 212, 213, 216, 220, 221, 225, 226, 227, 229, 234, 236, 238, 239, 240, 241, 242, 244, 245, 246, 247, 248, 258, 259, 260, 264, 268, 271, 272, 281, 286, 295, 297, 298, 301, 302, 303, 309, 310, 311, 314, 315, 317, 319, 322, 324, 325, 331, 333, 334, 335, 342, 350
McChesney, Claude 243
McCoy, Eugene 323
McKenzie, Alex 149
Mediterranean Sea 1, 62, 109, 149, 151
Military Valor Cross XXX
Miller, Virgil .. 83, 155, 156, 293
Min, Yong-ik V
Minami, Yoshio 4, 5, 44, 73, 89
Miyaki, Mike 29
Mizuha, Jack 61

Monaco..............149, 150, 151
Monte Cassino.40, 68, 73, 74, 75, 76, 78, 80, 81, 166, 288, 360
Moon, Kwan-ook................339
Moran Medal of Korea.....XXII
Moses, Lloyd........................342

N

Nanjing Massacre................19
National Security Agency174
Neal, Sam...........335, 336, 337
New Korea...................... XI, 15
Normandy Landings..............1

O

Operation Shingle................81
Operation Showdown.......351

P

Park, Chung-hee...............356
Park, Yong-man..................VIII
Patterson, Robert.....VI, VII, 96
Pearl Harbor.5, 23, 26, 28, 31, 36, 145, 148, 364
Pence, Charles 84, 85, 88, 90, 91, 92, 94, 95, 112, 121, 122, 123, 127, 128, 129, 134, 135, 149, 155
Pidgin English........................35
Pisa..XXVII, 101, 102, 105, 106, 151, 204
Purcell, Alfred... 179, 180, 182, 183, 184, 185
Purple Heart Battalion.........81
Pye, William................ 126, 132

Q

Quinn, Bill.............................221

Quinn, William . 183, 201, 202, 313, 314

R

Reagan, Ronald 364
Rhee, SyngmanIX, XII, 15, 147, 172, 187, 253, 284
Roh, Baek Rin.......................... X
Roh, Moo-hyun 370
Rome . XXVII, 1, 12, 39, 73, 82, 85, 97, 98, 100, 102, 106, 142, 278, 370
Rutledge, Pual W. 101, 103, 107, 108
Ryder, Charles... 2, 11, 44, 85, 86, 116

S

Sa-ee-gu .... XVII, XVIII
Sakamoto, Samuel......78, 133
Salerno............................39, 52
Santa Maria Olivetto 4, 74, 76
Sassetta 88, 90, 94, 95
Second Spring Offensive 258, 269, 283, 311
Shihan, Tom 323
Shon, Lee Mary XII
Singles, Gordon2, 3, 9, 10, 82, 84, 85, 86, 87, 88, 90, 96, 97, 102, 103, 105, 106, 107, 112, 116, 121, 122, 123, 125, 127, 129, 130, 131, 134, 135, 149, 150, 155, 171, 176, 177, 178, 179, 180, 181, 183, 184, 185, 186, 187, 188, 191, 201, 202, 284, 333
Sink, Robert213, 214, 216, 242, 310, 318
Smith, Frank........................203
So, Kwang-bom V
Song, Alfred .... II, XIII, 15

Special Service for Groups 366
Steigermolt, Lincoln 222
Stevens, Durham IX
Suzuki, Taro .40, 41, 45, 46, 47, 48, 49, 52, 53

T

Taeguk Order of Military Merit ....XXX, 370
Takahashi, Sakae .. 5, 6, 9, 59, 67, 68, 69, 78, 86, 87, 98, 99, 113, 118, 119, 120, 134, 135, 142, 143, 156, 172, 173, 320
Takata, Shigeo......................41
Takeba, Masaharu 42, 49, 52, 53, 55, 57, 60, 61, 73, 74, 76, 156, 359
Tanaka, Ernest 33
Texas Division 109
Treaty of Amity, Commerce and Navigation V
Turner, Farrant..29, 38, 41, 42, 51
Tuskegee Airmen.................38

U

United Way of Los Angeles III

V

Van Fleet, James.....207, 208, 246, 311, 332
Volturno River... 40, 45, 51, 76
Vosges Mountains .. XIX, XXIX, 110, 112, 127, 142

W

Walker, Tom 231
Walker, Walton..................249
Warden, I.D........................299
Weisenberg, Charles........224
Westmoreland, William...342, 343, 344, 345
Willecke, Harold 230, 231, 232, 233, 238, 256, 264, 273, 287, 289, 308, 325
Wise, Frank 223, 224, 254

Y

Yost, Israel 136, 137, 138
Yu, Kil-jun V

Z

Zedong, Mao 332
Zoot Suit Riots.....................366

BIBLIOGRAPHY

Asia, Munhwasa. *The New Korea.* 4/26/1907-12/28/1961. Seoul: Asia Munhwasa, 1972.

Bonacich, Edna and John Modell. *Economic Basis of Ethnic Solidarity: Small Business in the Japanese American Community.* Berkeley, University of California Press, 1980.

Chae, Myung Shin. *Chae Myung Shin's Memoires: Sa sun ul num go num eo.* Seoul: Maeil Business Daily, 1994.

Chang, Do Young. *Manghyang: Former Army Chief of Staff of Korea Do Young Chang's Memoires.* Seoul: Supsok eui kkum, 2001.

Chang, Edward T. "What Does it Mean to Be Korean Today?: One Hundred Years of Koreans in America and More." *Amerasia Journal.* Vol. 29 No. 3, 2003-2004.

Chang, Edward T. and Jeannette Diaz-Veizades. *Ethnic Peace in the American City: Building Community in Los Angeles and Beyond.* New York: New York University Press, 1999.

Choi, Bong-youn. *Koreans in America.* Chicago: Nelson Hall Press, 1979.

Chung, Il Kwon. *Il Kown Chung's Memoires.* Seoul: Korea Book Inc., 1996.

Clark, Mark. *From the Danube to the Yalu.* New York: Harper & Brothers Publishers, 1954.

Duus, Masayo Umezawa. *Unlikely Liberators: The Men of the 100th and 442nd.* Honolulu: University of Hawaii Press, 1987.

Jung, Ho. *Yeomyung: Secrets behind the military coup d'état of Korea.* Seoul: Hongik Press, 1967.

Kim, Elaine H. and Eui-Young Yu. *East to America.* New York: The New Press, 1996.

Kim, Hyung-Chan (ed.). *Korean Disapora* Santa Barbara, ABC-Clio, 1977.

Kim, Hyung-Chan. "Ethnic Enterprises among Korean Immigrants in America," in *Korean Diaspora*, 1977.

Kim, Ill-Soo. *New Urban Immigrants: The Korean Community in New York*, Princeton, New Jersey: Princeton University Press, 1981.

Kim, Jin. *Chungwadae Biseosil.* Seoul: Joongang Daily, 1992.

Kim, Kwang-Chung and Won Moo Hurh. "Korean American and the "Success" Image" *Amerasia Journal*, (1983) Vol.10 No.2.

Lee, Sang Woo. *Birok: Park Chung Hee Sidae(1)*. Seoul: Joongwonmunwha, 1984.

Moses, Lloyd R. *Whatever It Takes: The Autobiography of General Lloyd R. Moses.* Vermillion, South Dakota: Dakota Press, University of South Dakota, 1990.

Moulin, Pierre. *U.S. Samuraïs in Bruyères*. Luxemburg: Rapidpress, 1993.

Murphy, Thomas. *Ambassadors in arms.* Honolulu: University of Hawaii Press, 1954.

Nakasone, Edwin M. *The Nisei Soldier.* 2nd Edition. White Bear Lake, Minnesota: J. Press, 1999.

National Defense of Korea's Military History Compilation Committee. *The Korean War: Excerpts.* Seoul: National Defense of Korea's Military History Compilation Committee, 1986.

National Defense of Korea's Military History Compilation Committee. *Pyungyang Talhwan Jakjeon.* *Seoul:* National Defense of Korea's Military History Compilation Committee, 1986.

National Defense Military History Institute of Korea. *The Korean War: I, II, III.* Seoul: National Defense Military History Institute of Korea, 1996.

National Defense Military History Institute of Korea. *The Korean War: I, II.* Seoul: National Defense Military History Institute of Korea, 1997.

Paik, Sun Yup. *Guilgo guin yeorumnal 1950.6.25.* Seoul: Gigoochon, 1999.

Tom, Sheehan. *Cool Cool Kim.* Sheehan's unpublished essay written in mid-1950s.

Silvestri, Ennio. *The Long Road to Rome,* 1994.

Song, Gun Ho. *Suhr Jae Pil and Rhee Seung Man.* Seoul: Jungwoo Press, 1980.

Takaki, Ronald. *Strangers from a Different Shore: A History of Asian Americans.* New York: Back Bay Books, 1998.

Tanaka, Chester. *Go For Broke: A Pictorial History of the Japanese American 100th Infantry Battalion and the 442nd Regimental Combat Team.* Richmond, California: Go For Broke, Inc., 1982.

U.S. Army. *Command Reports. 31st Infantry, U.S. Army.* 11/1/1950-9/15/1952.

U.S. Army. *Command Reports. 7th Division, U.S. Army.* 11/1/1950-9/15/1952.

U.S. Army. *Command Reports. U.S. Eighth Army.* 4/1/1951-6/15/1951.

U.S. Army. *Command Reports. 100th Battalion / 442nd RCT, U.S. Army.* 9/1943-10/31/1944.

U.S. Army. *Hour Glass. 7th Division, U.S. Army.* 5/1/1951-11/30/1951.

Wampler, Molly Frick. *Not Without Honor: The Story of Sammy Lee*. Santa Barbara: California: Fifthian Press, 1987.

Weglyn, Michi. *Years of Infamy*. New York: Morrow, 1976.

Wilson, Arthur W. and Norman L. Strickbine. *Faces of War*. Portland, Oregon: Artwork Publications, 1996.

Yu, Eui-Young; Phillip Earl; Eun-Sik Yang (eds). *Koreans in Los Angeles, Los Angeles*, Koryo Research Institute, 1982.

Zaffiri, Samuel. *Westmoreland: A Biography of General William C. Westmoreland*. New York: William Morrow and Company, Inc., 1994.

About the Young Oak Kim Center for Korean American Studies, UC Riverside

The nonprofit Young Oak Kim Center for Korean American Studies at UC Riverside is dedicated to understanding what it means to be a Korean American in the 21st century, the history of Korean Americans, the Korean diaspora in the United States and globally, and the role of Korean Americans in the reunification of South and North Korea.

The Center hopes to also study the impact of the 1992 Los Angeles Riots on the Korean American identity. Through cultural and academic study, the center aims to empower the Korean American community and bridge ethnic and generational gaps.

The YOK Center hopes to lead the United States in studying issues related to Korean diaspora and Korean American identity issues, encourage and facilitate the free exchange of ideas and perspectives on topics related to Korean American studies and benefit surrounding KA communities by sharing leadership and academic knowledge.

If you would like contact the YOK Center, please feel free to e-mail or call Director Edward Chang at:

Edward.Chang@ucr.edu
(951) 827-5661

How to Order

If you would like to pick up a copy of the paperback book for $25, please visit the center at the address listed below. Or please send a $30 check, ($25 for the book and $5 for S&H), made payable to UC Regents with YOK Center written in the memo to the address listed below. Please include the address you would like the book shipped to. You may also order a copy of the book online at Amazon.com; Lulu.com or at www.yokcenter.ucr.edu.

The Young Oak Kim Center for Korean American Studies
UC Riverside
900 University Avenue
4031 CHASS INTN (Interdisciplinary Building North)
Riverside, CA 92521

Order Form

Name:_____
Address _____
_____
_____

No. of Hard Back Copies: _____
No. of Paper Back Copies: _____

Please make checks payable to Regents UC.
Include $50 + $5 for S&H for a Hardback Copy.
Include $25 + $5 for S&H for a Paperback Copy.
If you would like to order multiple copies, please contact the YOK Center at (951) 827-5661.

ISBN 978-0-615-47372-7

CPSIA information can be obtained at www.ICGtesting.com
226918LV00001B/73-1998/P